THE RECORD

THE RECORD

*The Trial of Adolf Eichmann for
His Crimes Against the Jewish People
and Against Humanity*

Lord Russell of Liverpool

ALFRED · A · KNOPF : NEW YORK

1963

L.C. catalog card number: 62-15570

THIS IS A BORZOI BOOK,

PUBLISHED BY ALFRED A. KNOPF, INC.

FIRST AMERICAN EDITION

Originally published in Great Britain by William Heinemann Ltd. as THE TRIAL OF ADOLF EICHMANN.

PREFACE

T HE OBJECT of this book is to give a reliable account of
the trial of Adolf Eichmann. It is unlikely that the
voluminous official record of the trial will be published for a
considerable time and, when it is, few will have time to read it.

Some difficulty has arisen, in writing this account of the
trial, by reason of the fact that the only English version of the
proceedings at present in existence, and likely to be available
for a considerable time, is the unrevised transcript of the
simultaneous translation from the Hebrew or German.

It has, therefore, sometimes been necessary to change the
actual wording of the translation, where quoted, for gram-
matical reasons, but whenever this has been done great care
has been taken to ensure that the general sense has in no way
been impaired.

CONTENTS

PROLOGUE

O N 23 MAY 1960 David Ben Gurion, Prime Minister of Israel, made the dramatic announcement in the Knesset, the Israel Parliament, about the arrest of Eichmann, the man who once admitted that he would be considered one of the main German war-criminals, for he had millions of Jews on his conscience. The news spread like fire across the world and there was much speculation as to where it was that he had finally been brought to bay.

Within a few days there appeared to be little doubt that he had been kidnapped in the suburbs of Buenos Aires, and on 1 June the Foreign Minister of the Argentine asked the Israeli Ambassador whether these reports had any foundation. It was proved that there had been a violation of international law, the Foreign Minister stated, and his Government would take the necessary steps to obtain redress.

On 3 June the Government of Israel replied to this demand, through their ambassador, admitting all the facts and, on the same day, Ben Gurion sent the following letter to the President of the Argentine Republic, Señor Frondizi:

Dear Mr. President
At this hour, as a result of the capture of the Nazi war-criminal Adolf Eichmann, and his transfer to Israel, misunderstandings may arise in the relations between the Republic of Argentina and the State of Israel, and I therefore regard it as my duty to send you this direct message. I take the liberty of doing so precisely because

the relations between our two Governments and our two peoples are dear to our hearts and because we should regard it as a matter for profound sorrow and regret if they were to be in any way impaired as a result of recent happenings in connection with Adolf Eichmann.

I understand that you personally are at the present time giving due consideration to the Diplomatic Note which our Ambassador at Buenos Aires delivered to your Minister for Foreign Affairs on Friday, 3 June. In that Note you will find all the elements of our case in this matter. There are, however, certain points touching the very core of the issue which transcend the confines of a Diplomatic Note. It is on these points that I wish briefly to enlarge, and I do so in the conviction that only by fully appreciating them is it possible to pass judgment on the issue involved.

During the Second World War this man Eichmann was the person directly responsible for the execution of Hitler's orders for the "final solution" of the Jewish problem in Europe, i.e. the murder of every single Jew on whom the Nazis could lay their hands throughout the territories of Europe which they had occupied at that time. Six million of our people were murdered in Europe, and it was Eichmann who organised this mass murder, on a gigantic and unprecedented scale, throughout Europe.

I need not explain to you, Mr. President, what it means for any people on earth to be the victims of such a satanic murder campaign, and what profound scars such an experience must leave on a people's soul.

Never, even in the age-old annals of our martyrdom, has there been such a fiendish atrocity. Not only were millions murdered—including a million infants—but the cultural and spiritual centre of our people, which until World War II had its seat in Europe, was extirpated. There is hardly a Jew in the world who does not have a member of his family among the victims of the Nazis. Hundreds of thousands of the survivors are living in our midst, and hundreds of people in Israel and abroad would not rest since the end of the war until they had found the man who had been in charge of this appalling campaign of extermination. They regarded it as their mission in life to bring the man responsible for this crime, without precedent in history, to stand trial before the Jewish people. Such a trial can take place only in Israel.

I do not underestimate the seriousness of the formal violation of Argentine law committed by those who found Eichmann, but I am convinced that very few people anywhere can fail to understand their feelings and appreciate the supreme moral validity of their act. These events cannot be approached, Mr. President, from an exclusively formal point of view. Though I do not question for a moment the duty of every State to respect its neighbour's laws— and we regard the Argentine Republic, of which you are the head, as an outstanding example of a State founded on respect for law—yet we can appreciate the over-riding motives whose tremendous moral and emotional force underlay the determination to find the chief murderer and to bring him, with his consent, to Israel.

I am convinced that Your Excellency will give full weight to the transcendental moral force of these motivations, for you yourself have fought against tyranny and shown your deep regard for human values. I hope you will understand our feelings, accept the expression of our sincere regret for the violation of your country's laws, which was the result of an inner moral imperative, and associate yourself with all the friends of justice in the world, who see in the trial of Adolf Eichmann in Israel an act of supreme historic justice, and that the friendly relations between Israel and your country will not be impaired.

DAVID BEN GURION

Diplomatic exchanges between the two countries concerned went on for several days, but, although the Premier of Argentina was understood to have realised the moral force of Ben Gurion's appeal for understanding, the Argentinian Ambassador to the United Nations, on behalf of his Government, asked for an urgent meeting of the Security Council to consider the violation of the rights of sovereignty of the Argentine Republic resulting from the illicit and clandestine transfer of Adolf Eichmann from Argentine territory to the State of Israel.

Article 34 of the United Nations Charter, under which the request was made, states that the Security Council "may investigate any dispute or any situation which might lead to international friction or give rise to a dispute, in order to determine whether the continuance of the dispute or situation is *'likely to endanger the maintenance of international peace and security.'* "

It is difficult to understand how, in any circumstances, anyone could imagine that the capture of this Nazi war-criminal, so that he should be brought to trial for his misdeeds, could possibly endanger the maintenance of international peace and security, and this, doubtless, explains the very mild resolution which was carried without a dissentient, although Poland and the U.S.S.R. both abstained.

At the hearing of Argentina's complaint, Mrs. Golda Meir, the Israel Minister for Foreign Affairs, presented her Government's case with great persuasion and cogency.

Her Government deeply regretted, she told the Council, that the Argentine Government had found it necessary to bring the question before it, because Israel had always had the most friendly relations with the Argentine people and their Government. She hoped that this "isolated violation of Argentine law" would be seen in the light of the exceptional and unique character of the crimes attributed to Eichmann on the one hand, and the motives of those who acted in this unusual manner, on the other hand. These men belonged, as she did herself, Mrs. Meir continued, to a people whose tragedy in the Second World War was unmatched in history. No people in modern times had ever mourned the loss of one third of its number in so short a period. Six million of Europe's Jewry were gassed and murdered, among whom were one million children.

Referring to the opening address of the Argentinian representative, Mrs. Meir then said:

A considerable part of the address we heard this morning was devoted to elaborating the charge that the State of Israel has violated the sovereignty of Argentina. I emphatically deny this charge. The State of Israel has not violated the sovereignty of Argentina in any manner whatsoever, and there is nothing in the record to enable the Security Council to make any such finding. The Government of Israel has made clear in official communications to the Argentine Government, which appear now on the record of the Security Council, that certain of its nationals in the course of their efforts to bring Eichmann to justice, may have committed infringements of the law of Argentina, and it has already twice expressed its regret for this. I wish to repeat in all solemnity before this Council my Government's regret for any infringements of the law of Argentina which may have been committed by any Israel nationals. But, with the greatest respect for the distinguished representative of the Argentine, I think that he is in complete error, as a basic legal proposition, in confusing the illegal action of individuals, for which regrets have been expressed, with a non-existent intentional violation of the sovereignty of one member-State by another. This distinction is so fundamental, and so well-established in international law, that I am at a complete loss to understand how it could be expected that the Security Council should make so far-reaching a finding, as is implicit in the statement we heard this morning, without any adequate basis in fact and in law, and again I want to stress that if Israeli citizens broke the law of Argentina, they broke it not in tracking down any ordinary criminal but in tracking down Adolf Eichmann. And here I must ask: would Argentina have admitted Adolf Eichmann into its territory had it known his true identity? Would asylum have been accorded him? Surely not. The distinguished delegate of Argentina expressed anxiety that this, if not dealt with by the Security Council, might constitute a precedent. But modern history knows of no such other monster as an Adolf Eichmann. The distinguished representative of Argentina has sought to construct the means of ordinary legal procedure on the one hand with resort to lynchings and mob violence on the other. Insofar as he sought in the latter connection to draw an analogy to the apprehension of Eichmann, there is no analogy. Far from lynching Eichmann or hanging him on the nearest tree, those who pursued him for over fifteen years and finally seized him have handed him over to the processes and judgment of the courts of law. The reference to mob passions and lawless justice in this context is unwarranted and provocative. This is not only my view and that of the Government of Israel. It is also shared by prominent Argentinians. In an article by the well-known publicist, Ernesto Sabate, in the important newspaper *El Mundo* of 17 June, published under the suggestive title "Sovereignty for Butchers," we read: "How can we not admire a group of brave men who have, during the years, endangered their lives in searching throughout the world for these criminals, and yet had the honesty to deliver him up for trial by judicial tribunals instead of being impelled by an impulse of revenge to finish him off on the spot?"

Finally, the Israel Minister for Foreign Affairs returned to the question of whether this was a proper matter to be brought before the Council, a body that was created to deal with threats to peace. How could this possibly be a threat to peace: Eichmann being brought to trial by the very people to whose total physical annihilation he had dedicated all his energies, even if the manner of his apprehension violated the law of Argentina? Did not the threat to peace lie, rather, in Eichmann at large, Eichmann unpunished, Eichmann free to spread the poison of his twisted soul to a new generation?

Mrs. Meir ended her speech with these words: "We value the friendship of the Argentine people, we fully understand its concern for its sovereignty, but we also respect it for its sense of justice. It is because we know that no threat to the sovereignty of the Argentine or of any other country has or will come from Israel, because of the sense of justice we both share, that we say in real friendship that this is not an item that should divide us any longer."

The Council's resolution referred to the universal condemnation of the persecution of the Jews under the Nazis and of the concern of people in all countries that Eichmann should be brought to justice for the crimes of which he is accused. Noting, at the same time, that the resolution should in no way be interpreted as condoning the odious crimes of which Eichmann was accused, the Council declared that acts such as that under consideration, which affected the sovereignty of a member state, *might, if repeated,* endanger international peace and security; requested Israel to make appropriate reparation in accordance with the Charter of the United Nations and the rules of international law; and expressed the hope that the traditionally friendly relations between the two countries would be advanced.

The only thing which had not yet been settled was the question of what would constitute "appropriate reparation." This was finally settled amicably, after the Israeli Ambassador in Argentina had been declared *persona non grata* and left the country as a result of negotiations conducted between Dr. Pardo, legal adviser to the Argentine Foreign Minister, and his opposite number in Israel, Shabtai Rosenne. These two international lawyers knew each other very well and had been on friendly terms for some years. The spade-work was done over innumerable cups of coffee in a small café in Buenos Aires, and the final result of their labours was the following joint communiqué which was published simultaneously in both capitals on 3 August:

The Governments of Israel and the Republic of Argentina, animated by the wish to comply with the resolution of the Security Council of 23 June 1960, in which the hope was expressed that the traditionally friendly relations between the two countries would be advanced, have decided to regard as closed the incident that arose out of the action taken by Israel nationals which infringed fundamental rights of the State of Argentina.

It had, indeed, been "much ado about nothing."

The reaction of the world press to Israel's action, and her declared intention of bringing Eichmann to trial before an Israeli Court was, on the whole, favourable. The main opposition came from the U.S.A. and, not surprisingly, from Israel's inveterate and implacable Arab enemies. Elsewhere the majority of newspapers were convinced that Eichmann could be assured of a fair trial in Israel, and all apparently felt that it was only historic justice that it was to be in Israel that he would, at long last, have to answer for his alleged crimes.

The London *Times* considered that there was no "moral

case" against Israel's action. The charges against Eichmann included crimes against the Jewish people and against humanity, all of which came within the category of "persecutions on political, racial or religious grounds" for which, by Article 6 of the Nuremberg Charter of 1945, individuals may be held responsible "whether or not in violation of the domestic law of the country where perpetrated."

The *Guardian* called it "Old Testament Justice," but considered that there appeared to be no grounds in international law why Eichmann should not be tried in Israel.

There were, however, not a few in Israel itself who feared that the trial of Eichmann by Jewish judges might resuscitate anti-Semitism, and that the spectacle of the Jews, as one of them put it, "stripping and shewing their scars to the world, like old beggars, years after the sores have healed," would be unedifying and might have a bad effect on many young Israelis who were already inclined to despise many of their elders who, in their opinion, in Germany and in Central and Eastern Europe should have resisted their fate with more vigour. The evidence which would be given at the trial, however, was more likely to have the opposite effect, for many of those young people would learn for the first time that whenever there was a possibility of resistance, as in the Warsaw Ghetto, the Jews did so gallantly, and that those who had no opportunity to offer resistance, because they were neither armed nor organised, went to their death with dignity and undiminished faith. Might it not be a good thing for the young citizens of Israel, gathered together from the four corners of the world, to be made aware of the fact that the young State, of which they were such proud and useful members, owed its very existence to the centuries of persecution which preceded its formation?

The most important consideration, in the opinion of nearly all unprejudiced foreign observers and commentators was not who should try Eichmann, but would he get a fair trial before an Israeli Court? If the trial were to be by jury there might have been more reason for doubting this, but it was not. The three judges who were to try him would be judges of fact, as well as of law, and it would be they who would say whether or not Eichmann was guilty.

Anyone knowing little or nothing of the quality of the Israel judiciary, or the character of the three of its members who were to try him, might be excused for doubting whether Eichmann could receive a fair trial at their hands, were it not for one reason.

The trial, everyone knew, was going to be conducted in the full glare of publicity. The court-room would be crammed to overflowing with journalists from all over the world, more than 450 of them. Everything would come under their scrutiny and nothing could escape their notice. Every minute of the proceedings was to be televised and could be shown to millions of television viewers. Was it conceivable that an Israeli Court of three eminent judges, in the presence of this world-wide audience, would discredit themselves and the whole legal system of their country by acting unfairly? It is now almost forgotten, but it is interesting to remember in this context, that at the Reichstag trials in 1933 a court composed of entirely subservient Nazi judges, much against their own inclinations and to their Führer's intense disgust, were forced to acquit the accused Dimitrov, because it had become obvious that he was not guilty.

If Eichmann is to be judged by Jews, the critics said, justice will not be seen to be done. There was a simple answer to that criticism. With the eyes of the whole world upon the trial, if any *injustice* were done it would be clearly seen.

Another criticism made before the trial opened was that it was "a vast irrelevance." The crimes with which Eichmann is charged, these critics said, are beyond retribution. The trial is, therefore, for revenge and those who have set the wheels of justice in motion against him have forgotten God's injunction, "To me belongeth vengeance and recompense." Israel is already receiving recompense in the form of reparations, these critics said; she has also had the judgment of the International Military Tribunal. What more does she want?

There was also a good answer to the question, why Israel was not satisfied with the Nuremberg proceedings as a permanent historical record of Hitler's crimes against the Jews? At the trial of major German war-criminals the Tribunal was dealing with very much wider issues, and in a very long judgment only one small sub-section of not more than six pages dealt with the persecution of the Jews, and there were only three short references to Eichmann. There were still many gaps to be filled in, as the picture was, by no means, complete. The trial of Eichmann, therefore, would serve a historical purpose.

The most impressive support of Israel's decision to bring Eichmann to trial before an Israeli court, however, came from West Germany itself where all the leading newspapers gave it their blessing.

Should Eichmann be brought before a German court? This question was put to the Federal Minister of Justice, Herr Schäffer, who gave the following reply: "German justice cannot address a demand for extradition to the Israel Government since the necessary basis for such a move, according to international legal practice, is lacking. On the other hand German justice will do everything possible to contribute to the just punishment of Eichmann's misdeeds. It will, on request, render Israel justice every legal assistance and place any available material at its disposal. Moreover, it will dispatch observers to Israel, in order that use may be made of the knowledge gained there concerning Eichmann's accomplices in West Germany."

The dramatic capture of Eichmann in the Argentine ended a hunt which had been going on incessantly since the unconditional surrender of Germany after her defeat in 1945. Many took part in it and contributed, in some measure, to its final success.

It was Simon Wiesenthal, however, who provided the Government of Israel, as long ago as 1953, with the one vital piece of information which was to lead his captors to Eichmann's hiding-place more than six years later.

When the American forces liberated Mauthausen Concentration Camp on 5 May 1945 Wiesenthal was one of the inmates. He had been there for a number of years, and at that time he was lying seriously ill in what was known as the Death Block. Shortly after his release he obtained employment in the War Crimes Office of the American Army and almost at once began his long search for Eichmann. He had never heard of Eichmann during the war and only came across his name while checking the lists of wanted Nazis involved in anti-Jewish atrocities. It intrigued him to learn that Eichmann was formerly a resident of Linz because, shortly after the war ended, Wiesenthal went to live there.

In the list of wanted Nazi war-criminals issued by the Jewish Agency, Eichmann had been described as having been born in Palestine at Sarona. This was found afterwards to be quite untrue when Wiesenthal checked the old police registration-forms in Linz only to discover that no member of the Eichmann family had ever been born in Palestine. The source of this information is not definitely known but it is thought to have come from Eichmann himself who, wanting to impress people that he had special knowledge of Jewish affairs, told them that he came originally from Palestine. For the next eight years Wiesenthal spent most of his time, all his energy, and quite a lot of money following up trail after trail, but without success.

Meanwhile, he had become an enthusiastic stamp-collector. In 1948, when the long nightmare of Mauthausen was still uppermost in his mind, Wiesenthal found it impossible to sleep at night and consulted his doctor about this insomnia. The doctor told him that unless he took up a diverting hobby the strain would gradually wear him down, mentally and physically. The hobby which he chose was stamp-collecting. He had little or no knowledge of it but the new interest took his mind off other things. He would sit up late at night bent over his stamp albums. It may not, at first, have cured his insomnia but it did stop those terrible nightmares. After a time he became, like so many other collectors, almost an addict. He took in all the principal philatelic periodicals and corresponded with others interested in the same hobby at home and abroad.

One of these enthusiasts was an elderly Austrian baron. Wiesenthal first met him at a stamp exhibition in Innsbruck in 1953. He was a typical member of the Austrian nobility, owned a castle in the Tyrol, and had a very valuable collection of stamps which, for some reason or other, he wanted to sell. He invited Wiesenthal to his place and showed him the collection. He was a charming old gentleman, had travelled all over the world, and he asked Wiesenthal what he was then doing. Wiesenthal told the Baron that he had been in several concentration camps during the war, was Chairman of the Jewish Central Refugee Committee in Austria, and had been working for years tracking down wanted German war-criminals.

"That reminds me," the old man said, "I had almost forgotten that there is something I want to show you which might be of interest. I have a friend in the Argentine, formerly a major in the German Army, with whom I exchange stamps and I always send him Austrian first issues. He was a regular German officer but not like other Germans. He was never a Nazi, has been living in the Argentine for years, and is a decent respectable fellow. Two or three months ago he wrote about someone in whom you might be interested." The old man got up from his chair, went over to his desk and fumbled about in a pile of letters from which he eventually picked out one, held it under the light and then said, "Here it is, read it." It was quite a long letter but this is one of the paragraphs which Wiesenthal read: "Among the acquaintances whom I have recently met out here is the former Deputy of Fritsch, Major B, who belonged to a Berlin regiment, and another person, whom I have already seen twice and with whom a friend of mine has even spoken, is none other than that dastardly swine Eichmann who deported all the Jews. He is living in the vicinity of Buenos Aires and works for a water-supply company." The letter then dealt with other subjects.

When Wiesenthal finished reading that paragraph the Baron said, "Well what do you think of that? The man is alive."

Wiesenthal did his best not to let the old man see how excited he really was, and said casually, "He is not the only war-criminal at large in the Argentine."

Wiesenthal said this so as to make sure that the Baron would not write quite casually to his friend saying that he had told some Jew in Austria that Eichmann was living near Buenos Aires. One could never be sure how people reacted, and if such a letter had been written the information might have got round, by devious means, to Eichmann himself.

On his way back to Linz Wiesenthal kept saying to himself that the information was obviously a hundred per cent authentic. There could be no mistake regarding the form in which it was presented to him. Later, Wiesenthal learned from a different source that Eichmann was in the Argentine, but he was equally certain that the Argentine Government would never agree to Eichmann's extradition. It was common knowledge that Peron had many ex-Nazis around him, and huge German capital investments had been made in the Argentine since 1944, when several of the Nazi high-ups were trying to get their money out of Germany before it was too late.

A few months later Wiesenthal received a visit from the Israeli Consul-General in Vienna who told him that the President of the Jewish World Congress, Dr. Nahum Goldmann, had approached the Israeli Government with a request for material which could be helpful in the search for Eichmann. Dr. Goldmann had also said that there was someone in Israel who would like to continue the search and Wiesenthal was asked to send a full report and enclose with it any relevant documents in his possession.

Nothing could have pleased Wiesenthal more than to know that he could, at long last, pass on to someone else the result of the heartbreaking efforts of the last eight years; hand them over to someone who could bring them to a satisfactory conclusion.

In his report to Dr. Goldmann, Wiesenthal described in detail all the attempts so far made to track down Eichmann in order to ensure that all these fruitless trails would not be followed a second time. Finally he wrote, "I am convinced that Eichmann now lives in Buenos Aires and works for a water-supply company." He wished his successor more luck than he, Wiesenthal, had experienced and enclosed Eichmann's personal SS file, some photographs of him, a specimen of his handwriting and a full list of the members of his own family and that of his wife. All this information was forwarded on the 30 March 1954, and a copy of the report was sent to the Israeli Consul-General in Vienna.

Wiesenthal waited anxiously for a reply from Goldmann but he received nothing until May, when a letter arrived from a rabbi, named Kalmanowitz, who wrote to say that Dr. Goldmann had forwarded the report on to him and that he was much impressed by it. At the same time Dr. Goldmann had also given the rabbi information obtained from some American source to the effect that Eichmann was living in Damascus. The rabbi wanted to know whether Wiesenthal could obtain Eichmann's exact address in Buenos Aires.

Wiesenthal replied that it was now only a question of money, and not very much of that would be needed, but someone would have to be sent there to verify his information. All that was required were the travelling expenses, which would not be more than 500 dollars. A reply was received from Rabbi Kalmanowitz, a few weeks later, regretting that he was unable to do anything further, and informing him that the report together with its enclosures had been sent to the United States State Department in Washington.

This letter so depressed Wiesenthal, who was convinced that Eichmann's exact whereabouts could be definitely determined with the expenditure of very little money, that he entered into negotiations with Yad Washem for the transfer to that organisation of his entire collection of documents, including the archives of his Documentation Centre in Austria. A representative of Yad Washem visited Wiesenthal in Linz, inspected the archives, and in 1955, 500 kilograms of documents, many of them concerning Eichmann, were shipped to Jerusalem. Four years passed by, and Wiesenthal did not want to be reminded of Eichmann.

In the summer of 1959, however, the German illustrated weekly *Stern* organised a treasure-hunt in Lake Toplitz. All sorts of wild rumours were circulated. In August, while Wiesenthal was on holiday with his family in Switzerland, a telephone call was made to him from Linz. It was from a local newspaper editor who told him, in confidence, that Eichmann had just been seen in the Aussee region. Wiesenthal packed his bags next day and returned home but, before leaving, he telephoned the Israeli Ambassador in Vienna and told him what he had just learned. Within a fortnight, however, it was established that the rumour was quite unfounded.

Eichmann was not in Austria and the treasure-hunt in Lake Toplitz was called off. The whole incident, however, had revived Wiesenthal's interest in the subject, and he began to check all his old notes on the Eichmann hunt. Once again he decided to try and trace Frau Vera Eichmann and, for this purpose, he assumed that her husband was living in the Argentine. She had brothers and sisters and a mother who lived in Germany. Wiesenthal wanted to find out if she was corresponding with any of them. The members of the Eichmann family, who still lived in Linz, said that Eichmann's wife had remarried although none of them knew her whereabouts.

In the spring of 1959 Eichmann's stepmother died, and an announcement in one of the local newspapers included the name of Vera Eichmann in the list of mourners. If she had really remarried it was unlikely that she still bore the name of Eichmann.

At this time Oberstaatsanwalt Dr. Wolf [1] was preparing the dossier for the new Auschwitz trial, and Frau Eichmann's mother and sister were interrogated about her whereabouts. They stated that she had moved with her children to a little village near Heilbronn, where she lived for some time before disappearing without leaving an address. Wiesenthal went to the village and questioned Vera Eichmann's mother who told him that her daughter had remarried and that her new husband had a name which she could not recall but it sounded English, something like "Clem" or "Clems." [2] She had not received any letters from her daughter for some years. This information was immediately conveyed to the Government of Israel by Wiesenthal, and representatives of the Government were sent over to see him. The hunt for Eichmann was, once more, in full swing.

By the end of September 1959 Israeli secret agents had discovered Frau Eichmann's address near Buenos Aires. It was reported that she was living with a strange man, to whom she was not really married but whose name she used.

About the same time Wiesenthal received information that the notorious Dr. Mengele of Auschwitz was also living in the Argentine. Wiesenthal knew that a warrant had been issued for Mengele's arrest and that the German Legation in Buenos Aires had asked for his extradition which the Argentine Government had refused on the grounds that the address was incorrect and his crimes were of a political nature.

Wiesenthal thought that this would be an ideal test case to prove the Argentine Government's utter disregard for justice.

---

[1] Dr. Wolf is one of the chief prosecutors working in Frankfurt-am-Main, under Dr. Bauer, on the preparation of war-crime cases to be tried in 1962.

[2] It was, of course, under the name of Klements that Eichmann was living incognito in the Argentine.

Mengele had been responsible for the death of at least 100,000 men, women and children in Auschwitz camp and there were hundreds of witnesses who could give evidence against him. It was not difficult for Wiesenthal, through one of his friends who lived in the Argentine, to obtain Mengele's new address. He did so, and communicated the address to the German Legation in Buenos Aires on 30 December 1959, and a renewed demand for Mengele's extradition to Germany was made. The Argentine Government, however, refused to change its mind. It was now clear that Eichmann would never be extradited. The Argentine Government, in this respect, had forfeited its goodwill, and this was of great importance in view of what the Israelis decided to do in May 1960.

On 5 February 1960 Adolf Eichmann's father died, and one of the Linz newspapers carried an announcement of his death and funeral in which the name of Vera Eichmann again figured among the mourners. This was the second occasion on which the story of her remarriage had been proved to be untrue.

Meanwhile, however, more news about Eichmann had been coming through from other sources, and it became almost certain that Vera's fictitious second husband was none other than Eichmann himself disguised under a false name.

Wiesenthal then had another idea. Perhaps Eichmann's family had told him of his father's death and he might want to attend the funeral. It was most unlikely that he would take the risk, but it could not be excluded as a possibility. The funeral was scheduled to take place five days after father Eichmann's death, and it was reported that some members of the family, living far away, were expected to attend it. It would have been physically possible for Eichmann to have got there in time had he travelled by air.

Wiesenthal arranged for two photographers using telescopic lenses to take up unobtrusive positions overlooking the ceremony, and take several snapshots of the funeral party. By the evening he was in possession of photographs of nearly all

Eichmann's relatives, but Adolf Eichmann himself was not among them. But Wiesenthal then had yet another idea. The photographs of Eichmann which were in Wiesenthal's possession were twenty-four years old. His face must have undergone the same changes as those of his brothers. Up-to-date photographs of the brothers could be useful in identifying the "wanted" Eichmann in the Argentine. A few days later Wiesenthal handed these photographs to two Israelis with whom he kept in touch. That was in the middle of February 1960, and he later learned that these pictures played an important role in the identification of Eichmann three months later. This was the last contribution which Wiesenthal made to Eichmann's eventual capture, but he had worked to this end unceasingly and unremittingly for several years, and when the momentous news was announced by the Prime Minister of Israel on the 23 May, that same year, Wiesenthal had every reason to be satisfied.

The machinery for trying Eichmann had been in existence since 1950. On 27 March of that year Mr. Pinhas Rosen, the Israel Minister of Justice, introduced in the Knesset the Nazi and Nazi Collaborators (Punishment) Law under which the indictment against Adolf Eichmann was drawn.

When moving the first reading of the measure Mr. Rosen admitted that the new law involved certain departures from the accepted rules of criminal law. Like the Prevention and Punishment of Genocide Law, which was then under discussion by the Knesset at the second reading stage, Mr. Rosen said, the measure again brought before the Israel Parliament the most tragic story in the annals of the Jewish people, the campaign of destruction and extermination in which six million of them had been destroyed. The passing of these laws could neither give any consolation nor restore the dead. The only consolation possible was by turning their hearts to creative and constructive achievements in the new State, and the reception and settlement of Jewish exiles which had been taking place in Israel since its formation.

Nevertheless, by enacting these laws, Israel was fulfilling a natural and elementary duty, for it was inconceivable that any legislature which spoke in the language of law should totally ignore the Nazi crimes which staggered the world with their brutality and led to a drastic revolution in juridical thought and to new developments in the law for which there were no legal precedents. In the Nuremberg Charter and at the Nuremberg trials new legal principles were laid down, and in the Nazi and Nazi Collaborators (Punishment) Law there were departures from legal principles, hitherto regarded as sanctified, which no act of criminal legislation would have found it easy to ignore, had it not been for the Nazi crimes.

First, the law was intended to punish acts some of which were not yet defined as offences at the time they were committed; secondly, under the new Bill, offenders would be brought to trial for offences committed outside the borders of the State of Israel; thirdly, the Bill was retroactive.

There was a distinction, Mr. Rosen said, between this Bill and the Prevention and Punishment of Genocide Bill. The latter provided for the future, and was designed to prevent the repetition of acts similar to the crimes committed by the Nazis under their Führer. The former, on the other hand, applied to the past, to a particular period in history which began with Hitler's rise to power and ended with the destruction of his régime.

The decision to make these changes in the law was done deliberately. The new Bill proclaimed that Israel would never forget or forgive the past. Therefore, it rescinded the principle of limitations with regard to the more serious crimes, those that have been included in this Bill as war crimes against humanity. It is interesting to note that in this respect it resembles, to some extent, the German statute of limitations regarding war-crimes which created a time limit of twenty years except in the case of murder.

The Bill also demonstrated a revolutionary transformation that had taken place in the political status of the Jewish people. While other peoples passed suitable legislation for the punishment of the Nazis and their accomplices soon after the end of the war and, in some cases, even before it was over, the Jewish people, whose account with the Nazis was the longest and gravest of all, had no political authority to bring the Nazi criminals to justice until the establishment of the State of Israel. It had no political authority to demand that those criminals should be handed over for trial by its own Courts. The Bill, then being presented to Parliament for the first time, proposed to change all that.

When the principal Nazi criminals and their accomplices, whose offences were not committed in any one country, were tried by the International Military Tribunal in Nuremberg, it was assumed that other war-criminals would, in due course, be brought to trial in the countries where they had committed their crimes, or before the courts of those nations against whom their crimes were committed. The Jews were one of those peoples and, indeed, suffered from such crimes more than anyone else. The countries in which the Nazis committed their war-crimes passed special legislation to ensure their punishment. In some countries, such as Czechoslovakia, Rumania, Holland, Austria, Bulgaria, Hungary, and Poland, special courts were set up for the purpose. In others, such as Norway, Denmark and Yugoslavia, the trial of Nazi war-criminals was entrusted to the ordinary criminal courts. Military Courts for the punishment of Nazi war-criminals were used by Britain, Australia, Canada, Italy and Greece.

Since then, the Jews, always a race, have become once again a nation. It may be a new principle of law that a nation by means of retroactive legislation can try offences committed against its people before they became a State, but without it Israel would have had no means of retribution whatsoever and this, in all the circumstances, would seem inequitable.

Part 1

THE CASE FOR
THE PROSECUTION

I

The Trial Opens

THE FIRST three days of the trial, which opened on 11 April 1961, were occupied by legal arguments regarding the jurisdiction of the Court to try the accused, Adolf Eichmann. Apart from the purely legal question of jurisdiction, Dr. Servatius, leading Counsel for the Defence, challenged the right of the three judges to sit in judgment upon a man who had brought such evil upon the Jewish people; they might be prejudiced by reason of the fact that some of their relatives had been victims of the "final solution" or even because the whole Jewish nation was involved. To this submission the Attorney-General duly replied. When the Court reassembled, after adjourning for the week-end, the Presiding Judge, Judge Moshe Landau, rejected the submission in these words:

Counsel for the Defence fears that the judges will not be able, in this case, to be without prejudice. The fear is not in respect of any one judge in particular but against the three judges, being members of the Jewish nation and citizens of Israel. Counsel for the Defence says that he fears that the memory of the catastrophe and the holocaust which exterminated their people, which is the background of the various offences in the indictment, may influence the judges and impair their ability to do justice. He also asked each one of them to examine himself and ask whether his personal suffering or the suffering of his relatives during the years of the catastrophe does not invalidate him from sitting in judgment on Eichmann.

Mr. Justice Landau then said that what they would be called upon to decide was the responsibility of the accused for the acts alleged in the indictment, and when that was being determined it would not be difficult to safeguard the interests of the accused for the simple reason that, according to the Criminal Code Ordinance of Israel, everyone appearing before a criminal court was innocent until proved guilty. The verdict would be in accordance with the evidence brought before the Court.

We are professional judges, used and accustomed to weighing evidence brought before us and to doing our work in the public eye and subject to public criticism. The accused is defended by eminent Counsel. So far as the affairs of the accused regarding the background of this case are concerned, we can only repeat what holds good in every proper court of law. When a court sits in judgment, the judges who compose it are human beings, are flesh and blood, with feelings and senses, but they are obliged by the law to restrain those feelings and senses. Otherwise no judge could ever be found to try a criminal case where his abhorrence might be aroused, such as treason, murder, or any other serious crime. It cannot be denied that the memory of the Nazi holocaust stirs every Jew, but while this case is being tried before us it will be our duty to restrain those feelings, and this duty we shall honour.

Judge Landau also announced that the Court had decided that it had jurisdiction to try the accused, but that their reasons for this decision regarding the Defence's submission would be given in their final judgment.[1]

The Accused then pleaded "not guilty" to each count in the indictment, a summary of which is given below.[2]

All the charges were brought under the Nazi and Nazi

---

[1] As the legal grounds upon which this submission was made are fully discussed in the Court's judgment, details of them have not been given in this chapter.

[2] The indictment itself is of great length and it has not been thought necessary to give it in full.

Collaborators (Punishment) Law, 1950, and (except for Counts 13–15 inclusive) under Section 23 of the Criminal Code Ordinance, 1936.

FIRST COUNT
Committing a crime against the Jewish people.

This count alleged, *inter alia*, that Eichmann, together with others, caused the death of millions of Jews by gassing and other means in the extermination camps of Auschwitz, Chelmno, Belzec, Sobibor, Treblinka and Maidanek; and that he also co-operated with the four *Einsatzgruppen* A, B, C and D, which in Russia, between June 1941 and November 1942, exterminated not less than 363,000 Jews.

SECOND COUNT
Committing a crime against the Jewish people.

This count alleged that the accused, together with others, for the purpose of executing the final solution of the Jewish problem took steps to put millions of Jews to work in forced-labour camps, sent them to ghettos, transit camps and other concentration points, deporting them and conveying them by mass transportations under inhuman conditions.

THIRD COUNT
Committing a crime against the Jewish people.

This count contained allegations with regard to the organising of mass persecution of some 20,000 Jews on the night of 9–10 November 1938 (The Night of Broken Glass), the social and economic boycott of the Jews in Germany, the application of the Nuremberg Laws to them, and their mass arrest and deportation to camps like Dachau and Buchenwald.

FOURTH COUNT
Committing a crime against the Jewish people.

This count dealt with the measures which the Accused was alleged to have taken in Theresienstadt and certain other ghettos in the East, with regard to the sterilisation of Jews and gypsies, and the forced interruption of their pregnancy by artificial abortion with the intention of destroying the Jewish people.

FIFTH COUNT
Committing a crime against humanity.

Namely, between 1931–45, causing the murder, extermination, enslavement, starvation and deportation of the civilian Jewish population in Germany and other Axis countries.

SIXTH COUNT
Committing a crime against humanity.

Namely persecuting the Jews, as described in Counts 1–5 above, on national, racial, religious and political grounds.

SEVENTH COUNT
Committing a crime against humanity.

In Germany and other Axis countries he established various organisations for the purpose of robbing Jews in those countries of their property, depriving them of their livelihood and even robbing the dead and those about to die of their hair, gold teeth, clothing, artificial limbs, etc., and sending them to Germany. The extent of the success of such robbery is reflected by the fact that when the Germans, at the time of their retreat in January 1945, burned 29 stores of personal effects and valuables, out of 35 such stores which had been erected in the extermination camp at Auschwitz, the 6 stores saved from the fire were found to contain, *inter alia:* 348,820 men's suits; 836,255 women's dresses; 38,000 men's shoes.

EIGHTH COUNT
Committing a war crime.

During the period of the Second World War, in Germany and other Axis States and in the countries occupied by them, caused

the ill-treatment, deportation and murder of the Jewish inhabitants of such areas.

NINTH COUNT

Committing a crime against humanity.

Caused the deportation of over half a million Polish civilians from
their places of residence with intent to settle German families in
those places.

TENTH COUNT

Committing a crime against humanity.

Committing a similar offence, as alleged in Count 9, in respect of
the inhabitants of Yugoslavia.

ELEVENTH COUNT

Committing a crime against humanity.

Causing the deportation of tens of thousands of gypsies to extermination camps for the purpose of their being murdered.

TWELFTH COUNT

Committing a crime against humanity.

In 1942 caused the deportation of approximately 100 children
from Lidice in Czechoslovakia to Poland and their murder there.

The last three counts of the indictment (13, 14 and 15) al-
leged that during the period of the Nazi régime in Germany, the
Accused had served in various capacities in the SS, SD and the
Gestapo, all of which were declared criminal organisations by the
International Military Tribunal at Nuremberg on 1 October
1946, in accordance with Article 9 of the Nuremberg Charter.

II

The
Criminal Conspiracy

T HE ATTORNEY-GENERAL then began his opening speech.
The history of the Jewish people, he said, was steeped
in suffering and tears. Almost from time immemorial they
had been persecuted. Pharaoh in Egypt decided to "inflict them
with their burdens and to throw their sons into the River Nile.
Haman's decree was to destroy, to slay, and to cause them to
perish." Yet never before had any man arisen who dealt the
Jews such grievous blows as did Hitler. In all history there had
been no other example of a man against whom it would be
possible to draw up such a bill of indictment as that which had
been read out at the commencement of the trial. The terrible
crimes of Genghis Khan, Attila, and Ivan the Terrible, seemed
almost to pale into insignificance when contrasted with Hitler's crimes against European Jewry.

In the Dark and Middle Ages there had been many years of
extermination in which one nation had attacked another with
intent to destroy it and, in the heat of battle, large masses had
been massacred. But only in this generation had a nation attacked an entirely defenceless and peaceful population, men
and women, young and old, children and infants, locked them
up behind electrified fences, imprisoned them in concentration
camps and planned to destroy them entirely. Murder was nothing new, but it was not until the twentieth century that a new

kind of murder came to light, not the outcome of a momentary outburst of hatred but the result of a calculated decision and careful planning. Not through the evil design of an individual but through a criminal conspiracy involving thousands, not against one victim but against an entire nation. On this occasion Eichmann was the executioner but of a different kind. He carried on the killing from behind a desk. Only one incident is known in which Adolf Eichmann actually killed someone with his own hand and that was the occasion when he beat to death a Jewish boy who had dared to steal fruit from a peach tree in Eichmann's garden in Budapest. Nevertheless, although he was not himself a killer, it was his word of command that put the gas-chambers into action. He lifted the telephone receiver and railroad cars left for the extermination centres. It was his signature that sealed the doom of tens of thousands of Jews. He had but to give the order and, at his command, German troops took the field to round up Jews in their homes, beat and torture them, crowd them into ghettos, pin the yellow star on their breasts, steal their property, until finally, when everything had been taken from them, when even their hair had been shorn off and their clothes and possessions removed, they were transported *en masse* to the slaughter. Even then their corpses were still of value. Their gold teeth were extracted and sent to fill the coffers of the Reichsbank.

Eichmann took pride in the fact that he was just a white-collar worker in charge of the administration of wholesale butchery. To him Hitler's decree for the extermination of the Jews was just another written order to be carried out; nevertheless, it was he who planned it, and organised it, it was he who instructed others to spill this ocean of blood.

He bore the same, if not a greater, responsibility than those who actually carried out the extermination. He is just as guilty, if not more so, than those who with their own hands knotted the hangman's noose, who beat the victims into the gas-chambers, who shot them in the back and pushed them into open graves. Yet his accomplices in the crime were neither gangsters nor men of the underworld, many of them were leaders of the nation. They included professors and scholars, doctors and lawyers, bankers and economists, many of the intelligentsia, so-called men of enlightenment.

Hitler's decision to exterminate a whole nation and remove it from the face of the earth was taken deliberately and in cold blood. There were no adequate words to describe it, and it eluded human intelligence, said the Attorney-General. The fact that millions were condemned to death, not for any crime, not for anything they had done, but only because they were Jews.

This unprecedented crime, carried out by so-called civilised Europeans in the twentieth century, had led to the adoption of a new concept of crime unknown in history, even during the darkest ages, now embodied by the United Nations in "The Convention on the Prevention and Punishment of Genocide." This was adopted by the General Assembly in December 1948 and signed by twenty-five States. It has now become operative. The Convention qualifies as genocide specific acts such as killing, with intent to destroy, wholly or in part, a national, ethnical, racial or religious group. In Article I of the Convention the parties confirmed that genocide, *whether committed in time of peace or in time of war*, is a crime under International Law which they undertake to prevent and to punish.[1]

Until this Convention was adopted crimes against humanity were not punishable under International Law *if committed in peace-time*. The International Military Tribunal at Nuremberg, in its judgment, dealt with Article VI(c) of its Charter which brought crimes against humanity within the jurisdiction of the tribunal, whether committed before or during the war, provided they were committed in execution of, or in connection with, any crime within the jurisdiction of the tribunal.

[1] Oppenheim's International Law by Lauterpacht, vol. II, 7th edition, page 585.

The Attorney-General then went on to explain why this trial was necessary. Although Hitler's persecution of the Jews had been the subject of consideration at a number of war-crime trials conducted immediately after the war, in none of those trials was the tragedy of Jewry as a whole the main concern. It was one of the matters dealt with but it was never the crux of the trial, as the accused at those trials were indicted for crimes committed against members of many nations. There was only one man whose official life had been almost entirely concerned with Jewish affairs, whose business had been their destruction. That man was Adolf Eichmann. If at this trial he was also charged with crimes against non-Jews it was purely coincidental. Throughout this trial it should never be forgotten that the Accused's mission, his destiny, and his calling, to which he devoted himself with such enthusiasm and zeal before and throughout the war, was the "final solution" of the Jewish question.

A number of factors contributed to the rise of Nazism: the defeat of Germany and the Treaty of Versailles, the ensuing economic difficulties, and lack of leadership and political party strife. All of these encouraged the German people to look around for a dynamic leader. Thus did Hitler come to power. But he would not have been able to remain in power, and to consolidate the majority of Germans behind him, had he not been supported by a large number of intelligent men, university professors, professional men, the civil service and the German General Staff and Officer Corps. There are many such persons, who today vehemently declare that they had nothing to do with the Nazis, but who sung Hitler's praises and willingly gave him their support during the years immediately preceding the Second World War.

In a book entitled *The German Question* written after the Second World War, Professor Wilhelm Röpke of the University of Marburg wrote: "There have been Hitlers everywhere and at all times, but it is Germany's shame that so miserable a figure could become her leader. In order to germinate, the seed of Nazism had to find a favourable soil: it found it in the German Reich and the Germans, such as they had become in their political, spiritual, economic and social history." Long before Hitler was ever thought of, Goethe, in his *Poetry and Truth*, gave a prophetic description of the kind of demoniacal personality that Hitler turned out to be. "Against him, no union of moral forces can make a successful stand. In vain will men of enlightenment seek to scorn him or unmask his true character as a cheat and deceiver. The masses are drawn after him. . . ."

The party which Hitler was eventually to lead and which was only dissolved in 1945, when Germany surrendered to the Allies unconditionally, was originally called the German Labour Party, and it had been formed less than two months after the Armistice of 11 November 1918, eight months before Hitler joined it. At that time it had very few members. On 24 February 1920, at the Party's first political meeting in Munich, Hitler announced its programme which consisted of twenty-five points, one of which has special significance in the context of this trial: *Point IV* which said: Only a member of the race can be a citizen. A member of the race can only be one who is of German blood without consideration of creed. Consequently no Jew can be a member of the race.

The Aryan race was to be supreme—the Master Race—destined to rule the world, and Hitler wrote thus about it in *Mein Kampf:* "All that we see before us today of human culture, of the achievements of art, science, and technology, is almost exclusively the creative product of Aryan man. This fact leads to the well-based conclusion that he alone represents what we understand by the word 'Man' . . . He is the Prometheus of humanity, out of whose brow the divine sparks of genius sprang forth for all the ages, to be ever rekindled at that fire which, as knowledge, illuminated the night of the silent mysteries, and so enabled men to rise and be sovereign over the other creatures of this earth. It is thus no accident that the first cultures developed where the Aryan, encountering inferior peoples, subjugated them and made them subordinate to his will. . . . So long as he mercilessly maintained the position of master, he remained not only master, but also the upholder and propagator of culture. . . . But when the peoples he had subjugated began to raise themselves up and to approach the level of the conqueror, the definite barrier between master and slave fell. . . . The Aryan surrendered the purity of his blood and thereby lost the Paradise that he had created for himself. In the interbreeding of the races he declined, and was gradually and increasingly bereft of his cultural capacities. . . ."

Who were the Aryans? According to Hitler they had certain distinct characteristics. Their skulls were oblong, their complexion bright and splendid. (Hitler and Goebbels were undoubtedly two of the exceptions which proved the rule.) Furthermore, the word Aryan in Sanskrit means "master." They were of Indo-Germanic stock and the Teutons, and hence the Germans, were the most highly developed off-shoot of this magic strain. They were to rule the world with an iron hand and they must, at all costs, avoid pollution by contact with other races.

As Germany was still a Christian country, and the time for the persecution of the Churches was not yet ripe, it became necessary to make it clear that Jesus Christ was not Jewish but Aryan. This presented no problem to the Nazis whose scientists, physicists and biologists were prepared to bend their learning to Hitler's will. In the words of the popular song, *Anything you can do I can do better,* Professor Lenard, who had already won the Nobel Prize, undertook to establish a German physics in opposition to the Jewish science represented by Einstein. According to such theorists of racial doctrine as Hermann Gauch and others, non-Nordic man is closer to the animals than to the human race. Those who believe in this strange racial doctrine invented the term "subman" (*Un-*

termensch) to describe those who were not Aryans. Another well-known German professor discovered that it was only the Nordic peoples who had the aptitude for leadership.

Hitler's dislike of the Jews appears to have begun when he was still quite young, despite his subsequent denials, and it eventually developed into an almost pathological hatred. One of his boyhood friends, in a book entitled *The Young Hitler I Knew*, wrote that in their school days at Linz his friend's "anti-Semitism was already pronounced. . . . Hitler was already a confirmed anti-Semite when he went to Vienna. And although his experiences in Vienna might have deepened this feeling they certainly did not give birth to it."

According to Hitler himself, however, he had no inhibitions or prejudices about the Jews before his arrival in Vienna. He only thought of them as belonging to the Jewish religion, not the Jewish race. Indeed he even mentioned in *Mein Kampf* that he considered that the anti-Semitic tone adopted by much of the Viennese Press was "unworthy of the cultured traditions of a great nation."

Linz possessed very few Jews and they, Hitler wrote, "throughout the centuries had become European in externals like other people; in fact, *I looked upon them as Germans*," which indeed they were. It was only later that he realised his mistake. One day when he was walking through the "inner city" of Vienna, he suddenly came across a being in a long kaftan with black side-locks. His first thought was: "Is that a Jew?" In Linz they had not looked like that. He watched the "creature" stealthily and cautiously, but the longer he stared at that strange countenance and studied it feature by feature, the more insistently did the question go round in his brain in a different form: "Is that a German?" To help him solve this enigma he bought some anti-Semitic pamphlets, but they were so extreme that he still retained some doubts and, in his own words, "was tortured by the fear of doing an injustice." He did not remain in this state of unhappy uncertainty for very long, however, and soon began, like others before him, to see the Jew behind everything that was unsavoury, unclean and unpatriotic. At last he recognised the Jews as the leaders of social democracy and, as he wrote in *Mein Kampf*, "the scales, as it were, began to fall from my eyes. My long mental struggle was over. . . . From being a feeble world-citizen I became a fanatical anti-Semite."

Nor did this loathing of the Jews abate during the First World War, and, having seen Jewish youths helping to lead the revolution in November 1918 "none of whom had ever been to the front," he anathematised them as "miserable depraved criminals." "With the Jews there is no bargaining, there is merely the hard either-or," he wrote, "so I decided to become a politician."

This and other similar vapourings fill the pages of *Mein Kampf*, and it was clear from the very start that no Jew was to share in the Nazi millennium. How many Jews read the book, though they all had, of course, to buy it, nobody knows. Those who did read it can have had little doubt that the only wise thing to do was to go while the going was good, though many of them left it too late. The conviction amongst many Jews in Germany that Hitler, in building up his brave new world, would have need of their brains, their skill, their industry and, above all, their money, was one of the most tragic misjudgments in history.

Many of them, however (for the most cultured people in Germany were Jews), must have been aware of the teaching of Hegel and Nietzsche and their amoral philosophy, and even if Hitler's own views were not based on their doctrine, they were not at variance with it. Hegel argued that "private virtues" and "irrelevant moral claims" should not deter great men from carrying out their plans and that all opposition must be ruthlessly stamped underfoot. For such a man the concentration camp and the gas-chamber had no horrors. Nor had they any horror for Hitler. The Jews were "the enemy," he told an adoring audience, in his old haunt the Bürgerbräu Keller in Munich in February 1925, just after his release from

Landsberg Prison, and in the forthcoming struggle there were only two possible results: "either the enemy passes over our bodies or we pass over theirs."

The next twenty years was going to see the struggle develop and end, but not until some five million Jews had been exterminated in the final destruction of the Third Reich and all the beastliness that was part and parcel of it. Hitler, however, had learnt nothing, and in his so-called *Political Testament*, written just before he died, he tried to pass on the torch of anti-Semitism to those whom he was leaving behind. "Above all," he wrote, "I enjoin the Government and the people to uphold the racial laws to the limit and to resist mercilessly the poisoner of all nations, international Jewry."

The Court were reminded, however, by the Attorney-General that anti-Semitism was not invented by Hitler. It had been in existence for centuries. But the Nazis streamlined it into an offensive weapon. They turned it into a doctrine of hatred which began with hostility and ended in murder.

The weapon was there to his hand. The Jew had, for centuries, been the eternal scapegoat. It was only necessary to play up this natural antipathy to the Jews and form it into a consuming hatred. It must be admitted that, although his speeches and his writings betray an appalling ignorance, Hitler was able to persuade the mass of Germans that the Jews were a national menace.

Otto Strasser, who was eventually expelled from the Nazi party and went to live in the United States of America but has since returned to his homeland, wrote of Hitler: "I have been asked many times what was the secret of Hitler's extraordinary power as a speaker. I can only attribute it to his uncanny intuition which infallibly diagnoses the ills from which his audience is suffering. If he tries to bolster up his argument with theories or quotations from books which he has only imperfectly understood, he scarcely rises above a very poor mediocrity. But let him throw away his crutches and step out boldly, speaking as the spirit moves him, and he is promptly trans-

formed into one of the greatest orators of the century. . . .
"Adolf Hitler enters a hall. He sniffs the air. For a minute
he gropes, feels his way, senses the atmosphere. Suddenly he
bursts forth. . . . His words go like an arrow to their target.
He touches each private wound on the raw." [2]

Even before Hitler came to power the Jews were unpopular. They could do nothing right. They were easy meat and
fair game. As supporters of communism they were condemned as the enemy of the German people. As capitalists they
were the enemy of the workers. It was "heads I win, tails you
lose." They were even envied by non-Jewish Germans because
of their cultural attainments, and this was so even before the
First World War. Lord Balfour once told Dr. Weizmann of a
conversation which he had had with Frau Wagner, the composer's widow, during the Bayreuth musical festival in 1912
regarding the position of German Jews. Frau Wagner had
complained how Jews had captured the stage, the press, the
universities and commerce and expressed resentment at being
obliged to receive all culture at Jewish hands. Dr. Weizmann
replied that her sentiments revealed the very crux of the Jewish
tragedy, namely that the Jews who were giving their energy
and brains to Germany were doing so as Germans, not as Jews.
They were enriching Germany not Jewry, and most were
sinking their Judaism to put their brains at Germany's disposal.
The Zionists could not accept them as Jews, yet the Germans
did not recognise them as Germans.

But the outside world, so long as it was only the Jews whom
the Nazis persecuted, was not perturbed. It was too blind to
see that this was the shape of worse things to come, that Hitler's ultimate objective was world domination. In the same way
many Jews failed to see the red light. It could never happen
to us, they thought. Few of them are still alive and most of
those who are dead have Eichmann to thank for it.

There were, however, as the Attorney-General took care

[2] *Hitler and I* by Otto Strasser.

to point out, many who risked their lives to help their Jewish compatriots. "Thousands of them," he said, "scientists, ecclesiastics, statesmen, writers and ordinary people who refused to bow their heads to Nazi tyranny and even rebelled against it. Thousands of opponents of the bloody régime were imprisoned and were later destined to suffer terribly in concentration camps before the Nazi monster was beheaded. Thousands of these died without seeing the day of victory. Hundreds of ecclesiastics were arrested and imprisoned. There were also examples of personal bravery—like that of the pastor who was sent by Eichmann to a concentration camp for intervening openly on behalf of the Jews.[3] There were Germans who concealed Jews and shared their rations with them, at the risk of their lives, and helped to obtain "Aryan" papers for them. There were others who built up and maintained an anti-Hitler resistance movement. During the war there were also Germans who protested to Hitler at the disgrace the Gestapo was bringing on the German people by acting like "beasts of prey," as they described the extermination of the Jews. There were, moreover, soldiers who tried to prevent some of the killings by direct intervention.

But after all is said and done, they were a small minority. The decisive majority of the German people made peace with the new régime, and were unprotesting witnesses of the most terrible crime ever perpetrated in human history. And when Goebbels, the Nazi Propaganda Minister, made a public bonfire of the creations of men of the spirit, Jewish and non-Jewish—the works of such men as Thomas Mann, Wassermann, Einstein, Freud, Upton Sinclair, H. G. Wells, Zola, Havelock Ellis, and scores of others—because they were "in opposition to the German spirit," he proclaimed:

The soul of the German people can again express itself. These flames not only illuminate the final end of an old era; they also light up the new.

[3] Dr. Heinrich Grüber, now Dean of St. Mary's Cathedral in Berlin. Extracts from his evidence appear on pages 210 ff.

"The majority of German intellectuals were ready to warm themselves at these bonfires," the Attorney-General said, "and to accept as their spiritual guide the false glitter of the flames."

It was not enough, however, to blame the Jew for all the ills from which post-war Germany was then suffering. The Jew was the devil incarnate, and the Nazis denounced him and all his works.

The Protocols of the Elders of Zion, that forgery which suddenly came into existence towards the end of the First World War and purported to reveal a Jewish conspiracy to rule the world, was resurrected, used as anti-Semitic propaganda and taught in the schools. The spearhead of this anti-Semitic attack was Julius Streicher, "Jew-baiter Number One," as he liked to be known. He was an obvious choice for the post for he had been Jew-baiting since before 1922 when he first published *Der Stürmer,* a weekly anti-Semitic journal. A flood of abusive literature of all types and for all age-groups was published and circulated throughout Germany by him. Not even the Bible escaped. In an article in this newspaper, entitled *The Chosen People of the Criminals,* Streicher wrote: "The history book of the Jews, which is usually called the Holy Scriptures, impressed us as a horrible criminal romance which makes the shilling shockers of the British Jew, Edgar Wallace, grow pale with envy. The 'holy' book abounds in murder, incest, fraud, theft and indecency."

Another of Streicher's publications was called *Der Giftpilz* (*The Poisonous Fungus*), a *Stürmer* book for young and old. In this way young Germans, from the moment they started going to school, were taught to loathe and despise all Jews as being revolting and disgusting. In one lesson they were taught to recognise a Jew in these words, illustrated by sketches drawn on the black-board: "One usually recognises a Jew by his nose. The Jewish nose is crooked at the end. It looks like the figure 6. Therefore it is called the 'Jewish Six.' Many non-Jews have crooked noses too but their noses are bent not at the end, but farther up. Such a nose is called a hook-nose or

eagle's beak. It has nothing to do with a Jewish nose. . . .
But the Jew is also recognised by his lips, which are usually
thick. Often the lower lip hangs down. His eye-lids are usually thicker and more fleshy than ours and his look is cunning
and more sinister." The children would then chant a little
rhyming chorus to the effect that the Devil looked out from
inside every Jew, and they would only remain free if they
struggled to subdue the Jewish devil.

There was also that fantastic nonsense about what the Nazis
called "race pollution." "It is established for all time: alien
albumen is the sperm of a man of alien race. The male sperm
in cohabitation is partially or completely absorbed by the female and thus enters her blood-stream. One simple cohabitation of a Jew with an Aryan woman is sufficient to poison her
blood for ever. Together with the alien albumen she has absorbed the alien soul. Never again will she be able to bear
Aryan children . . . they will all be bastards. . . . Now we
know why the Jew uses every artifice of seduction in order
to ravish German girls at as early an age as possible: why the
Jewish doctor rapes his female patients while they are under
an anaesthetic. . . . He wants the German girl and the German woman to absorb the alien sperm of the Jew. She is never
again to bear German children!" It is difficult to believe that
the above extract is from an article which appeared in a semi-
medical journal called *The German People's Health Through
Blood and Soul*, but it is less incredible when it is known that
Streicher was its editor.

In addition to writing pages of this poisonous nonsense
Streicher travelled round the country talking to young German girls at school prize-givings. The following is an account
of one such occasion which appeared in a German newspaper
in March 1934 under the headline, DO NOT BECOME LA-
DIES BUT REMAIN GERMAN GIRLS AND WOMEN.
"At a celebration at the Preisslerstrasse, Julius Streicher spoke
to the girls at the passing-out ceremony after finishing their
course. A celebration, unique of its kind, was experienced on

Saturday morning last by the girls of District 7 in the school-room of the technical school. Julius Streicher spoke about his life and told them about a girl who at one time went to his school. She fell for a Jew and was finished for the rest of her life. 'German girls,' Julius Streicher continued, 'when you go out into the world you are in great danger. The Jew to whom, according to his laws, you are free game will try to approach you in various ways. Repulse him, stay honest and good. It is not beautiful frocks, lipstick and the powder box that make you into German women. See that you remain clean spiritually, and eventually become good German mothers.' "

Then Julius Streicher gave a few typical examples of how the Jew carefully plans to break up the lives of the people; how he tries, by raping German women and girls, to lower the level of the race so as to render it unable to offer any resistance and thus helps to establish his world domination. At the end of his speech Herr Streicher requested the girls, in a truly fatherly manner, to come to him whenever they should be in need of help.

On 30 January 1933 the aged Field-Marshal Hindenburg handed over the reins of government to Hitler, and the fate of the Jews was settled. As the Attorney-General said:

Even before the power was firmly in their hands, the Nazis ini-tiated official measures of persecution against the Jews. On 1 April 1933, only two months after the inception of their rule, they organised the "Day of Boycott," to give symbolic form to the goal of uprooting the Jews and driving them out of the German Reich. Jews were beaten and imprisoned in concentration camps; Aryan customers were forbidden to enter Jewish places of business.

The economic boycott of the Jews continued, and was kept up until their final extermination. At a later stage it was enforced by means of legislation. Thus a series of laws excluded Jews from a number of professions. Law, medicine and teaching were closed to them. They were dismissed from the Army. In 1935, the Nuremberg laws were enacted, which forbade Jews to intermarry with Gentiles and deprived them of German citizenship. Later, they were driven out of industry and expelled from the entire German economy.

After the Nazis had succeeded in using anti-Semitism as an important instrument for securing their power in Germany itself, they planned to use the same poison of hate in order to unite the enemies of the Jews throughout the world, and to undermine by this means the opposition to the hegemony of Nazi Germany. And while German military might cast its shadow of terror on peoples and lands, silencing the voice of reason, anti-Semitism was exploited as a deliberate expedient to undermine the conscience of the nations, to excite the basest of passions, and to encourage Quisling and other collaborators. The Jew was described, in the official publications of the Party and the German Reich, as an enemy to the peace of the world, and it was suggested that all nations should join an alliance against Judaism.

Wherever the Nazi conqueror set foot, there awaited him a prepared group of adventurers, traitors to their country, underworld characters—sometimes plain assassins, who cast lustful eyes on Jewish property and lent their unclean hands to the destructive work. Wherever the German legions trod, they introduced the suppression of human freedom and the whipping up of Jew-hatred.

So far, however, there had been no public talk of exterminating the Jews, whatever else may have been in Hitler's mind. As the Attorney-General told the Court, the Nazis were still sensitive to world opinion, and the solution of the Jewish problem was forced emigration. Later, before it was considered safe to turn on the green light for annihilation, there was a transitional stage in which they planned a territorial solution which will be described later.

Large-scale Jewish emigration began shortly after the Nuremberg Laws and other wholesale restrictions had come into force, the economic boycott had started, and many thousands of Jews had been taken into so-called protective custody (*Schutzhaft*). The Nuremberg Laws, so-called because they were approved by a special session of the Reichstag assembled in the Nazis' "Holy City" in September 1935, deprived Germans with Jewish blood in their veins of their citizenship, prohibited marriages between Jews and nationals of German or kindred blood, and forbade the employment of German female servants in the household of a Jew.

The wholesale emigration of Jews to other countries was, nevertheless, turned to profitable account by the Nazis, for all Jewish emigrants were obliged to pay a tax amounting to a quarter of their income before they left the country, and to exchange the balance for "frozen marks" which automatically dropped to a small fraction of their nominal value.

The next step was to get rid of all Jews resident in Germany who had previously been Polish citizens. "These Poles," the Attorney-General said, "had cancelled their passports, but the Nazis decided to take advantage of their position and get rid of them. They were arrested on the orders of Reinhardt Heydrich, then head of the Security Police and the SD. Thus the first mass Jewish expulsion took place. The Jews were permitted to take only what they could carry, and were ordered to leave the rest of their property behind. Crowded into freight cars, they were transported to a point near the border, ordered out, and then chased through the fields in the direction of the Polish border. Men and women stumbled and fell, but were forced by kicks to rise and run on. Some lay dead where they had fallen.

"The Polish border-guard, unprepared for this sudden invasion, were helpless. The human flood broke through: the first expulsion had been a success."

These wholesale deportations provoked an incident in Paris only a few days later, which was to have tremendous repercussions in Germany and lead to an increase in the tempo of Jewish persecution. It is best described in the Attorney-General's own words.

Among those unfortunate deportees was a Jewish cobbler, Sendel Grynszpan. He too was expelled, in a state of utter destitution, with his wife and children. In bitter despair, the family wrote a postcard from Poland to their son, Herszel, who was then in Paris. This young lad of 17 decided that he would not remain silent in the face of such injustice. Though the entire world seemed indifferent to these crimes committed in broad daylight, he, Herszel Grynszpan, would not be still; he would at least try to avenge the injustice to his parents and family. On the morning of 7 November he bought a pistol, and that very day showed up at the German Embassy in Paris. He had determined to kill the Ambassador, but was ushered in to the Counsellor of the Legation, Ernst vom Rath, who asked him what he wanted. The young man's revolver barked twice, and vom Rath fell, severely wounded. To the Paris police Herszel Grynszpan declared: "I resolved to kill a member of the German Embassy as a sign of protest. I had to avenge the Jews, to draw attention of the world to what is happening in Germany."

Grynszpan did not know then that his sacrifice would be in vain. Not even the despairing act of this young Jew could shock the world. He himself was imprisoned in Paris and, after the invasion, fell into German hands. He was sent to Berlin for special investigation by the accused; no further trace of him has ever been found.

Vom Rath died of his wounds after two days. Immediately Heydrich issued emergency instructions to all units of the Gestapo to the effect that, following the attack on vom Rath, "anti-Jewish demonstrations may be expected." He therefore ordered the police to cooperate in the organisation of the demonstrations, to guide them, and to permit the destruction of Jewish property and the burning of synagogues—so long as it was possible to ensure that the flames would not spread to other neighbourhoods. All the property of the Jewish communities was to be confiscated.

Thus Nazi Germany revived in Europe the burning of the synagogues, which until then had been known only in the darkest days of the Middle Ages.

That night of terror, between 9 and 10 November, came to be known as the *Kristallnacht*.[4] The Nazi hooligans broke into Jew-

---

[4] The Crystal Night, sometimes called "The Night of Broken Glass."

ish homes, pillaged, destroyed and plundered. Thousands were imprisoned in concentration camps, in order to protect them from the wrath of the people. This was the first time the Nazis arrested Jews in large numbers at one time and put them in concentration camps. One hundred and one synagogues were burned and seventy-six destroyed; seven thousand and five hundred places of business were plundered. These figures are taken from an official report submitted by Heydrich to Goering at a meeting of Ministers devoted to Jewish affairs two days later, the minutes of which will be submitted to the Court. The damage to shop-windows alone came to six million marks, and what most bothered the participants in the meeting was the problem of the compensation for damages that the insurance companies would normally have to pay the Jews. It was thereupon decided quite simply that these companies would make their payments to the German Treasury, and the Jews would have to repair the damage at their own expense. Goering complained that a great deal of property had been destroyed; and when Heydrich also reported the deaths of thirty-five Jews, Goering said: "It would have been better if you had killed two hundred and not destroyed so much property."

There was a further exchange of opinions about the compelling of Jews to wear a distinctive badge. Towards the end of the meeting, Goering said: "I shall find an appropriate formula to force the Jews to pay a collective fine of one billion marks for their base criminal acts, etc. etc. That will hit them where it hurts. The swine won't carry out another murder so quickly. And in general, I must repeat: I wouldn't like to be a Jew in Germany."

The fine was imposed, and brutal legislation went into effect to deprive the Jews of all sources of livelihood.

On the *Kristallnacht* Eichmann was still in Vienna where he had been since March 1938.[5] It was not until he was appointed

---

[5] He was posted there immediately after the Anschluss with Austria with an *Einsatzkommando* of the SD under the command of Heydrich. When Heydrich, soon afterwards, was appointed Chief of the *Sicherheit Polizei* (SIPO) Eichmann became responsible for all Jewish questions in that office.

head of Amt IV B 4 in the Reich Security Head Office, always known by the initials RSHA, that he became the "managing director" of Jewish extermination. Nevertheless, at this Council of Ministers presided over by Goering, Heydrich gave a glowing report of the Accused's activities in Austria where, thanks to his zeal and efficiency, no less than 50,000 Jews had already emigrated. It was then decided to set up a central authority for Jewish emigration in Germany itself, and in January 1939 Goering put Heydrich in charge of it with an economist named Wohlthat as administrative assistant. Emigration was to be speeded up in Germany and in German Czechoslovakia, and as the Jews were expelled they were also plundered. Previously Goering had expressed doubts about the wisdom of getting rid of the geese that laid the golden eggs. This new scheme insured that the policy of Jewish emigration could be pursued without damaging the German economy. Ribbentrop caused an announcement to be made in a Foreign Office circular issued on 25 January 1939 that the final objective was the emigration of all the Jews in Germany. It had already proved quite profitable. According to Walther Funk, the Minister for Economics, two billion marks of the estimated seven billions of Jewish-owned property in Germany had already been paid over to the Treasury, and the transfer of the remaining five billion was not expected to be long delayed.

As the Attorney-General said:

These two aims—the physical liquidation of the Jews by expulsion or killing, and the pillage of their property—were thereafter fixed pillars of German policy. First expulsion and robbery, then murder and robbery—these were to remain closely associated, accompanying one another through all the phases of the holocaust, soon becoming so indistinguishable that one is at a loss to say which was the more important, which was being put into the service of the other. Henceforth, they are both to be part of the "final solution": to kill *and* to take possession were the two fundamental principles of the evil German plan. At all stages of the holocaust, in official reports filled with shocking details of cruel killings by strangulation, burning, hanging, and unimaginable tortures, there will always be found a twin section telling of the plunder of Jewish property.

He then proceeded to trace the course of the "final solution" through its various stages from the outbreak of war in September 1939. The pressure on German Jews to emigrate was not discontinued, he told the Court, and the plan was only changed as and when decisions were reached regarding their ultimate physical fate. At first it was not clear what was to be done with them.

They were to be got rid of (said the Attorney-General), but not completely; to be expelled, but a certain number had best be left to serve as hostages, so that the threat of their destruction might bring pressure on the world's rulers to submit to the German will. Hitler gave expression to this idea in one of his conversations with Rauschning, President of the Danzig Senate, and on 30 January 1939, he delivered his famous speech in the Reichstag predicting that, if the Jews controlling international world capital would again bring the nations to a world war, the result would not be the spread of Bolshevism and the subsequent victory of Judaism, but rather the annihilation of European Jewry.

Within the framework of this policy of expulsion, two schemes for a territorial solution of the problem were prepared. They both proved abortive. One was to deport all Jews to Madagascar, and in July 1940 the German Foreign Office was working on a memorandum suggesting that France, which had just signed an armistice with Hitler, would have to hand over Madagascar as one of the terms of the Peace Treaty and that a German military base would be established on the island and the Jews settled there, under a German mandate, as a hostage for the future good behaviour of their kinsmen in the U.S.A. Dannecker, who was later Eichmann's representative in Paris, had a hand in preparing this memorandum and he proposed that the resettlement should be carried out at the rate of a million Jews a year. No active steps, however, were ever taken to put this plan into execution, and it has not yet been satisfactorily established whether there was ever any intention to implement it or whether it was not merely camouflage for a much more sinister solution of the Jewish problem.

An attempt was made, however, to carry out the other scheme, known as the "Nisko Plan," for concentrating Jews into an area, called the Lublin zone, between the San and Vistula Rivers. Eichmann himself was implicated in this, for he expelled thousands of Jews from Vienna, Moravia and Bohemia, during the winter of 1939, as part of the scheme; and evidence of eye-witnesses was given, later in the trial, of the brutal treatment to which these unfortunate people were subjected en route to the zone, and how they were left there destitute. Eichmann dealt personally with the Nisko Plan and evidence was given that he actually visited the area and spent some days there. The plan was later called off by Goering, at the request of Hans Frank, the Governor-General of Poland, who complained that it was hindering the German war effort. Its abandonment, however, did not save the wretched refugees who all subsequently met their deaths in Belzec extermination camp.

According to the case for the prosecution, the invasion of Russia in June 1941 and the entry of America into the war six months later were turning points in the development of the Nazis' plans for the extermination of the Jews in Europe. The idea, however, was not a new one, and the minutes of a meeting called by Heydrich in September 1939, at which it was mentioned, were produced in evidence as a documentary exhibit later in the trial. A number of high-ranking SS officers were present including Eichmann himself. Heydrich made a distinction between the "long-range solution" of the Jewish problem, by which he undoubtedly meant extermination, and the immediate steps which were to be taken against the

Jews in Poland, large areas of which were already under occupation. In the country areas they were to be rounded up and concentrated in or near the larger cities and towns where there were good railway communications. This was to be carried out with the co-operation of the Councils of Elders which the invading Germans set up as they advanced farther into the country. In order to furnish some pretext for these measures it was claimed that the Jews had been looting and taking part in other illegal activities in opposition to the German forces.

Demanding that periodical situation-reports on the rounding-up operation should be forwarded to him, Heydrich told the delegates to the conference, before it dispersed, that in order to achieve these objectives he would order the immediate mobilising of all the forces of the Security Police and Security Services. "The Chiefs of the *Einsatzgruppen* active in the same neighbourhood," he said, "will keep in close touch with one another so that all the possible areas will be completely covered by the network."

In less than seven weeks after Hitler's armies invaded the Soviet Union, Goering gave Heydrich the following instructions:

> In order to complete the mission imposed on you by the order of 24 January 1939, to solve the problem of the Jews by means of emigration or evacuation in the way most likely, in the circumstances, to lead to the possible solution, I hereby instruct you to make all the necessary organisational, practical, and material preparations for a comprehensive solution of the Jewish question within the German area of influence in Europe.
>
> In so far as the other central authorities are concerned, they are to co-operate.
>
> I hereby instruct you further to submit to me without delay a comprehensive plan with respect to the organisational, practical, and material means necessary for the execution of the desired final solution of the Jewish question.

This appears to have been the first official mention of a *final* solution, but Heydrich regarded this directive as the signal to go ahead with the planning of extermination, and he put the accused, Eichmann, in charge of it.

Meanwhile, large deportations of Jews from Germany to the East were being carried out, and Eichmann prepared the general plan in his Berlin office. In August 1941 he wrote to the Foreign Office suggesting that it would be advisable to stop emigration having regard to "the preparations for the final solution of the problem of European Jewry." Before the year was out these "preparations" had been completed, and Eichmann was already writing about "the imminent final solution."

During the summer he had paid his first visit to Auschwitz on the instructions of Himmler. Rudolf Höss had been summoned to Berlin by the *Reichführer SS* and was interviewed alone. "The *Führer*," Himmler said, "has ordered me to solve the Jewish question once and for all and we, the SS, are to carry out the order." The existing extermination centres in the East were not large enough to cope with the operation, Himmler continued, and he had, therefore, decided that Auschwitz should be enlarged and modernised. Himmler had chosen Auschwitz because it had good railway communications and the whole area could easily be isolated and camouflaged. Himmler told Höss that he had been selected to be in charge of this important project, that it would be onerous and require absolute devotion to duty, whatever difficulties might arise, and that *Sturmbannführer* Eichmann, the head of Amt IV B 4, would call on him in the near future. Höss was to regard this information as top-secret, even from his superiors, and after discussing all the details on the spot with Eichmann, he was to submit plans for the new "installations." Himmler brought the interview to an end with these words: "The Jews are the sworn enemies of the German people and must be eradicated. Every Jew we can lay our hands on is to be destroyed now during the war without exception. If we cannot now obliterate the biological basis of Jewry, the Jews will one day destroy the German people."

Höss, in his autobiography, has given a detailed account of Eichmann's promised visit, which took place very shortly after the above interview.

He disclosed to me the plans for the operations as they affected the various countries concerned. I cannot remember the exact order in place. First was to come the eastern part of Upper Silesia and the neighbouring parts of Polish territory under German rule, then, depending on the situation, simultaneously Jews from Germany and Czechoslovakia, and finally the Jews from the West: France, Belgium and Holland. He also told me the approximate numbers of transports that might be expected, but I can no longer remember these.

We discussed the ways and means of effecting the extermination. This could only be done by gassing, since it would have been absolutely impossible to dispose by shooting of the large numbers of people that were expected, and it would have placed too heavy a burden on the SS men who had to carry it out, especially because of the women and children among the victims. Eichmann told me about the method of killing people with exhaust gases in lorries, which had previously been used in the East. But there was no question of being able to use this for these mass transports that were due to arrive in Auschwitz. Killing with showers of carbon monoxide while bathing, as was done with mental patients in some places in the Reich, would necessitate too many buildings and it was also very doubtful whether the supply of gas for a vast number of people would be available. We left the matter unresolved. Eichmann decided to try and find a gas which was in ready supply and which would not entail special installations for its use, and to inform me when he had done so. We inspected the area in order to choose a likely spot. We decided that a peasant farmstead situated in the north-west corner of what later became the third building sector at Birkenau would be the most suitable. It was isolated and screened by woods and hedges, and it was also not far from the railway. The bodies could be placed in long, deep pits dug in the nearby meadows. We had not at that time thought of burning the corpses. We calculated that, after gas-proofing the premises then available, it would be possible to kill about 800 people simultaneously with a suitable gas. These figures were borne out later in practice. Eichmann could not then give me the starting date for the operation because everything was still in the preliminary stages and the *Reichsführer SS* had not yet issued the necessary orders.

Eichmann then returned to Berlin to report to Himmler, and a few days later Höss forwarded detailed plans together with a full description of the "installations."

Towards the end of November 1941 a conference was held in Eichmann's office in Berlin, at which Höss was present, and reports were made by all Eichmann's representatives throughout occupied Europe on the present stage of the operation in their own areas and the difficulties which had arisen, such as the problem of housing the prisoners, the provision of adequate railway transport, and the proposed timetable. "D"-day could not yet be fixed as Eichmann had not yet discovered a suitable kind of gas. Eventually, however, this was found. It was known as Zyklon B and had been supplied by the firm of Tesch and Stabenow and was in constant use in Auschwitz for the destruction of vermin. During Höss's absence it had been used by one of his camp staff, on his own initiative, for killing a number of Russian commissars. He crammed them into the detention cells which were underground and, himself protected by a gasmask, discharged the Zyklon B into the cells killing the victims instantly. During a second visit to Auschwitz, which Eichmann made shortly after the November conference, Höss told him about this new use of the gas and it was then decided to use it for the mass-extermination programme. All was now arranged and Eichmann was ready to make a start. As the Attorney-General put it, "the plans had been formulated, the means had been determined. Instead of the Jews emigrating, they would in future be murdered." [6]

[6] Bruno Tesch and two others were tried by a British Military Court in Hamburg from 1–8 March 1946 for committing a war-crime in that they "at Hamburg, Germany, between 1 January 1941 and 31

Meanwhile a difficulty had arisen. Rosenberg, Minister in the occupied Eastern territories, had issued a directive on severe repressive measures to be taken against the Jews in the Baltic States, East Poland and various parts of the Soviet Union. These measures did not, however, include extermination. "The problem of the Jews," it was stated in the directive, "will find a solution in the whole of Europe at the end of the war." When a draft of this directive was seen by Heydrich he wrote at once to Rosenberg insisting that it should be altered. In this letter, written on 10 January 1942, Heydrich wrote, "in view of the fundamental policy for dealing with the Jewish problem which has been formulated by the Reich Security Head Office and is to be put into execution by *SS Sturmbannführer* Eichmann, I *must ask you to reprint your instructions.*" This letter was followed a few days later by a list of proposed amendments to Rosenberg's directive drawn up by Eichmann.

The Attorney-General quoted at length from this important document.

All measures in connection with the Jewish question in the occupied territories in the East are to be considered from the point of view that the Jewish question must be generally solved for the whole of Europe. Hence, such measures in the occupied territories in the East as contribute towards the final solution of the Jewish question and thereby the liquidation of Jewry must in no way be hindered. In the occupied territories in the East in particular, efforts are to be made to bring about an immediate solution of the Jewish question. . . . Any measures taken by the local population against the Jews are therefore not to be hindered. . . . So long as measures that will contribute to the liquidation of Jewry have not yet been taken, the local Jews are to be strictly separated from the rest of the population. . . . Free

March 1945, in violation of the laws and usages of war did supply poison-gas used for the extermination of allied nationals interned in concentration camps well knowing that the said gas was to be so used." The accused pleaded not guilty, but Tesch and one of the accused were found guilty. He was sentenced to death by hanging and the sentence was confirmed and put into effect.

movement is to be immediately stopped for all Jews. A transfer
to ghettos is to be carried out. . . . The watching of the boundaries between the ghetto and the outside world is the affair of
the police. . . . The measures that contribute to the liquidation
of Jewry are to be carried out without any consideration for economic needs. . . . All Jewish property is to be registered. Trans-
fers of property by Jews are to be prevented. . . .

Rosenberg, however, was not the only one who was inter-
fering. Hans Frank, the Governor-General of Occupied Poland, also wanted to solve the Jewish problem in his own way
and to take it out of the hands of the Gestapo. Other difficulties
had been met with elsewhere and some co-operation was obviously needed. Eichmann, therefore, proposed to his chief that
a conference should be called to settle all the points at issue, and
Heydrich agreed. The preparatory work for this conference
was all done by Eichmann, who also drew up the agenda and
decided who should attend. Those invited were asked to make
a special effort to be present "in view of the exceptional importance of the problem and the need to arrive at a unified
point of view."

The Attorney-General summarised the proceedings of the
conference, which assembled in the Berlin suburb of Wannsee
on 20 January 1942, in these words:

The conference took place on 20 January 1942, in the suburb
of Wannsee, near Berlin. The participants were the leading personalities, with the rank of Director-General, of the Ministries for
the Occupied Territories in the East, the Interior, Law, Foreign
Affairs, Economics, Race and Settlement; representatives of the
Party, the RSHA and the *Reichskanzlei*, and, of course, Eichmann. Heydrich delivered the main speech, from a brief prepared by the Accused. He recalled Goering's order and established at the outset, in order to prevent any doubts, that it was
his Ministry that was centrally responsible for the execution of
"the final solution" everywhere, without any geographical limitations. He mentioned "the practical experiments" that had been
carried out in the East, the lessons from which were of the ut-

most importance for "the final solution." After having briefly outlined the steps taken thus far "in the battle against this enemy" for the purpose of forcing the Jews out of the areas in which the German people lived and which constituted its *Lebensraum*, he stated that a halt had been called to this emigration at the order of Himmler, and that now would begin, according to the *Führer's* orders, the evacuation of the Jews to the East, the ultimate goal being "the final solution."

Heydrich then listed the countries to be considered for this "final solution," including, besides all the countries under Nazi occupation, Britain, Ireland, Sweden, Switzerland, Spain, Turkey, and the entire area of the Soviet Union, and arrived at a total of eleven million Jews to be included in it. In this list, Estonia already appeared as *"Judenrein"* (clear of Jews).

And this is how the problem would be solved: "Under suitable management, the Jews will be brought, in the course of the final solution, in a convenient way to labour units in the East. The Jews capable of working will be transported in long labour columns, men and women separate, to build roads in that region; as a result of which, no doubt, a large part of them will fall out through natural losses. Those who will ultimately remain, who will surely be those who will have great powers of resistance, must be given special treatment (*Sonderbehandlung*), because they will constitute a nucleus for the building of a new Jewry.

"For the practical execution of the final solution, Europe will be combed from West to East. In the occupied territories and the countries within our sphere of influence in Europe, the officer designated by the Security Police will work in co-ordination with the appropriate representative of the Foreign Ministry."

We shall prove (the Attorney-General continued) that this was none other than Adolf Eichmann, and we shall prove that the meaning of "special treatment" was murder.

There was discussion, further, of what to do with children of mixed marriages. This problem troubled the exterminators. The principle was established that children of mixed marriages of the first degree—namely, in which one of the parents was Jewish—would be classified as full Jews, excluding men who had married German women and had children, or those with respect to whom there were exceptional circumstances and for whom the higher institutions of the Party and the State had specially interceded; but such circumstances were to be examined with great care.

These exceptional cases were to be permitted to stay in Germany on condition that they gave consent to their own sterilisation.

Instructions were also given with respect to children of mixed marriages of the second degree, the mixed couples themselves, and various categories of borderline cases.

The Economics Ministry asked that, for the time being, Jews working in vital war industries should not be evacuated, and Heydrich agreed. Dr. Bühler, representative of the Polish General-Government, gave notice that there the final solution had already begun, asked that the problem be solved with all possible dispatch, and declared that the majority of the Jews in his region, about two and a half million, were quite incapable of working. He agreed that the implementation of the final solution be entrusted to the Gestapo, and promised full support from the General-Government. He asked only for the work to begin as rapidly as possible.

The decisions made at the Wannsee conference enabled the programme of extermination to get into its stride and from then on Eichmann was in sole charge. He and his representatives abroad began combing Europe from the Pyrenees to the Urals to herd the Jews together and drive them to destruction.

There is reason to believe that Eichmann had in his possession a written order from Hitler for the extermination of the Jews, but the prosecution admitted that no such order had ever been found and that it could not, therefore, be produced in evidence. Nevertheless, his assistant, Wisliceny, in evidence at the Nuremberg trial of major German war-criminals, testified that Eichmann had shown him a letter from Himmler giving the substance of the missing order:

The first time I learned of any order (Wisliceny said) which directed the annihilation of all Jews was from Eichmann in the summer of 1942. In the spring of 1942 about 17,000 Jews were taken from Slovakia to Poland for slave labour. This was the result of an agreement made with the Slovakian Government which had also asked whether the families of these workers could also be taken to Poland. At first Eichmann refused this request, but early in May 1942 he told me that in future entire families could be taken to Poland, and at the same time he gave the Slovakian Government an assurance that these Jews would be humanely and decently treated in the Polish ghettos. This was the special wish of the Slovakian Government. As a result of this assurance about 35,000 Jews were sent to Poland from Slovakia. The Slovakian Government made every effort to ensure that these Jews would be humanely treated, and the Prime Minister asked Eichmann to allow a Slovakian delegation to enter the areas to which the Jews had been sent in order to inspect them and see that they were being properly treated. At the end of July or early in August I went to see Eichmann in Berlin and begged him to grant this request. I pointed out to him that there were already rumours abroad that all the Jews in Poland were being exterminated and I reminded him that the Pope had intervened with the Slovakian Government on their behalf. I told Eichmann that if these rumours were in fact true it would seriously injure our prestige abroad. After a long discussion he told me that this request for a delegation to visit the Polish ghettos could not be granted under any circumstances whatsoever, and in reply to my question, "Why?" he said that most of these Jews were not alive. I asked him who had given him instructions for them to be killed and he referred me to an order of Himmler. I then begged him to show me the order because I found it impossible to believe that there could be a written order of this kind. Eichmann told me that if it would salve my conscience he could show me the order. He took a small file of documents from his safe, turned over the pages and showed me a letter from Himmler to the Chief of the Security Police and the SD. The gist of the letter was roughly as follows: That the *Führer* has ordered the final solution of the Jewish question. The Chief of Security Police and SD and the Inspector of Concentration Camps have been entrusted with the execution of this final solution. All Jewish men and women who are able to work will be temporarily exempted from the final solution and so long as they are fit for work they will be used for work in the concentration camps. This letter was signed by Himmler. I am certain of this, for I am familiar with his signature.

Eichmann then went on to explain to me what the final solution meant. He said that it was a euphemism for the planned biological annihilation of the Jewish race in the Eastern territories. He also told me that within the RSHA he was personally entrusted with the execution of the order and had received full authority from the Chief of the Security Police to enable him to carry it out. It was perfectly clear to me that this order meant death for millions of people and I said, "God grant that our enemies never have an opportunity of doing the same to the German people." Eichmann told me not to be sentimental, it was a *Führerbefehl* and must be carried out. The order remained in force until October 1944 when Himmler issued a counter-order forbidding the further annihilation of the Jews.

Wisliceny is no longer alive, having been hanged in Bratislava after his trial there in 1948, and no corroboration of his evidence is, therefore, available. But it is beyond question, as the Attorney-General told the Court, "that the unusual character of his appointment raised Adolf Eichmann to a unique position invested with tremendous authority, enabling him to contact directly heads of Governments and Ministers, and to issue orders and instructions in all matters relating to the destruction of the Jewish people."

Everything relating to the programme of extermination and the plans to implement it were his direct concern, few details were so minor as to be beneath his notice. Yet, although he attended all the important conferences on the final solution, and did most of the donkey work in connection with them, he never appears to have addressed the delegates at any time according to the minutes which have been preserved. The possible reasons for this were dealt with by the Attorney-General.

It may be because his superiors, Himmler and Heydrich, who had chosen him after careful consideration to do the work of butchery, did not want to have him speak in the company of the professors and university graduates who usually took part in such consultations. It may be that he himself took no great interest in talking, having devoted himself to his work with complete fanaticism, zeal and single-mindedness. To achieve his goal, he would not hesitate to come into conflict with, and sometimes even to mislead, men in positions higher than his own in the Nazi hierarchy. But this did not bother him at all, since he sheltered behind the all-powerful Himmler. Ministers and envoys of occupied States he treated with open contempt. By means of persuasion, threats or force, he got from them what he wanted, the enactment of laws depriving the Jews of human and civil rights, their rounding up and their concentration in ghettos and finally their eventual deportation to the extermination centres. Everywhere he adapted himself to the needs and circumstances of the moment. We shall see him visiting and inspecting the ghettos in Warsaw and Lodz. We shall follow him as he travels in the autumn of 1939 to visit Globocnik, Chief of the SS and Police in the Lublin region, to convey to him personally the secret order for the physical extermination of the Jews. He was also in Treblinka and Chelmno, where gas was used to kill the Jews. In the latter camp he witnessed the parade of naked Jews who had been stripped of their clothing and were waiting their turn to enter the vans into which exhaust pipes pumped gas. He looked on as gold teeth were extracted from the mouths of his dead victims. When in Minsk he saw his SS men shooting their victims in the back so that they fell into graves which they had first been made to dig. He saw these SS units murdering women and children. He saw them operating against the Jews in the vicinity of Lwow where, to use his own words, blood spurted from the mass grave "as from a spring."

But these rough and ready methods did not satisfy him. They were not, as he once said, "elegant" enough for the purpose. A more "elegant" method of extermination was soon put into operation: the gas-chambers and crematoria of Auschwitz and other camps which he visited on a number of occasions to inspect the "installations" as they were euphemistically called.

It was also from his department of RSHA that all the directives were issued regarding the death transports. This was the name by which the convoys of Jews en route to the gas-chambers were known. All Jews were included, unless exempted by Eichmann's office, and full reports were rendered to him after each convoy had arrived at its final destination. Eichmann, therefore, knew at any given moment who had been sent to Auschwitz, who were ear-marked for execution and who had already been killed.

His office became the central authority for all the Reich Ministries in respect of Jewish affairs. There is ample evidence that in regard to such matters everyone had to apply to Eichmann and accept his decision. When the German Foreign Office wished to save 30,000 Jews of foreign nationality from death so that they could be exchanged for Germans living in their respective countries, it was to Eichmann that the application had to be made. When, at one stage, Eichmann considered that many wealthy Jews were managing to leave Rumania unharmed, he wrote to the German Foreign Office protesting that if this continued there would soon be none but impoverished Jews left in Rumania.

In order to implement the final solution of the Jewish problem according to plan, and without interruption, I must request that suitable means be taken to stop this practice and that I be kept notified of the position from time to time.

The Attorney-General then dealt with the effort made by Eichmann, aided and abetted by the Mufti of Jerusalem, to prevent Jewish emigration to Palestine. Eichmann had travelled to Palestine before the war in order to contact the Mufti, but the visit had not been successful and ended ignominiously, some forty-eight hours after it had begun, with the expulsion of Eichmann by the British authorities. From 1942 onwards, however, these two anti-Jewish fanatics met quite frequently, for the Mufti was leaving no stone unturned to ensure that no Jews were allowed to emigrate to Palestine and that they should all be sent to the gas-chambers. Shortly after his arrival in Germany, the Mufti had visited Amt IV B 4 in Berlin and had been shown round it by Eichmann. Haj Amin el Husseini had been greatly impressed by Eichmann's statistical information about the Jewish population in the various countries of Europe. It was, without doubt, information obtained from Eichmann that prompted the Mufti to write the following letter from Rome to the Hungarian Foreign Minister in June 1943, almost nine months before the Germans occupied Hungary.

ROME, 28 JUNE 1943

His Excellency
The Minister of Foreign Affairs for Hungary.

Your Excellency,

You no doubt know of the struggle between the Arabs and Jews of Palestine, what it has been and what it is, a long and bloody fight, brought about by the desire of the Jews to create a national home, a Jewish State in the Near East, with the help and protection of England and the United States. In fact, behind it lies the hope which the Jews have never relinquished, namely the domination of the whole world through this important, strategic centre, Palestine. In effect, their programme has, among other purposes, always aimed at the encouragement of Jewish emigration to Palestine and the other countries of the Near East. However, the war, as well as the understanding which the members of the Three-Power Pact have of the responsibility of the Jews for its outbreak and their evil intentions towards these countries which protected them until now—all these are reasons for placing them under such vigilant control as will definitely stop their emigration to Palestine or elsewhere.

Lately I have been informed of the uninterrupted efforts made by the English and the Jews to obtain permission for the Jews living in your country to leave for Palestine via Bulgaria and Turkey.

I have also learned that these negotiations have been successful, since some Hungarian Jews have had the satisfaction of emigrating to Palestine via Bulgaria and Turkey and a group of these Jews arrived in Palestine toward the end of last March. The Jewish Agency, which supervises the execution of the Jewish programme, has published a bulletin which contains important information on the current negotiations between the English

Government and the Governments of other interested states to send the Jews of Balkan countries to Palestine. The Jewish Agency quotes, among other things, its receipt of a sufficient number of immigration certificates for 900 Jewish children to be transported from Hungary, accompanied by 100 adults.

To authorize these Jews to leave your country under the above circumstances and in this way would by no means solve the Jewish problem, and would certainly not protect your country against their evil influence—far from it—for this escape would make it possible for them to communicate and combine freely with their racial brethren in enemy countries in order to strengthen their position, and to exert a more dangerous influence on the outcome of the war, especially since, as a consequence of their long stay in your country, they are necessarily in a position to know many of your secrets and also about your war-effort. All this comes on top of the terrible damage done to the friendly Arab nation which has taken its place at your side in this war and which cherishes for your country the most sincere feelings and the very best wishes.

This is the reason why I ask your Excellency to permit me to draw your attention to the necessity of preventing the Jews from leaving your country for Palestine; and if there are reasons which make their removal necessary, it would be indispensable and infinitely preferable to send them to other countries *where they would find themselves under active control,* for example, in Poland, in order thereby to protect yourself from their menace and avoid the consequent damage.

Yours, etc.

What the Mufti expected to happen to these Jews when they got to Poland is left in no doubt by a document which was discovered after the war amongst the official papers which he left behind when he fled from Germany. It was the draft of an official joint declaration which the Mufti wanted Hitler and Mussolini to make. It was, in effect, a Balfour Declaration in reverse. Clause 7 reads as follows:

Germany and Italy recognise the illegality of the "Jewish Home in Palestine." They accord to Palestine and to other Arab countries the right to resolve the problem of the Jewish elements in Palestine and other Arab countries in accordance with the interests of the Arabs, *and by the same method that the question is now being settled in the Axis countries.* Under this agreement no Jewish immigration into the Arab countries should be permitted.

Again, a year after his letter to the Minister of Foreign Affairs for Hungary, the Mufti wrote to Ribbentrop on the same subject.

BERLIN, 25 JULY 1944

His Excellency, Minister for Foreign Affairs.

Your Excellency,

I have previously called the attention of your Excellency to the constant attempts of the Jews to emigrate from Europe in order to reach Palestine, and asked your Excellency to undertake the necessary steps so as to prevent the Jews from emigrating. I had also sent you a letter, under date of 5 June 1944, in regard to the plan for an exchange of Egyptians living in Germany with Palestinian Germans, in which I asked you to exclude the Jews from this plan of exchange. I have, however, learned that the Jews did depart on 2 July 1944, and I am afraid that further groups of Jews will leave for Palestine from Germany and France to be exchanged for Palestinian Germans.

This exchange on the part of the Germans would encourage the Balkan countries likewise to send their Jews to Palestine. This step would be incomprehensible to the Arabs and Moslems after your Excellency's declaration of 2 November 1943 that "the destruction of the so-called Jewish national home in Palestine is an immutable part of the policy of the greater German Reich," and it would create in them a feeling of keen disappointment.

It is for this reason that I ask your Excellency to do all that is necessary to prohibit the emigration of Jews to Palestine, and in this way your Excellency would give a new practical example of the policy of the naturally allied and friendly Germany towards the Arab nation.

Yours, etc.

The Attorney-General gave many other examples of the complete authority with which Eichmann was invested and the thoroughness with which he did his job. He was forever urging his staff to step up the rate of deportation and he accepted no excuses for failure.

He also dealt personally with all applications for exceptional treatment made by foreign governments, by the German Foreign Office or by individuals. Almost invariably he callously rejected them. On occasions, when the German Foreign Office interceded with him to save individual Jews in whom, for some reason, the occupation authorities were interested, his answer was always that for reasons of principle the request could not be granted. Sometimes other reasons were given. Two Jewesses living in Poland were not allowed to leave because they knew too much about the methods used to carry out the deportations. A report by General von Stulpnagel, commanding the German Occupation Forces in France, for permission to allow the entry of German Jews to join their relatives in occupied France was also turned down by Eichmann. The Jews, he wrote, must not be allowed to evade deportation to the East. The German delegate to the Serbian Puppet Government, Herr Benzler, asked Amt IV B 4 for instructions regarding the treatment of Serbian Jews. He said that it was dangerous to keep them in camps because of the threat of partisan attacks, and there was a shortage of trains for transporting them to Poland and Russia. A photostat of this letter was produced as a documentary exhibit at the trial, and in the margin there was written in Rademacker's handwriting—*"Eichmann schlägt erschiessen vor"*—"Eichmann suggests shooting," and when Rademacker wanted to confirm this, and spoke to Eichmann on the telephone about it, all he heard was, "shoot them," and the telephone receiver was replaced.

"Thus with two words," the Attorney-General said, "he sentenced to death some 10,000 Jews. Such was the man and such was his power."

Eichmann stopped up every hole through which the "Jewish

vermin" might escape to freedom. Particularly callous was his handling of an application from the German Foreign Office in May 1943 regarding a certain Mario Sasson of Zagreb, who had been sent to Auschwitz and whose wife was a non-Jewish German with three brothers serving in the German Army on the Russian Front. As Frau Sasson was in desperate straits Eichmann was asked to have her husband transferred to Germany and re-united with his family. He evaded this request by delaying his answer for a long while until eventually he was able to write and say that Sasson was no longer alive.

No part of his bloody work was so shocking as the deportation of about one million children to the concentration camps where they were either murdered or died of starvation. Those who travelled with their parents, as some did, were often separated by force from them when the train reached its destination, torn to pieces before their mother's eyes, or had their heads smashed in against a wall. Speaking of this the Attorney-General said:

> You will hear evidence of deeds which the mind of man does not want to believe. You will hear about little ones thrown out of windows of hospitals when they failed to respond to orders that they report for parade.

We shall present to you the instructions issued by Eichmann and his office about the transport of children. One of these said that the children were to be divided among the transports intended for Auschwitz. Children of fourteen were considered "independent" for purposes of transport to the extermination camps. Nor can we say who suffered the more terrible fate; those who died, or those who concealed themselves in every conceivable hiding-place and crevice, who lived in perpetual terror of expulsion, who survived through the kindness of Christian neighbours who agreed to hide them. Children would come home from the schools and centres organised by the community to find their parents' home was empty, for they had been sent by some "*Aktion*" or "operation" to their deaths; and the apartment had in the meantime been occupied by others.

You will hear evidence of tender infants pressed by their

mothers to their bodies in the gas-chambers so that they should not inhale the poisonous gas, until the executioners came and threw them alive into the furnaces or the waiting graves.

Those unhappy children who lived for years in fear of the beating of a rifle butt on their door; who had been sent by their parents to the woods in an attempt to save them, who had been taught to choke their tears and sighs because a weeping child would be shot on the spot; who had been ordered to deny their origins and pretend to be Christians; who saw their fathers being lashed with whips before their eyes; in front of whom "discussions" would be carried on by the German executioners as to who should be killed first—the father or the son; who went to the open grave with "Hear, O Israel!" on their lips—these children and youths . . . are the very soul and hard core of the indictment. Those Anne Franks and Justine Drangers and a million others.

We shall present the pictures of some of those children swollen with hunger, frightened and crushed, with eyes frozen with terror. We shall show you the photographs of their starved bodies thrown into manure wagons, of the helpless little ones on the threshold of the extermination chambers.

It is no wonder that the German Foreign Ministry passed on for Eichmann's information the warning, broadcast by London Radio, that those responsible for the murders in Auschwitz would be brought to judgment. Even on the verge of the German collapse in April 1945, in that atmosphere of the twilight of the gods, when the Allies from the East, West and South were closing in—Eichmann still told a German Red Cross representative that he could not agree to the more humanitarian methods of dealing with Jews then being considered by Himmler.

Many millions of non-Jews also perished in the Great War. We shall not attempt to decide here, at this trial, which of the acts of hostility were contrary to the laws and customs of war as laid down by international law. But we shall say, with all the emphasis at our command, that the extermination of the Jewish people was not connected with any military action. It cannot be compared with the bombing of cities or with submarine warfare. These were acts of war, and whether they were legitimate or not they were carried out in connection with and in the process of waging war. The extermination of the Jews had no connection with the war effort of Germany and her allies. The extermination was carried out *at the time* of the war, when the battle-smoke to some extent covered and concealed the atrocities; but it was not done in pursuit of war, nor was it impelled by the needs or necessities of war.

Everything possible was done to keep the terrible secret from the rest of the world, and their ultimate fate from the victims themselves. Hitler's orders were that no single person should know more than was absolutely necessary to enable him to carry out his duties, and euphemisms were used to cover up the murderous activities of the SS. First and foremost was the expression *Sonderbehandlung* (Special Treatment) which meant murder in some form or other. The Court in the Wilhelmstrasse Trial, in Nuremberg, held that "special treatment," in the phraseology of the Third Reich, meant death, or at best, confinement in a concentration camp, the latter being, in most instances, the substitution of a lingering death for a quick one. The Wiener Library, however, which carefully examined all the available evidence on this subject, in response to an inquiry received from a court in Western Germany did not agree with the above view. The Library's reply to this inquiry stated that the expression "meant in all cases, *without exception*, enforced death," and that its meaning had never changed. The term was well-known to all senior SS officers, though it may well be that more junior officers and the rank and file were ignorant of its sinister meaning.

Many ingenious devices were used by the Nazis to delude their victims into believing that they were only being taken to labour camps. Some of these deceptions were described by the Attorney-General:

> The Nazis used to camouflage some of the gas-vans as caravans; they built a sham railway station at Treblinka so that it appeared to be nothing more than a transit point. Over the gates of Auschwitz camp there appeared the words *"Arbeit Macht Frei"* (Work Makes Free). The camp prisoners were made to

write postcards to their relatives saying that they were in good health, but the postcards usually reached their destination only after the senders had been gassed and burned in the crematoria.

But truth will out, and the dread secret could not be kept indefinitely. What did the German people know of these things? It has often been suggested that they knew nothing. That probability is as unlikely as its converse, that they knew everything. There is good reason to suppose that many Germans knew a great deal about what went on in concentration camps. There were still more who had grave suspicions, and perhaps even misgivings, but who preferred to lull their consciences by remaining in ignorance.

As the shortage of labour grew more acute it became the policy to free German women criminals and asocial elements from the concentration camps to work in German factories. It is difficult to believe that such women told no one of their experiences. In these factories the forewomen were German civilians who were in contact with the internees and able to speak to them. Forewomen from Auschwitz, who subsequently went to the Siemens sub-factory at Ravensbrück, had formerly been working at Siemens in Berlin. They met women whom they had known in Berlin and told them what they had seen in Auschwitz. Is it reasonable to suppose that these stories were never repeated? Germans who, during the war, indulged in careless talk used to be told: "You had better be careful or you'll go up the chimney." To what could that refer but the crematoria?

In many factories, where parties from concentration camps worked, the technicians were not members of the armed forces and the foremen were not SS men. They went home overnight after supervising the work of the prisoners every day. Did they never discuss with their relatives and friends when they got home what they had seen and heard during the day? And what of the SS executive-staff and guards? It is true that they had all signed statements binding themselves never to reveal to anyone outside the concentration camp service anything which they had seen inside their camp. But is it reasonable to believe that none of them was human enough to break that undertaking?

Höss himself said of Auschwitz, "The foul and nauseating stench from the continuous burning of bodies permeated the entire area and all the people living in the surrounding communities knew that exterminations were going on at the concentration camp." Day after day train loads of victims travelled in cattle-trucks over the whole railway system of the Reich on their way to extermination centres. They were seen by hundreds of railway workers who knew whence they had come and whither they were going. Whatever horrors remained hidden behind the damp walls, such things as these went on in broad daylight.[7]

How much of all this was known to Germany's enemies and in neutral European countries, and how soon, is not definitely known, but there is reliable evidence that detailed information about what was going on in the Polish extermination camps was given to Baron von Otter, the First Secretary of the Swedish Embassy in Berlin, in September 1942 by an SS Colonel Dr. Kurt Gerstein. The first time that the general public ever heard his name mentioned was on the occasion of the trial in Germany in 1955 of Dr. Gerhard Peters, the former managing director of the German Association for the Extermination of Vermin (generally known by the initials DEGESCH). Peters was tried for aiding and abetting mass-murder by supplying gas, well knowing the purpose for which it was to be used, and he stated during the proceedings that he had negotiated the sale with Gerstein who was then head of the Waffen SS Institute of Hygiene, but as he knew then that Gerstein was a member of the anti-Nazi resistance he naturally assumed that the gas would only be used for innocent purposes.

This was, unquestionably, true. Gerstein had been an anti-Nazi and had, in fact, in 1936 been imprisoned for an alleged

[7] See *The Scourge of the Swastika*, by the author, pages 183–185.

offence "against the security of the Reich." On 5 May, three days before the unconditional surrender of the German armed forces, Gerstein gave himself up to two officers of the American 6th Army Group. He admitted that he had formerly been the head of the Disinfection Service of the *Waffen SS*, said that he had some important information to give them, and handed in a statement written in French. He also handed over a set of invoices for the purchase of Zyklon B gas, which was used at Auschwitz and other extermination camps.[8]

These invoices were made out in his name. Gerstein, who later committed suicide in a French prison, always asserted that his only reason for joining the *Waffen SS* in 1941 was to find out the truth about the euthanasia programme. He had heard about the massacre of lunatics in Hadamar, and his one desire was "to gain an insight into this machinery and then shout it to the whole world." As he wrote to his wife in prison shortly before his death, "my activity in the Gestapo Head Office was from the first that of an agent on behalf of the Confessional Church." He then told his captors that on the way back from Warsaw, to report to Eichmann about a visit that he had just paid to Globocnik, an opportunity arose for him to get information over to a neutral Government about the terrible atrocities being committed against the Jews in Poland by the Nazis.

It so happened that the First Secretary of the Swedish Embassy in Berlin, Baron von Otter, was a fellow passenger on the Warsaw-Berlin train. Gerstein wrote an account of his meeting with von Otter:

Under the fresh impression of the terrible things which I had just seen I told him everything and asked him to report it at once to his own Government and, through diplomatic channels, to the Allies, as every day was bound to cost the lives of thousands more people. He asked me for a reference and I gave him the name of Dr. Otto Dibelius, an intimate friend of Dr. Niemöller and a member of the Church Resistance against the Nazis.

[8] These invoices were produced in evidence at this trial.

Gerstein met Baron von Otter twice again at the Swedish Embassy. The Baron had, meanwhile, reported to his own Government and told Gerstein that the information given had had a considerable bearing on Swedish-German relations. Gerstein had also tried to make a report to the Papal Ambassador in Berlin. He was asked at the Embassy whether he was a serving soldier, and on saying that he was he was requested to leave.

This statement made by Gerstein was confirmed in all essential details by several witnesses at the trial of Peters, including Dr. Dibelius. The Reverend Doctor, now the Protestant Bishop of Berlin, testified that he had known Gerstein before the war, when he was a member of the Protestant Youth Movement, as a profoundly religious young man and a Christian. He then went on to say that one day Gerstein, dressed in SS uniform, had visited him. When asked by the astonished Dibelius what on earth had made him join the SS, Gerstein had explained, although Dibelius must, at the time, have found it difficult to believe, that he had not done so from any "inner conviction," but because he considered it important that an authentic report should be given by "someone watching from the other side."

The Attorney-General then proceeded to deal in detail with the process of extermination carried out under Eichmann's direction in the various European countries under German occupation.

Eichmann's guilt, he said, lay in the planning, initiation, organisation and execution of the crimes specified in the indictment. The prosecution would prove his complicity in the final solution of the Jewish problem; the part he played in the implementation of this criminal policy and his role as administrator, director, and commander of the operation, in addition to the part he played as partner and accomplice of others in carrying out the extermination programme.

In support of these charges the Prosecution produced extensive documentary and oral evidence. The central archives of the Gestapo, including those of Eichmann's department, have never been found, but documentary evidence is to be found in the extensive archives of the German Ministry for Foreign Affairs and other Ministries of the Third Reich, in correspondence between the Accused and his partners in crime and in the offices of the Security Police throughout Germany and in occupied Europe. There are, in addition, many documents and reports published by War-Crime Commissions in Poland, France, Holland, Denmark and Belgium and a great deal of material is available from the records of the various war-crime tribunals, including the International Military Tribunal which tried major German war-criminals at Nuremberg. Documents have also been preserved by private individuals and many of them were placed at the disposal of the Prosecution.

Although millions of Jews were killed many survived, and several of them were called to describe what they themselves saw, heard and suffered. Nevertheless, when all the evidence had been called, both oral and documentary, the Prosecution would only have given, as the Attorney-General said, a "pale reflection of the colossal human and national tragedy which the Jews suffered at Hitler's hands."

III

The Final Solution
in Poland

THE FIRST COUNTRY with which the Prosecution dealt was, not unnaturally, Poland which was the first to bear the brunt of Germany's blitzkrieg methods at the outbreak of World War II.

Ever since the Treaty of Versailles Poland had been singled out by Hitler for special hatred. By this Treaty certain territory, which the Germans had annexed at the time of the second partition of Poland, was restored to the Poles. German hatred of the Poles was not only due to the fact that they objected to the separation of East Prussia from the rest of Germany by the creation of the Danzig corridor which justly gave Poland access to the sea, but also to the German attitude that the Slav people were inferior beings, whose historic destiny it was to serve the Master Race. It was the aim of Nazi policy, when Poland was over-run and conquered, to subjugate the whole nation and never allow it to recover. This object was stated by Hans Frank, the Reich Governor-General of Poland, in these words:

The Government-General will serve only as a reservoir of manual labour. Workers required by the Reich will be brought from the Government-General.[1] . . . There will be only one

[1] The Government-General of Poland, formed by a decree of Hitler of 12 October 1939, consisted of what was left of Poland, after

master for the Poles—the Germans. . . . and therefore all the representatives of the Polish intelligentsia are to be destroyed. . . .

We shall see to it that the Poles do not die of hunger, but they must not reach any higher level. . . . If once the Poles reach a higher level of development, they will cease to be the manpower reservoir which we need. . . . The humblest German worker or farmer must always be as least ten per cent higher than any Pole.

If that was to be the fate of all the Poles it is not surprising that there was still worse in store for the Polish Jews. There was never any doubt, from the very beginning, that they were to be exterminated. The only disagreement on this, between the Governor-General and Eichmann's department at RSHA, was when and how it should be done. Frank wished to destroy the Jews only after they had contributed toil and sweat to German industry. The orders from Berlin were for immediate extermination, and the Gestapo, acting on its own responsibility and without consulting the Government-General, proceeded to put them into effect.

Frank complained bitterly, at a conference which he held on 9 December 1942, that the Jewish labour force was being taken away from him:

It obviously makes our work very difficult when, in the middle of this war, an order comes to send all the Jews for extermination. The responsibility for this does not rest with the administration of the Government-General. The order to exterminate Jews comes from higher levels. . . . Taking the Jews away has caused immense difficulties in the labour field. . . . Now the order comes to take the Jews out of the munition factories.

He did not make this protest because he wanted to save them from destruction. His views on the Jews had been clearly expressed more than a year previously at another conference

Russia had taken her share and Germany had annexed her former provinces, plus some additional territory in West Poland.

when he said, speaking "as a veteran National Socialist," that if the Jewish community in Europe were to survive the war, after the Germans had sacrificed their dearest blood to hold Europe, then they would have achieved only partial success. He had, basically, only one expectation of the Jews, namely that they should disappear. "What are we to do with the Jews?" he said. "Do you think that we shall settle them in the Ostland? Why all this talk? We must liquidate them. We must take steps to exterminate them. The Government-General must be as free from Jews as is the Reich." Later he was to make this apologetic note in his diary: "I could not, of course, eliminate all lice nor all Jews in only a year, but in the course of time this end will be attained."

The Nazis began to put their plan for the extermination of the Jews into operation from the first day of the invasion of Poland. Jews were first subjected to discriminatory legislation; their right to own property was taken away, and they had to wear special markings on their clothing; ghettos were instituted; valuables confiscated; and even the Jews' scale of rations was less than that of the other inhabitants. They performed forced labour and were habitually terrorised and severely punished for trivial offences. The persecution continued and increased in intensity as time went on. Hostages were taken, and the Jews were consistently derided and abused. Their synagogues were desecrated and set on fire. On one occasion after a synagogue in Wloclawek had been burned down, the local Jewish leaders were arrested and forced to sign a confession that they themselves had set it on fire, and the Jewish community in Wloclawek were fined 100,000 zlotys. Within the first three weeks of the Nazi occupation hundreds of synagogues had been burned down, blown up, or converted into prisons or public lavatories.

Their shops were looted and executions began. Jew hunts were organised, and when a rabbi was caught his beard was either cut off or pulled out by the roots. The Jews were made to perform the filthiest and most degrading tasks. To clean out latrines with their hands. To collect horse-droppings in the streets and fill their caps and pockets with them.

They were also made to make a pile of their holy books in the market-place of many towns, set fire to them and dance round the bonfires until the flames died down. Photographs of these spectacles were taken for publication in *Der Stürmer* and other Nazi papers.

Their women could be violated with impunity, for the Nazis' principles and their regulations concerning the purity of German blood did not prevent them from systematically raping young Jewish girls. When *Gruppenführer* Vende of the Gestapo in Warsaw was reminded by the Jewish Council of Elders of these decrees, he replied, "This is war and theories are dead for the time being." One disgusting orgy took place in the house of a leading Jewish citizen in a town named Szekeszswski. Forty young girls were abducted on a road in the Warsaw Ghetto and taken to his house which was a billet for German officers. There, after being forced to drink, the girls were ordered to undress and dance for the officers' amusement. After being beaten, abused, and raped they were eventually released in the early hours of the morning.

During the search of a Jewish shopkeeper's house in Warsaw the SS found a dresscoat in a wardrobe. The owner of the house, who was an old man, was made to put on the coat, pushed through the front-door and chased down the street while being beaten with horse-whips. On another occasion some Jewish girls were, for no reason, arrested in the street, taken to SS headquarters and there made to wash their captors' feet and then drink the water.

While taking part in incidents of this kind was meat and drink to the barbarians of the SS it did not find favour with the German High Command in Poland. The following is an extract from a report made by General Blaskowitz, a senior commander in the East, and submitted to Field-Marshal von Brauchitsch when he was still Commander-in-Chief of the *Wehrmacht:*

The methods and means of slaughter employed are most damaging to us, complicating the problem, and making matters far worse than they might have been if a sensible and systematic course of action had been taken. The results of this are:

(*a*) Enemy propaganda is provided with material far more effective than anything that could possibly have been invented. What foreign radio broadcasts have mentioned up to now is only a fraction of what has actually happened. There is a reason to apprehend that the protest from foreign countries will increase, resulting in serious political damage, all the more since the atrocities really have taken place and cannot be denied.

(*b*) The violence perpetrated against the Jews is not only provoking a deep feeling of disgust among the basically pious Polish people, it is also creating a profound pity for the Jewish population, to whom the police were previously more or less hostile. Our sworn enemies in the East, the Poles and the Jews, supported by the Catholic Church, will rapidly form a coalition on every front out of hatred for their tormentors.

(*c*) I need not again mention the unhappy lot of the *Wehrmacht*, forced to be a passive witness to these crimes, whose reputation with the Polish population has suffered irreparably.

(*d*) But the worst effect that the present situation will have on the German people is the unlimited brutalisation and moral depravity which will spread like an epidemic through the most valuable German material. If the high officials of the police and SS continue to call for violence and brutality, brutal men will soon reign supreme. With disconcerting speed depraved birds of a feather find one another out and band themselves together in order to satisfy their pathological and bestial instincts, as they are now doing in Poland. They can barely be kept in hand, for they have good reason to feel that they have official sanction to commit the most horrible acts.

All this and much more was done to the Polish Jews during a period of what was called "minor terror." The tragedy of the destruction of Polish Jewry was yet to come.

On 21 September 1939, only three weeks after the invasion of Poland had begun, Heydrich issued instructions regarding the treatment of the Jews in Poland. These instructions were in the form of a *Schnellbrief* (Special Delivery Letter) addressed to "The Chiefs of all *Einsatzgruppen* of the Security Police." The letter was headed, "The Jewish problem in the Occupied Zone," it was signed by Heydrich himself, and it is known that it was drafted in Eichmann's department.

The preamble referred to a conference which had been held in Berlin and it emphasised that the "ultimate goal" was to be kept strictly secret. Furthermore, a distinction must be made between the ultimate goal, which would require a long period of time, and the phases leading up to the ultimate goal, each of which would be carried out in a short period of time.

It was, of course, unnecessary to state in so many words what the ultimate goal was. All the recipients of the instructions knew that already. The first prerequisite of the ultimate goal was stated to be the concentration of all Jews from the country districts into the larger cities and towns, which was to be carried out with all speed. In principle, all Jewish communities of less than five hundred were to be disbanded and transferred to the nearest concentration centre.

In each Jewish community, a Council of Elders was to be set up composed of influential locals and the rabbis. These Councils were to be made "fully responsible" for carrying out all instructions given to them, and it was not considered necessary to explain what was the literal interpretation to be given to the words "fully responsible." A census of all Jews in their areas was to be made by the Councils, and when notified of the route to be taken they would also be held personally responsible for the evacuation itself.

The concentration in Poland presented no great difficulty because the majority of the Jewish population were town or city dwellers, but to facilitate the rounding-up an order was issued that all Jews must forthwith wear the Jewish badge, the Star of David, and anyone who did not do so was liable to the death penalty.

Hitler, Goering, and Keitel then issued orders on 7 October 1939 for the establishment of settlement areas for Germans in the East from which all the other "ethnic groups" were to be removed, and almost unlimited powers were given to Himmler to execute this order which he passed on to Heydrich who issued the following statement on 12 December:

> Important reasons make it necessary to centralise all police and security matters connected with the execution of the evacuation in the Eastern areas. I have, therefore, appointed SS *Hauptsturmführer* Eichmann as my special representative in Amt IV, RSHA.

The object of the exercise was to resettle certain Polish provinces with Germans, and the first people to be deported in order to make room for them were, naturally, the Jews. It became Eichmann's responsibility to draw up detailed plans for the deportation and implement them.

In January 1940 Eichmann presided over a special meeting held to discuss the methods to be used to transport these Jews to the Government-General. There had already been, it was reported to the meeting, some "difficulties": a hundred men in one convoy had frozen to death. It was decided that no Jew should be allowed to take more than 100 zlotys with him, and that reports on each convoy were to be submitted to Eichmann.

Hans Frank told a meeting of the Government-General, which had been called to discuss administrative matters, that this "modern migration of peoples," as he called it, had been a very troublesome time for him and his staff. Trucks kept arriving, he said, filled to the brim with corpses, and every district chief and every municipal officer had to chase round from morning to night to get rid of this influx of unwanted Jews from the Reich. "All this we had to endure." He might have saved some sympathy for the half-million Jews of all ages who had been forced to make the dreadful journey during which they had died like flies, falling by the wayside in a sea of mud or in the driving snow.

Eventually, however, Frank's protests were successful and

orders were given to Eichmann that there should be no more deportations from the Reich to Poland without the Governor-General's consent.

Meanwhile the concentration of Jews in Poland, in accordance with the master plan of September 1939 mentioned above, continued. Before the German occupation, the Jews in many parts of Poland lived in a particular district in most of the towns, but there was no distinct ghetto in the mediaeval sense. No part of a town was set aside by law for the Jews, nor were they barred from anywhere. Quite soon after the Nazi occupation of Poland began they decided to herd all Jews together in special walled-off parts of the towns and cities. One of Dr. Goebbels' assistants who accompanied him on a visit to Warsaw and Lodz in the early days of the occupation said of the Jews: "They are ulcers which must be cut away from the body of the European nations. The inhabitants of these ghettos must be completely isolated. This is not merely a problem of forbidding marriage between them and members of other races, it is not a question of a single individual who commits a crime, but of the focus from which all crimes have their origin. These people must be completely isolated or the whole of Europe will be poisoned."

Despite this announcement, which was made over the German wireless, ghettos were not immediately established for there was still a more drastic alternative plan under consideration, i.e. to set aside a special district of Poland in which all the Jews were to be confined. It was for this reason that the "Lublin reservation" had been created, but it was found that it would take too long to resettle the Jews in this way and it was, therefore, finally decided to establish a series of ghettos.

When the ghetto idea was finally adopted it was carried out with typical German thoroughness. At first, a few weeks after the occupation, the occupation forces had tried to drive all the Jews in Warsaw into a ghetto but the Warsaw Jews, by payment of a heavy fine, avoided this. But it was only postponing the evil day, and in October 1944 the Warsaw Ghetto, later to

become distinguished for its famous rising, came into existence.[2] In the spring the Germans had already begun to build
walls in one of the worst quarters of Warsaw, thus isolating
blocks of houses, and this became the nucleus of the ghetto.
Gradually a large area of the city was cut off in this way. The
total number of Jews shut off from the outside world in this
ghetto is not accurately known but there is good reason to
suppose that by 1942 there were not less than four hundred
thousand of them.

Owing to the frightful overcrowding, the complete lack of
sanitation and an acute shortage of medical stores, epidemics
were rife and the ghetto itself became an instrument of extermination. One outbreak of typhus in 1941 carried off 15,749
victims. The Germans deliberately cut the Jewish rations
down to a minimum, and such things as fish, meat, fresh vegetables and fruit were not included. People died in the streets in
large numbers and passers-by used to cover the bodies with
newspapers until they could be moved away. The following is
an eye-witness' description of the Warsaw Ghetto in its early
days:

. . . On Yom Kippur, 1940, the German radio announced the
order for the setting up of a ghetto in the city of Warsaw. Within
a few days the Jews had to leave their homes outside and to
enter the quarter without being told into which part they were
to go. Thus about 100,000 Jews entered the Jewish quarter
which was already overcrowded. They became refugees, carrying their worldly goods by hand or on a cart, wandering through
the streets, stopping at a house, standing confused, not knowing
where to go. At that time the ghetto was still open and there was
contact with the outside world. It was still possible to go to work
outside the Jewish quarter.

After a short while, and without previous notice, the ghetto
was isolated and walled off, and German or Polish police stationed at every gate or exit. From then on it was cut off from all

---

[2] For an account of the liquidation of the Warsaw Ghetto by SS
Brigadeführer and Major General of Police Stroop, see pages 64–65.

sources of livelihood, from places of work, and from all the possibility of obtaining essential commodities, and its inhabitants felt as though the prison walls had closed in upon them.

During this period, tens of thousands of Jews were brought into the Warsaw Ghetto from nearby provincial towns. They were ordered to wind up their affairs at two hours' notice, to take with them what they could carry in their hands and on their backs, and they were all brought on foot into the ghetto. Anyone who faltered or stumbled, or who stopped for a moment, was generally shot dead. Still more refugees came into the ghetto, and people could be seen standing or sitting in the street without roof or food, waiting for salvation. Life became an unbearable hell. There was frightful overcrowding with tens of people to a room. The sanitary conditions were appalling, which led to epidemics and disease.

Since it was impossible to find work, except for slave labour, or to obtain food, starvation soon followed. Entire Jewish families, men, women, and children, could be seen sitting on the pavements swollen with hunger. During the curfew hours, when it was quiet in the streets, the voices of little children could be heard on all sides begging for a piece of bread, but all they could get were a few crumbs from Jews who had pity upon them. In the morning, corpses, especially those of children, were found lying naked on the pavements near the gates, for during the night even their clothing had been taken.

Of course, the most difficult plight was that of the refugees who had come in from the neighbouring towns, as it was impossible to find any unoccupied space for them within the ghetto, and they were packed into refugee houses. In these it was almost impossible to move, for there was not an inch of space unoccupied. The food consisted only of a plate of soup and a piece of bread per day. Every day, hundreds of Jews died.

Another ghetto which was established early in the occupation was that at Lodz where 160,000 persons were crowded together in an area of four square kilometres. The conditions there, also, were terrible. As the Attorney-General told the Court:

People lived six to a room. In the first 15 months about 15,000 of them died. Nevertheless, in spite of this Eichmann drafted another 20,000 Jews and 5,000 gypsies from Germany into the city. The District Commissioner wrote complaining to Himmler that Eichmann had given incorrect facts with regard to the capacity of the ghetto which was being swept by epidemics. . . . When the District Commissioner wrote his letter on 9 October 1941 he did not know that a decision had already been taken to exterminate all the Jews and that it did not matter by what method this end would be achieved.

The general idea of exterminating the Jews was, by 1941, beginning to attract adherents, although the method by which it should be done had not yet been determined. One of Eichmann's staff in Poland, *Sturmbannführer* Heppner, wrote to the Accused suggesting, amongst other things, that about 300,000 Jews from the Warthegau area should be concentrated in the district where they could work in the coal-mines. He thought that in this way he could overcome the danger of epidemics that had broken out in Lodz and other ghettos. In this camp all the Jewish women would be sterilised so as to finish off the Jewish problem for at least one generation.

There is a danger that this winter we shall be unable to feed all the Jews. It is worth considering seriously whether it would not be more humane to finish off those who are not fit for work by some quicker method. At all events this would be more pleasant than to let them die of hunger.

Heppner stated that possibly his proposal might seem fantastic but it was, nevertheless, practicable. Apparently he did not know how advanced were the plans for this kind of solution of the Jewish problem.

In the summer of 1943 Eichmann visited the ghetto at Lodz and came to the conclusion, after consultation with those concerned, that it was no longer worth maintaining. It was, therefore, decided that it should be turned into a concentration camp in which only those fit for work would remain. The others would be "sent away."

Early in 1943 it was decided to "resettle" all the Jews from the Warsaw Ghetto in Lublin. Over 300,000 had already been moved some six months earlier, but by this time Lublin had got a bad name; 40,000 Jews had been massacred there and the news had leaked through to Warsaw. At last the Jews were going to show a spark of resistance which the miserable life of the ghetto appeared for so long to have extinguished. The SS, however, were determined to see the thing through and planned what amounted to a military operation to begin on 19 April 1943. In charge of it was SS Major-General Stroop and by 16 May he was able to report as follows to his supervisors: "Progress of large-scale operation on 16 May 1943. . . . 180 Jews, bandits and subhumans were destroyed. The former Jewish quarter of Warsaw is no longer in existence . . . the operation was terminated at 2015 hours by blowing up the Synagogue. . . . Total number of Jews dealt with: 56,605 including both Jews caught and Jews whose extermination can be proved. . . . Signed—Stroop."

On the title-page of his report of this "*Grossaktion,*" as the Germans called it, was inscribed in decorative Gothic lettering the words, THERE ARE NO MORE JEWISH DWELL-INGS IN WARSAW. Some seventy-five pages long, the report gave a bombastic account of what was nothing more or less than the annihilation of several thousand defenceless Jewish men, women and children, and the destruction of their homes. After giving the names of the murderers who fell "for the Führer and their country in the battle for the destruction of Jews and bandits in the former ghetto of Warsaw," the report went on to describe the operations day by day:

"The resistance put up by the Jews could only be broken by the relentless and energetic use of our shock troops by day and night. . . . I therefore decided to destroy the entire Jewish residential area by setting every block on fire. . . . The Jews then emerged from their hiding-places and dug-outs.

Not infrequently they stayed in the burning buildings until finally, through the heat and fear of being burned alive, they preferred to jump down from the upper storeys after having thrown mattresses and other upholstered articles into the street. With their bones broken they still tried to crawl across the street into buildings which were not alight. . . . They even took to the sewers, but after the first week their stay there ceased to be pleasant. Men of the *Waffen SS* and the *Wehrmacht* Engineers courageously climbed down the manholes to bring out the Jews and not infrequently they stumbled over Jews already dead . . . it was always necessary to use smoke-candles to drive them out. Thus one day we opened 183 sewer manholes, and at a fixed time lowered smoke-candles into them, with the result that the bandits fled from what they believed to be gas towards the centre of the former ghetto where they could then be pulled out of the sewer holes. A great number of Jews who could not be counted were exterminated by blowing up sewers and dug-outs."

Himmler and Eichmann, as they sat in their Berlin offices studying this report and watching the extermination graph going up and up, must have felt proud of their SS comrades when they read the following: "The longer the resistance lasted the tougher the *Waffen SS* and Police became. They fulfilled their duty indefatigably in faithful comradeship and stood together as models and examples of soldiers . . . considering that the greater part of the *Waffen SS* who took part in the operation had only been trained for three to four weeks previous to its commencement, high credit should be given for the pluck, courage and devotion to duty which they showed." The reaction of Colonel-General Alfred Jodl, Hitler's Chief of the Operations Staff of the German High Command, on being shown the same document, was not one of admiration. "The dirty arrogant swine," he said referring to SS General Stroop. "Imagine writing a seventy-five page boastful report on a little murder expedition, when a major campaign fought by soldiers against a well-armed army takes only a few pages."

The final sentence of General Stroop's report held a special significance for Eichmann, for it told him that the second extermination camp at Treblinka, which had only been in full operation for a few months, was proving its usefulness. "Of the total of 56,000 Jews caught, about 7,000 were exterminated on the spot and 6,929 others by transporting them to 'T.II,' which means 14,000 Jews were exterminated altogether. . . ." T.II was the short name for Treblinka Extermination Camp B which, together with its older companion, Camp A, is reliably assessed to have been the place of execution of not less than 600,000, most of them Jews.

Many young Israelis, who are not unjustifiably proud of the victories they gained against enormous odds during the War of Independence, are inclined to despise their elders, who were the victims of Nazi persecution in Europe during the last war, for not resisting their fate with more vigour. It was thought by some in Israel that the trial of Adolf Eichmann might increase this feeling. If has always been my opinion, as I wrote in the introduction to this book, that the evidence which would be given at the trial would very likely have the opposite effect, for many of these young people would learn for the first time that whenever there was a possibility of resistance, as in the Warsaw Ghetto, the Jews did so gallantly and that those who had no opportunity to offer resistance, because they were neither armed nor organised, went to their death with dignity and undiminished faith.

It was, probably, for this reason that the Attorney-General called Mrs. Lubetkin-Zuckermann as a witness, for she was able to testify to the gallant resistance of her fellow-members of the ghetto to Major-General Stroop's *Grossaktion*.

Just before the war broke out Mrs. Zuckermann was attending the Zionist Congress in Geneva and, shortly after the invasion of Poland by the Germans on 1 September, she returned to Warsaw. Many of the discriminatory measures against the Jews were already in force. In her evidence she described the preliminary steps leading up to the formation of the Warsaw Ghetto and the difficulty of life within it, but the most dramatic part of her testimony dealt with the events that took place between 18 April and 16 May 1943. Asked by the Attorney-General what happened in April 1943 before Easter, the witness replied:

18 April 1943 was the day before Pesach. Two days earlier the Gestapo man, Brund, walked into the Community Council Office and said that he had come to the conclusion that the Council did not take enough care of the Jewish children. They did not have enough food and he suggested that kindergartens should be established for them and it was necessary that they should be well cared for and happy, because the Jews who still remained in Warsaw were needed for the purposes of the war-effort and there was no danger that they would be deported. We already had sufficient experience of the Germans and their methods to regard this visit as a bad omen. During the last few days, therefore, rumours had been spreading throughout the ghetto that the Germans were preparing to liquidate it. On 18 April one of our Jewish policemen, who was a member of our underground organisation, told us that a Polish policeman had told him that they did not know exactly when, but something was going to happen during the night. By this time we had built up in the ghetto a Resistance Organisation with a plan of action and we immediately declared a state of emergency. Everyone was sent to his post. About midnight the same policeman came and told us that the ghetto had been surrounded. Everyone was told that those who had arms would fight, not only those who belonged to the Resistance Organisation but anyone who had the means of resistance. Those who were not armed, including the older women and children, were to go down into the bunkers. To the fighting groups we did not have to issue orders. These young men and young women had been waiting for months for this moment to come when they would be able to shoot Germans. Now that moment had arrived. When dawn broke on 19 April I was standing at my post, looking out of an attic window. I saw thousands of Germans surrounding the ghetto with machine-guns. All of a sudden they began to enter the ghetto armed as if they were going to the Russian Front, and we, young men and

women, numbered twenty. And what did we have for arms?
Some revolvers, a few machine-guns, some grenades, some
home-made bombs and Molotov cocktails. It was strange to see
these twenty young men and women, Jewish men and women,
standing up against these armed German forces, happy and
merry, although they knew that their end would come. We
knew then that the Germans would conquer us first, but we knew
that for our lives they would pay a high price. It is difficult to
describe. Many of you will not believe me but when the Germans approached our posts and we threw hand-grenades and
bombs at them and saw German blood pouring over the streets of
Warsaw, having previously seen so much Jewish blood running
in its streets, there was universal rejoicing. The morrow did not
worry us. The rejoicing amongst the Jewish ghetto fighters was
great and wonderful to see. It seemed like a miracle. Those
German heroes retreated, frightened from the Jewish bombs
and hand-grenades. After about an hour we saw a German
officer order his men to collect the dead and wounded and withdraw. They did not collect their dead and wounded but retreated
without them. We took their arms later, and thus on the first day
we, the few, with our miserable weapons had driven the Germans away from the ghetto. Of course they came back. They
had more arms, more ammunition and bread and water which
we did not have.

They came back on the same day once again, this time reinforced by tanks and we with our Molotov cocktails set fire to one
of them. The casualties in our group were very small, two killed
and a few wounded. And we know that on that day many more
Germans had been killed.

Major-General Stroop's report of the day's operation was as
follows:

PROGRESS OF GHETTO OPERATION
ON 19 APRIL 1943

Closing of ghetto 0300 hours. At 0600 hours, order to *Waffen
SS* to comb out the remainder of the ghetto. Hardly had the
units fallen in when there was a strong concentration of fire

by the Jews and bandits. The tank used in this action, and the two heavy armoured cars, were pelted with Molotov cocktails, the tank was twice set on fire. Owing to the enemy counter-attack we had at first to withdraw our units and reform. About 0800 hours a second attack was made under my command. Although the Jews counter-attacked again we succeeded in combing out the blocks of buildings according to plan. We caused the enemy to retire from the roofs and elevated prepared positions into the cellars, dug-outs and sewers. During this operation we caught only 200 Jews. Immediately afterwards raiding-parties were directed to the dug-outs known to us with orders to pull out the Jews and destroy the dug-outs. About 380 Jews were captured. We found out that the Jews had taken to the sewers. The sewers were completely inundated so as to make it impossible for them to remain there. About 1730 hours we encountered very strong resistance from one block of buildings including machine-gun fire. A special raiding party invaded the block and defeated the enemy but could not capture them. The Jews and criminals resisted from one position to another and escaped at the last moment through subterranean passages. About 2030 hours the external barricade was reinforced. All units were withdrawn from the ghetto and dismissed to their barracks. The barricade was reinforced by 250 *Waffen SS*. The operation will be continued on 20 April.

The fighting continued for a number of days (continued Mrs. Zuckermann). The Germans could not defeat us and from time to time retreated. But not all the days were like the first day. We suffered more casualties and we killed less Germans. During the days which followed, the Germans changed their tactics and this forced us to change ours. Instead of fighting by manning our posts in the streets we went over to a system of fighting in small groups. During the night we took up positions in the houses and laid in ambush for the Germans when they came. They no longer came in large numbers but, like us, in small groups. We had one advantage over the Germans. We knew the terrain well. We knew where to hide and the Germans did not know where to find us. Thus for days the fighting continued. Life in the ghetto during this time is difficult to describe. I lived in this ghetto for years. During the first few days of the battle we were all jubilant, although it was clear to everyone of us that there was little likelihood that we should survive. We had the satisfactory feeling of being alive and avenging our brothers and sisters. We fought for our lives, we fought back. This made life easier, and it also made it easier to die.

From the beginning of the operation we were looking for contacts with Jews who were outside the ghetto. We had a number of friends, amongst them Yitzhak Zuckermann, now my husband, whom I already knew. Through them we were able to smuggle in arms. This was done by the ghetto's undertakers. Our cemetery was not within the ghetto walls and when there was a funeral, the undertakers, on their way back, were sometimes able to smuggle in arms and ammunition. . . .

Mrs. Zuckermann stated that she herself managed to escape from the ghetto on 8 May and remained hidden in Warsaw until the suppression of the Polish uprising in August 1944. She then moved to a small town quite near Warsaw, and remained there until she was liberated by the Red Army in the middle of January 1945.

Another method used by the Gestapo to liquidate the Polish Jews was that of the slave-labour camps. According to the records of the Political Main National Office for the investigation of war-crimes in Poland, there were 300 of these camps. Every Jew in Poland between the ages of 14 and 60 had to be registered for work, and all of them were eventually drafted to these camps for forced labour.

One of them was situated in Cracow. There, work began at 4.00 a.m. and was continued well into the night. The living-quarters consisted of huts in each of which several hundred people slept in three-tiered bunks. Work was carried out at the double. Anyone who lagged behind received twenty-five strokes on his bare body. There was little to eat; a small quantity of bread, a weak brown liquid that was called coffee was served twice a day, and a cup of watery soup at mid-day. The inmates were always hungry but it was forbidden to bring any food from the outside and those who infringed this rule were either shot or hanged. Very often massed floggings took place on the parade-ground. Punishment parades were frequently held, and on these occasions the inmates were ordered to stand for hours without moving. Anyone who moved was shot on the spot. Hangings were carried out in the presence of the whole camp.

One eye-witness gave a description of one of these parades. 20,000 people were assembled in the square, surrounded by an electrified fence and covered by machine-guns mounted in the turrets of the observation towers. In front of them a youth of fifteen was being hanged. The rope snapped and the boy pleaded for his life but they hanged him a second time. The next person, waiting for sentence of death to be carried out, opened a vein in his wrist but he was, nevertheless, carried bleeding to the gallows. Another witness testified that dogs were set on to the inmates who were badly bitten and sometimes torn to pieces. SS men frequently went up to somebody and shot him just because at that moment they felt like doing it. The same witness described the parades on which the weak, the old, and the children were selected for dispatch to the extermination camps while nursery rhymes were played over the loud-speakers. No one was allowed to move. At the slightest movement the machine-guns opened fire.

The mortality rate in all these camps was very heavy. One of the survivors from the labour camp at Lwow gave evidence of two incidents which happened when he was an inmate there.

On 2 July 1941 I was arrested with about 5,000 other Jews. After three days of suffering a few of us escaped, all the others were killed. Two days later I was taken outside for work with 100 other Jews but in the evening only twelve of us returned; all the others had been killed. In February 1942 I was taken to the concentration camp at Janowska where I contracted typhus and pneumonia. On 8 June I was taken away to be shot. The Germans gave us spades to dig our own graves. When we had completed the task, everyone was called by name and, two by two, they went down into the pit, lay side by side, their faces to the ground and were shot. The next couple due to be shot sprinkled some soil over those who had gone before them and the same thing happened. . . . Just before it became my turn I escaped.

On 15 June 1943 I was taken to the Death Brigade Command Unit 1005. This Brigade was formed in order to wipe out all traces of the German atrocities in Poland. Our job was to open the graves, burn the bodies, after extracting any gold from them, and then scatter the ashes. Every day we collected about 8 kilograms of gold. When a new batch of victims arrived the Germans shot them and burned them on the spot. I was there until 19 November, when once again I managed to escape.

The testimony of the victims, however, is not the only evidence available of the persecution and atrocities carried out by the Nazis in Poland. A report is still in existence which was drawn up by SS *Gruppenführer* Katzmann who was responsible for carrying out the extermination programme in Eastern Galicia. In it he has described the establishment of these labour camps and the concentration of all Polish Jews in ghettos, and the "special treatment" given to all work-shy and asocial elements in the "Jewish mob," as he politely called them. All those who were in possession of labour-cards were kept at work until they were unfit for it, and were then sent to one of the extermination camps unless they had already died from starvation. It soon became evident that many Jews who would otherwise have been selected for "special treatment" were obtaining these cards from the Germans by bribery. This led to an increase in the number sent away for "special treatment." Tens of thousands were "dispatched" to the death camps by train but the organisation of these convoys, according to Katzmann, caused "unusual difficulties," for those selected to make their last and final journey in this way tried to hide in cellars, bunkers, ditches and in the most unlikely places from which the SS were only able to dislodge them by employing flame-throwers or gas. "Finally," wrote Katzmann, "I was compelled to take brutal measures, the remaining Jews in Lwow were exterminated by the burning or demolishing of their houses. At least 3,000 Jews committed suicide." Katzmann's report ended with a glowing tribute to the indefatigable spirit and devotion to duty of the SS under his command whose duty it was to send all these Jews to their death.

In spite of the extraordinary amount of work imposed on every member of the SS and the police during these operations, their spirit remained firm and praiseworthy from the first day to the last. Only because of the sense of personal duty felt by every officer and man was it possible for us to get control of this "plague" in the shortest possible time.

Whenever Katzmann used the words "expulsion" or "dispatched" he was, of course, referring to the deportation of Jews to the extermination camps where, between 1941 and 1944, Polish Jews were destroyed by the million.[3]

As head of the Gestapo department for Jewish affairs, and as Special Commissioner for the extermination of the Jews, the Accused cannot escape criminal responsibility. Evidence was given by the Prosecution of the part he played in initiating and controlling the ghettos and in establishing and operating the extermination camps. He implemented the Heydrich plan of 21 September 1939. He approached the Ministry for Foreign Affairs and requested its agreement for the application to holders of foreign passports in the Warsaw Ghetto of all police measures in force in respect of the general population of the ghetto. In addition to all these heavy commitments, however, he always seemed to find time to deal with minor matters and with many individual applications from the Ministry of Foreign Affairs requesting exceptional treatment for wealthy or important Jews. Instructions were also issued by his department

[3] See pages 77–103.

regarding Jewish property, most of which was confiscated from the Polish Jews before they were deported to the Lublin area, Auschwitz, or one of the other extermination camps. These instructions dealt with many things. Cash was to be sent to the central bank; watches, fountain-pens, torches, wallets and other personal belongings were first of all sent to be repaired and cleaned and were then sold cheaply to soldiers in the front-line. Men's and women's clothing was collected and issued to the "*Volksdeutsche*" in the Eastern areas. So were blankets, umbrellas, perambulators and many other useful articles. Linen and tablecloths were sent to the army, spectacles to the Ministry of Health and furs to RSHA.

The instructions stated that particular care must be taken to see that the Jewish badge was removed from all clothing and that the clothing be carefully examined to make sure that no valuables were hidden there.

Insult was added to injury by the employment of the Jews themselves in handling, cleaning and repairing the clothes. A special SS unit was employed for that very purpose in what was known as *Aktion Reinhardt*. This operation was named after Heydrich whose Christian name was Reinhardt. He had been assassinated at Lidice in June 1942, but had he lived he would have been responsible for its implementation through Eichmann's office. The concept of this plan was colossal, for there were not less than 3,200,000 Jews in Poland when the war started, and 1,600,000 of them still lived in the Government-General. All of them were to be "resettled."

Globocnik, the Chief-Police and SS Commander in the Lublin area, was appointed to take charge of this operation, the purpose of which was the general plunder of all Jewish property in Poland and the killing of its owners. He also supervised the running of the extermination camps at Chelmno, Belzec, Sobibor, Treblinka and Maidanek. Globocnik was not a pleasant personality. He had been the first Nazi *Gauleiter* of Vienna and was always drunk. This did not, however, affect his efficiency as a "liquidator," though it may explain why

Eichmann, who had known Globocnik in his Austrian days, now found him rather a thorn in the flesh, and it may also account for his exaggeration, although that appears to have been common to all the Nazi mass-murderers.

Höss described Globocnik as "a pompous busybody whose object was to put himself into the foreground and who described his fanciful plans as though they had, to a large extent, already been put into practice."

There was, undoubtedly, a great deal of jealousy between the various executioners who took some pride in having the largest turn-over, for Höss went on to say that, according to Globocnik, it was he and only he who could get things done properly, whether it was a question of exterminating the Jews, or resettling the Poles, or utilising sequestered property. Himmler and Goebbels, however, both seem to have had a high opinion of Globocnik and although he appears to have got up against everybody else, including Hans Frank who resented what he felt was interference from Berlin, it was Himmler, through Eichmann, who continued to keep him employed. Goebbels wrote this about Globocnik in his diary on 27 March 1942 when Belzec camp had not yet got into its full stride and Sobibor and the two Treblinkas were not even built.

Beginning with Lublin the Jews in the Government-General are now being evacuated eastward. The procedure is pretty barbaric and is not to be described here more definitely. Not much will remain of the Jews. About sixty per cent of them will have to be liquidated. Only about forty per cent can be used for forced labour. The former *Gauleiter* of Vienna, Globocnik, who is to carry out this measure, is doing it with considerable circumspection and in a way that does not attract much attention. . . . The ghettos that will be emptied in the cities of the Government-General will not be repopulated with Jews thrown out of the Reich. The process is to be repeated from time to time.

There has been some dispute in the past regarding the exact role which Eichmann's Amt IV B 4 played in carrying out

Aktion Reinhardt. He, of course, has always tried to shift the responsibility on to Governor-General Frank. There is no longer any reason to doubt that as the head of Amt IV B 4 he was, at the very least, the stage-manager of the final solution. He was responsible for the registration, arrest and transportation of the Jews to the places of execution, and his jurisdiction extended to all the European countries which were invaded or occupied by the German armed forces, and he had representatives in all of them.

Whatever measures were taken against the Jews, all of them had but one objective, the destruction of European Jewry. Even if the extermination camps had never existed the end would have been the same, but the process of killing would have been more delayed. Nevertheless, it would not have been very long before the inmates of the ghettos and forced labour camps died of starvation, exhaustion and disease.

But there was no time to lose. The time-table of extermination had to be advanced, consequently the death-camps came into existence.

The first major gassings were now about to begin. Death was to become an industry. The idea of exterminating the Jews by poison gas had already been in Hitler's mind when he wrote *Mein Kampf.* "If twelve to fifteen thousand Jews had been gassed during the First World War," he wrote, "a million Germans would have been saved."

Killing by gas was first resorted to by the Nazis very soon after the outbreak of the Second World War in order to carry out Hitler's euthanasia programme. As early as August 1941, the Bishop of Limburg wrote to the Reich Ministries of the Interior, Justice, and Church Affairs as follows:

About eight kilometres away in the little town of Hadamar there is an institution where euthanasia has been systematically practised for months. Several times a week buses arrive with a considerable number of victims. The local school-children know these vehicles and say, "There goes the murder box again." The children call each other names and say, "You're crazy, you'll soon be sent to the baking ovens in Hadamar." Those who do not want to marry say, "Marry? Never! What, bring children into the world so that they can be put into the pressure-cooker?" You hear old folks say, "Don't send me to a State hospital. After the feeble-minded have been finished off, the next useless eaters whose turn it will be are the old people. . . ."

This euthanasia programme had not been a great success, indeed it was one of Hitler's few failures, but the experience gained by those responsible for carrying it out was, later, very useful to Eichmann and his staff when they began to build the new camps. It had originally been his intention to locate them in Russia, and the first convoy of Jews from Germany to go East in 1941 had been sent there.

After a special meeting, called together by Eichmann immediately after his return from the Wannsee conference, however, it was decided to build the installations "on the spot," in Poland. An officer named Wetzel, whose speciality was euphemistically known as "demographic planning," which meant in ordinary language getting rid of the Jews, wrote the following letter:

The machines in question are not, at present, available in Germany in sufficient quantity and must be specially built. Brack, an official in Hitler's chancellery, thinks that their manufacture in Germany would create more difficulties than if they were made locally. . . . I should like to point out that Eichmann, a specialist on Jewish questions in RSHA, agrees with the procedure.

Eventually almost every concentration camp acquired a gas-chamber of sorts although there was difficulty in operating some of them. The extermination camp at Chelmno was a typical one for it was designed solely for killing all who were brought there. The only way in which it differed from any of the other camps in Poland was that very few people were aware of its existence or of what went on there. This may seem extraordinary, having regard to the fact that it was not very far away from Lodz, the second largest city in Poland with a pre-war Jewish population of 202,000. In the village of Chelmno, however, there was a small country house standing in its own grounds and almost surrounded by a pine forest, part of which was completely impenetrable. It was the property of the State and it was selected by the German occupation authorities as the site of the new camp. A high wooden fence round the park concealed everything that went on behind it. The local inhabitants were evicted from their homes, and only a few were left behind in order to perform the essential odd jobs about the camp. The whole area of the camp, where hundreds of thousands lost their lives, was less than six acres. The staff at Chelmno took pride in the fact that their camp was the most efficient of them all, although Rudolf Höss, the zealous Commandant of Auschwitz, would hardly have agreed with them. The main principles on which its organisation was based were precision, speed, and complete secrecy. This could be achieved only by means of keeping the victims unaware of their fate. Those who were brought to Chelmno for destruction were convinced, until the very last moment, that they were in transit on their way to be employed on some work in the East. They were told that before they entrained for their final destination they were to take a bath and have their clothes disinfected, and immediately upon their arrival in the camp they were taken to a large hall in the main building itself where they were told to undress. They were then shepherded along the corridor to the front hall where a large lorry, equipped as a gas-chamber, was waiting for them. This lorry, they were told, was going to take them to the bath-house. When the lorry was full, and the door locked, the engine was started and carbon monoxide gas was introduced into the interior through a special exhaust-pipe.

Then, after five or six minutes, when the cries and struggles of the suffocating victims had died down, the lorry was driven to a wood where the corpses were unloaded and buried. Later they were dug up and burned in the crematorium. It can be assumed that such precautions were taken to keep the victims in complete ignorance of their fate. The hall in which the victims were told to undress was heated in winter, and various notices indicated rooms where doctors were supposed to be available for consultation. All the victims were promised that they would be sent to good jobs with fair conditions of work, and they were advised to take a cake of soap and a towel with them to the bath-house.

Although the main task of this camp was to exterminate the Jews of Poland, many convoys of Jews were sent there by Eichmann from Germany, Austria, France, Belgium and Holland.

Altogether there were three gas-chamber lorries on the camp establishment of vehicles. They were listed as *"Sonderwagen"* (special wagons), and every day, from 7.00 a.m. until the late afternoon, the main corridor in this house at Chelmno was thronged with a crowd of Jews quietly walking to their death without for a moment suspecting such a fate. After the gassing, the rest of the unpleasant work was usually performed by Ukrainian guards. First of all the lorry doors were opened, and ten minutes was allowed for the fumes to disperse. The bodies were then unloaded and carefully searched for gold and valuables in case the victims should have managed to conceal these about them. Gold teeth were pulled out and rings wrenched off. Until the spring of 1942 the corpses were buried in huge graves, but the decomposition of the bodies caused a severe epidemic of typhus and after that two crematoria were constructed and all the dead were burned there. This post-gassing work must have been extremely unpleasant. It is even unpleasant to read about it, let alone to have to do it. The men who did this work must, indeed, have had strong stomachs. In the early spring of 1943 an order came from Eichmann's office to destroy all the corpses and to remove every trace of the camp. The bodies were to be burned. A special commission arrived from Berlin to inspect the camp and see that these orders were being obeyed. When the commission arrived smoke filled the air and a horrid smell of burning corpses hung about everywhere. The members of the commission were more squeamish than the Ukrainians, and appear to have been a source of great amusement to the latter. One of the guards afterwards told his wife, and she testified to this before the Polish War Crimes Commission, "The gentlemen from Berlin could not stand the smell, nor look at the open graves for more than five minutes, after which they fainted. My husband laughed when he told me about it."

Perhaps the most reliable evidence about the Polish extermination camps was given by SS Col. Dr. Kurt Gerstein and the way in which this information came into the hands of the Allies has already been described.

The following are extracts from a statement which Gerstein wrote about two months before his suicide:

In January 1942, I became chief of the *Waffen SS* technical disinfection service, which included a section for extremely toxic gases. . . . One day SS *Sturmbannführer* Günther of the RSHA came into my office, dressed in civilian clothing. I did not know him. (Günther was Eichmann's Deputy in Amt IV.) He ordered me to get him 100 kilos of prussic acid and to go with him to a place known only to the truck driver. When the truck was loaded, we left for Lublin. We took along with us Dr. Pfannenstiel, who occupied the chair of hygiene at the University of Marburg. SS *Gruppenführer* Globocnik was waiting for us at Lublin. He told us: "This is one of the most secret matters there are, perhaps the most secret. Anybody who talks about it will be shot immediately." He explained to us that there were three installations:

1. Belzec, on the Lublin-Lwow road. A maximum of 15,000 people per day.

2. Sobibor (I don't know exactly where it is), 20,000 people a day.

3. Treblinka, 120 kilometres NNE of Warsaw.

4. Maidanek, near Lublin (still under construction).

Globocnik said: "You will have to disinfect large piles of clothing coming from Jews, Poles, Czechs, etc. Your other duty will be to improve the workings of our gas-chambers, which operate on the exhaust from a diesel engine. We need a more toxic and faster working gas, something like prussic acid. The *Führer* and Himmler—they were here the day before yesterday, 15 August—ordered me to accompany anybody who wants to see the installation." Professor Pfannenstiel asked him, "What did the *Führer* say?" Globocnik answered, "The *Führer* has ordered more speed. Dr. Herbert Lindner, who was here yesterday, asked me, 'Wouldn't it be more prudent to burn the bodies instead of burying them? Another generation might take a different view of these things.' I answered, 'Gentlemen if there is ever a generation after us so cowardly, so soft, that it would not understand our work as good and necessary, then, gentlemen, National Socialism will have been for nothing. On the contrary, we should bury bronze tablets saying that it was we, we who had the courage to carry out this gigantic task!' Then the *Führer* said, 'Yes, my brave Globocnik, you are quite right.' "

The next day we left for Belzec. Globocnik introduced me to SS Major Christian Wirth (a favourite of Globocnik), who took me round the plant. We saw no dead bodies that day, but a pestilential odour hung over the whole area. Alongside the station there was a "dressing" hut with a window for "valuables." Further on, a room with a hundred chairs, designated as "the barber." Then a corridor 150 metres long in the open air, barbed-wire on both sides, with signs: "To the baths and inhalants." In front of us was a building like a bath-house: to the left and right, large concrete pots of geraniums or other flowers. On the roof, the Star of David. On the building a sign: "Heckenholt Foundation."

The following morning, a little before seven there was an announcement: "The first train will arrive in ten minutes!" A few minutes later a train arrived from Lemburg: forty-five trucks with more than 6,000 people. Two hundred Ukrainians assigned to this work flung open the doors and drove the Jews out of the cars with leather whips. Through a loud-speaker instructions were shouted: "Take off everything, even artificial limbs and glasses. Hand all money and valuables in at the 'valuables' window. Women and young girls are to have their hair cut off in the 'barber's hut.' " An SS *Untersturmführer* told me, "From that they make something special for submarine crews."

Then the march began. Barbed-wire on both sides, in the rear two dozen Ukrainians with rifles. They drew near. Wirth and I found ourselves in front of the death-chambers. Stark naked men, women, children, and cripples passed by. A tall SS man in the corner called out to these unfortunate victims in a loud parsonic voice: "Nothing is going to hurt you! Just breathe deep and it will strengthen your lungs. It's a way to prevent contagious diseases. It's a good disinfectant!" They asked him what was going to happen and he answered: "The men will have to work, build houses and streets. The women won't have to do that, they will be busy with the housework and the kitchen." This was a last ray of hope for some of these poor people, enough to make them march toward the death-chambers without resistance. But some of them knew well what was going to happen, the smell betrayed it. They climbed a little wooden staircase and entered the death-chambers, most of them silently pushed by those behind them. A Jewess of about forty, with eyes like fire, cursed the murderers. She disappeared into the gas-chambers after being struck several times with Captain Wirth's whip. Many prayed. Others asked: "Who will give us the water before we die?" (A Jewish rite.) SS men pushed the men into the chambers. "Fill it up," Wirth ordered. 700–800 people in 93 square metres. The doors closed. Then I understood the reason for the "Heckenholt" sign. Heckenholt was the driver of the diesel, whose exhaust was to kill these poor wretches. SS *Unterscharführer* Heckenholt tried to start the motor. It wouldn't start. Captain Wirth rose up. You could see he was afraid, because I was there to see the disaster. Yes, I saw everything and waited. My stop-watch timed it all: fifty minutes, seventy minutes, and still the diesel would not start! The men were waiting in the gas-chambers. You could hear them weeping "as though in a synagogue," said Professor Pfannenstiel, his eyes glued to the window in the wooden door. Captain Wirth, furious, struck with his whip the Ukrainian who was helping Heckenholt. The diesel started up after two hours and forty-nine minutes, by my watch. Twenty-five minutes passed. You could see through the window that many were already dead, for an electric light illuminated the interior of the room. All were dead after thirty-two minutes! Jewish workers on the other side opened the wooden doors. They had been promised their lives in return for doing this horrible work, plus a small percentage of the money and valuables collected. The men were still standing, like columns of stone, with no room to fall or even lean. Even in death you could tell the families, all holding hands. It was difficult to separate them while emptying the rooms for the next batch. The bodies were tossed out, blue, wet with sweat and urine, the legs smeared with excrement and menstrual blood. Two dozen workers were busy checking mouths which they opened with iron hooks. "Gold to the left, no gold to the right." Others checked anus and genitals, looking for money, diamonds, gold, etc. Dentists knocked out gold teeth, bridges, and crowns, with hammers. Captain Wirth stood in the middle of them. He was in his element, and, showing me a big jam box filled with teeth, said: "See the weight of the gold! Just from yesterday and the day before! You can't imagine what we find every day, dollars, diamonds, gold! You'll see!" He took me over to a jeweller who was responsible for all the valuables. They also pointed out to me one of the heads of the big Berlin store, Kaufhaus des Westens, and a little man whom they forced to play the violin, who led the Jewish workers' commandos. "He is a captain of the Imperial Austrian Army, Chevalier of the German Iron Cross," Wirth told me.

Then the bodies were thrown into big ditches near the gas-chambers, about 100 x 12 metres. After a few days the bodies swelled and the whole mass of bodies rose up 2–3 yards because of the gas in them. When the gas died down several days afterwards, the bodies settled down again. Wirth told me that later they poured diesel oil over the bodies and burned them on railroad sleepers to make them disappear.

The Treblinka camp was set up in the Warsaw district in an isolated region close to the small village of that name. It worked at full pressure during the whole of 1942–1943. Years after the Germans themselves had destroyed the camp, in November 1943, articles of domestic furniture, clothing and suitcases were still left scattered about the site of the camp, and it was still possible to find human ashes and bones in the sandy soil. From the moment the victims arrived at Treblinka every device was employed to make them think that it was just another camp. A sham railway station had been built with notices showing the way to an entirely imaginary restaurant, and a waiting-room. Dummy signals and railway points were erected to give the impression that Treblinka was an important railway junction and not a "dead end" in its literal form. Whatever impression may have been gained by the passengers on their arrival the elusion must soon have been dispelled. Waiting at the station to receive them were SS men and Ukrainian guards who lashed out at the unfortunate Jews with whips if they were slow in getting out of the cattle-trucks in which they had been travelling. Dawdlers were often shot on the spot.

Nevertheless, this game of deception continued to be played at the camp itself. Those who were sick, cripples, invalids, old people and children were put into special huts marked with the red cross and the word "Lazaret." [4] Inside there was a "waiting-room," furnished with upholstered couches and a door at the far end. Here an SS man stood and as each person entered he would shoot him in the back of the neck,[5] push him through the door into a pit outside. The bodies of those who had died in the cattle-trucks en route or who had been killed on arrival were also thrown into the lazaret.

At the station new arrivals were ordered to hand over all money and valuables in their possession. These effects were sorted out, repaired when necessary, and sent to Germany. It is known that at least 208 wagon loads of clothing alone were sent to the Reich in this way.

Before they were killed the women's hair was cut off, placed into sacks and also sent to the Reich. The men were then ordered to get undressed and were hustled into the gas-chambers. If they did not move quickly they were prodded in the back with rifle-butts. Thus they were herded together inside, stark naked, their hands above their heads so that more people could be squeezed into the room. The hatch was then

---

[4] Hospital.   [5] This was called "*Genickschüss*."

closed, the engine switched on, and the poison-gas released until they were all dead or dying. At Treblinka also, when the gas-chamber doors were opened the same procedure was carried out, as at Chelmno, by Ukrainian guards. When the camp was first opened the bodies were flung into pits, but later on crematoria were constructed. One man, who was thrown into the death-pit while still alive, succeeded in escaping, but the farmer from whom he sought refuge handed him back to the camp-commandant. One of the members of the SS staff, Kurt Franz, set his dog on him and then beat him to death.

To try to offer resistance was useless. One convoy of Jews which had come from Grodno put up considerable resistance when ordered to enter the gas-chamber, and one of their number threw a grenade at one of the Ukrainian guards. Fire was opened on them immediately from tommy guns and the whole party was chased fully clothed into the chamber. At least 7,550 wagon loads of Jews arrived at Treblinka during 1942 and 1943, and the number killed during those years is known to be not less than 730,000. All this was accomplished in about 15 months during the time the gas-chambers were in operation.

The extermination camp in Sobibor was opened in the spring of 1942 and it was specially designed for the destruction of the Jewish population of Central and Eastern Europe. Situated in the Province of Lublin, close to the railway station of Sobibor, the camp was bounded on the north, south and east by a pine forest.

The construction of the camp began in March 1942, under the supervision of an SS officer, and was carried out by Jewish workers who had been brought from the neighbouring villages and were guarded by SS men and Ukrainians. It took several months to build, but even before it was finished a hut with gas-chambers was erected and the extermination of Jews began early in May 1942, only a few weeks after construction had started. The camp was in operation until October 1943, when a revolt of Jewish workers broke out and several SS men and Ukrainians were killed and some of the Jewish prisoners escaped. In the following month the camp was razed to the ground. Around the camp was a barbed-wire fence, interwoven with pine branches, which made it impossible for anyone to see through. Behind the barbed-wire was a minefield.

The camp was divided into two parts. The larger of the two contained the administrative offices and the living quarters for the guards, which bore high-flown names such as *Schwalbennest* (swallow's nest) and *Gottesheimat* (Home of the Lord). It also contained the yard in which the victims were stripped, and the huts where their belongings were stored. The smaller section of the camp consisted of the building fitted with the gas-chambers, the place where the corpses were burned, and the huts in which the Jewish workers were housed. Altogether there were some twenty huts in the camp. There was no crematorium proper, for the bodies were simply thrown on to iron bars held together with reinforced concrete and burned.

By October 1942 convoys of Jews were arriving at Sobibor at the rate of about twenty a month. As each of these convoys contained approximately 3,000 persons the most conservative estimate is that about a quarter of a million men, women and children were killed there.

Although the camp, as has already been stated, was intended mainly for the liquidation of Jews from Eastern Poland and from territory in the Soviet Union, which was then under German occupation, many convoys also arrived from Czechoslovakia, Austria, Holland and France as well as a large number of gypsies.

A witness named Noshe Bahir, who spent some time in Sobibor extermination camp, gave evidence about the camp itself and a visit which the accused, Eichmann, made in July 1942.

When this witness arrived at the railway-siding in a train which carried about 2,500 others he noticed some of his travelling companions saying their prayers and making confession to God. He had previously no idea of what went on in Sobibor camp, but when he saw this he realised that something terrible was going to happen. As the doors of the railway wagons were opened the Germans were waiting for them in their SS uniforms, some in black and some in green. With a great deal of shouting and screaming everyone was brought to camp No. I where the women and children were put on one side and the men on the other. He was only fourteen and a half years of age at the time, but he was forced to do very hard work. One day in July 1942 a party of important senior officers was expected to visit the camp. Bahir heard about this because about two hours before the visiting party arrived he was sent for, together with one of his friends, to polish the shoes of the officers on the camp-staff. About 11.30 a.m. he saw what he called in his evidence a "Luxury train" puffing its way into Sobibor siding.

Q: Why did you think it was a luxury train?

A: The victims who arrived at the camp always came in goods-trucks, but this was quite different. It was a passenger train with modern railway coaches. A group of high-ranking officers got out of the train, headed by Himmler, wearing that greatcoat of his. There were about eight officers, among whom was Eichmann, and there were also three civilians with them.

Q: How did you know it was Eichmann?

A: I did not know at the time, and I did not recognise Himmler either. The Jews were not working that day and when I came back to the camp I told my friends what I had seen. They knew that the first one was Himmler because they had seen him before. But they had never seen Eichmann. Even when I left the camp I still did not know that it was Eichmann, but in 1945, when half Poland had already been liberated, I was in Lublin. I was being interviewed by a Dr. Emil Sommerstein, the only Jew in the first provisional Polish Government who came from Russia. I was telling him about my experiences in Sobibor and he said: "There is a documentation centre in Lublin and as you say that you remember these officers so well perhaps you could identify them from photographs." I visited the documentation centre and was shown a number of photographs and in one of them I pointed out a man whom I had seen walking with Himmler and four others and I then saw a man and pointed him out as being there in the party, I had no idea that this was Eichmann, but I was then told: "The man you are pointing to is Adolf Eichmann." The man who said this told me not to think that Himmler was the only one who dealt with the Jewish question. There were, in addition to him, Heydrich and Eichmann, the latter of whom was responsible for the deportations to all the extermination camps.

Q: Did you ever see this man again at Sobibor after July 1942?
A: I saw him a second time in February 1943.

Maidanek camp, which was established in 1941, was situated near Lublin. Originally prisoners-of-war were detained there but later, as the camp grew in size, Jews began to arrive from Czechoslovakia, France and Greece. In the spring of 1942 gas-chambers were installed and two ovens in which to burn the bodies. In the summer of that year Jewish convoys began to arrive in large numbers.

In the spring of 1943, Jewish deportees from Warsaw arrived in Maidanek and the rate of killing was increased, reaching a climax in November when, in one day, 18,000 Jews were shot.

The conditions in the camp were such that even without the facilities for direct execution the prisoners would have finally perished from hunger, disease or pure physical exhaustion, for the food provided was about one-third of the necessary minimum.

At the parades on which the inmates were selected for extermination the procedure was as follows: males to the right, females to the left, children and the aged in the centre. Mothers who clung to their children were separated from them by the guards armed with whips. Evidence was given at the trial by a woman who obstinately refused to let go of her baby. An SS man came up to her, smashed the child's head on the ground and handed the woman the blood-stained body with the words: "Now you can take your child." Some of the mothers who had their babies torn from their arms went out of their minds with horror. In Maidanek there was only one place where the children were treated kindly. This was at the entrance to the gas-chambers where each child was handed a sweet before it entered.

According to the estimate of the Polish National War Crimes Commission, at least 200,000 Jews were destroyed in this camp.

Of all these terrible extermination camps, however, Auschwitz was by far the worst.

Late one afternoon in March 1946 two officers of the British War Crimes Investigation Unit were called to Minden to interrogate a German war criminal who had just been brought into the Investigation Centre which was situated in a former German Army Detention Barracks. His name was Rudolf Höss, the former commandant of the Auschwitz concentration camp, and he had been on the wanted list for some months. The two officers did not ask him many questions that evening, for they already had quite a formidable dossier about him, but after making sure of his identity one of them asked how many people he had been responsible for putting to death by gassing during the time he was commandant. After some thought he finally admitted to two million, and signed a statement to that effect. On being asked whether the number was not larger, he agreed that it probably was, but he had left Auschwitz at the end of 1943 and could not be held responsible for what happened after that.

His statement, which was made entirely voluntarily, read as follows: "Statement made voluntarily at (the name was not included) gaol by Rudolf Höss, former Commandant of Auschwitz concentration camp, on 16 March 1946. I personally arranged, on orders received from Himmler in May 1941, the gassing of two million persons between June–July 1941 and the end of 1943 during which time I was Commandant of Auschwitz. Signed, Rudolf Höss."

About three weeks later he stated, when giving evidence in

defence of Kaltenbrunner before the International Military Tribunal at Nuremberg, that he could not say for certain what the total number of gassed people was, for he had not been allowed to keep any figures. The whole of his information, he said, was obtained from a man by the name of Eichmann who had the task of organising and assembling these people. Eichmann had told him that in Auschwitz a total of two million Jews had been destroyed.

Höss met Eichmann for the first time in the summer of 1941 when he was summoned to Berlin by Himmler, when he had already been Commandant for Auschwitz for a little more than a year. This interview between Himmler and Höss has already been described.

The Polish town of Oswiecim (Auschwitz) with a population of 12,000 was situated about 160 miles south-west of Warsaw. It lay at the bottom of a flat basin and was surrounded by a series of stagnant ponds and marshland. It was damp, smelly and pestilential and it is not surprising that no one lived outside the town itself. As someone once said, "It was avoided by life for a thousand years, as death kept watch there." As I wrote in *The Scourge of the Swastika*, "If death kept watch there for a thousand years, it was not in vain, for it was here that the Germans established '*Konzentrationlager Auschwitz*' where at one time 10,000 were passing through the gas-chamber daily and not less than two million people, according to the commandant's own calculation, were killed in this and other ways."

The wholesale extermination of Jews at Auschwitz began some time in September 1942, the first victims coming from Upper Silesia. As the numbers of convoys began to increase, and the new crematoria had not yet been completed, these new arrivals had to be gassed in temporary gas-chambers and then burned in pits. For this purpose two old farm buildings, situated in an out-of-the-way spot, near the adjoining camp of Birkenau, were made air-tight and provided with strong wooden doors. The trains of Jews were unloaded on a siding in Birkenau and those who were fit for work were taken off to the camps at Birkenau and Auschwitz itself. All those who were not fit to work and were, therefore, due for gassing were marched, if they could walk, to the gas-chamber which was less than one kilometre from the siding at which they had detrained. The sick and any others who were unable to march were taken there in vans. When they reached these farm buildings they were all made to undress behind a screen of hurdles. On the door of the barn was a notice *"Desenfektionraum"* (disinfecting room). This was to mislead the prisoners into thinking that they had been brought there in order to be deloused.

When they were completely undressed they were then herded into the room, generally about 250 at a time, the doors were locked and one or two tins of Zyklon B were thrown in through specially constructed holes in the walls. The time it took to kill the victims varied, according to Höss, on the state of the weather, but it was seldom longer than ten minutes.

After waiting for half an hour, other camp inmates who were specially employed for the purpose, opened the doors, removed the bodies and burned them in the pits. Before this was done all gold teeth and jewellery were removed. Firewood was stacked between the bodies and when approximately 100 corpses were in the pit the wood was lit with rags soaked in paraffin. When the flames had taken hold more bodies were piled on top of the others. The fat that collected at the bottom of the pits was poured on to the fire to keep it alight. It used to take six to eight hours to cremate a pitful of corpses and the smell of burning flesh was noticeable in the camp at Auschwitz even when the wind was blowing away from it. After the pit had been emptied the bones were broken up. This was done by other Jews in the camp who placed the bones on the cement floor and pulverised them with heavy wooden hammers. What then remained was loaded on to lorries, taken to the River Vistula and thrown in.

The above description is taken from a statement which Höss

himself made in March 1946 during his interrogation by
the two officers of the War Crimes Investigation Unit at Minden already described. It was produced in evidence at the trial
of the Accused.

By the end of 1942, however, great improvements had been
made. During that year Eichmann had paid several visits to
the camp to see how the work and reconstruction was going
on, for he was anxious to step up the rate of extermination.
Eventually the new installations were ready. Before they
could be taken into use, however, Himmler paid another visit
to Auschwitz. He found that not all the bodies had been
burned. Over a hundred thousand had been buried in mass
graves. This did not meet with his approval, and shortly after
his return to Berlin, one of Eichmann's assistants, a certain
Standartenführer Blobel, arrived at Auschwitz with orders
from Eichmann to open up all the graves and burn the corpses
or what remained of them. Furthermore, the ashes were to be
got rid of in such a way that it would be practically impossible
for anyone to calculate, from their quantity, how many
corpses had been burned.

The following details of how the gassing was carried out,
after the completion of the new crematoria, are also taken
from Höss's original statement. Mass transports from Belgium, Holland and Greece were now beginning to arrive and
arrangements for their reception were as follows:

The train drew up alongside a specially built camp situated
midway between the camp store and Birkenau camp. On this
ramp the prisoners were sorted out and their baggage taken
away. As before, those who were fit for work were taken to one
of the two camps, and those who were unfit and were to be exterminated were taken to one of the new installations.

These victims were first taken to a large underground dressing-
room next to the gas-chamber. This room was fitted with
showers and coat-hooks, and the prisoners were told by inter-
preters that they were going to have a bath and be deloused,
and to be sure to remember where they had hung up their

clothes. From there they went to another room which was fitted with showers in order to keep up the illusion. These precautions were intended to prevent any panic, and two NCOs remained with the prisoners until the last moment in case anything untoward should happen. Despite these precautions, however, the prisoners sometimes sensed what was about to happen, particularly if they had come from Belsen. In Belsen there were no gas-chambers, and when prisoners from Belsen found themselves travelling many hundreds of miles eastward towards Poland their suspicions were, not unnaturally, aroused. From previous experience, therefore, whenever a convoy arrived from Belsen, special safety measures were taken and the prospective victims were split into smaller groups than usual and sent to different gas-chambers. On these occasions the SS guards were there in strength and used to push resisting prisoners into the gas-chambers. Nevertheless, there was seldom much trouble, though when there was it was not very pleasant.

In the same statement, given by him at Minden, Höss described one of these occasions in the following words:

I remember one incident specially well. One train from Belsen had arrived and two-thirds of the convoy, mostly men, were in the gas-chamber and one-third still in the dressing-room. When three or four armed NCOs entered the dressing-room to tell the prisoners to hurry up and get undressed, mutiny broke out, the lighting cables were torn down, the SS men were overpowered and disarmed and one of them was stabbed. As the room was then in complete darkness wild shots were exchanged between the sentry at the exit and the prisoners inside. When I arrived I ordered the doors to be shut and I had the process of gassing the first party finished, and then went into the room with the guards carrying small pistols where we forced the prisoners into one corner and then they were taken out one by one into another room and shot on my orders.

In accordance with the first instructions given by Eichmann to Höss all the Jews sent to Auschwitz were to be got rid of immediately after their arrival. When, however, a little later the first convoy of Jews arrived from Germany Eichmann gave orders that all those who were fit enough to work, irrespective of sex, were to be separated from the unfit and employed on war work. Eventually Auschwitz was to become a purely Jewish camp and all the other inmates were to be transferred elsewhere.

For those who in this way, temporarily at any rate, escaped the gas-chamber, remaining alive in Auschwitz was not much better. Over the gateway was a metal archway bearing the words: *ARBEIT MACHT FREI* (WORK MAKES FREE), but the description of Dante's Inferno would have been more appropriate: "Abandon hope all ye who enter here."

The following is a description of the camp by one of the SS guards who was employed there:

The mere view of the tightly drawn, barbed-wire fence with sign boards marked "Attention!" and "Danger!" the doors manned by sentries with machine-guns and sten-guns and the lifeless, bleak, brick blocks, reduced every newcomer into a hopeless state of mind as he began to realise that from there he would never return to freedom. And there were, indeed, few who did not come to a tormented end there. Many committed suicide after a few days. When out on a working-party they would run through the chain of sentries in order to be shot, or they "went into the wire," as it was termed in camp jargon. A high-voltage shock, a burst from a machine-gun, and death spared them from the tortures to come. Whenever shots were heard during the night everyone knew that once again despair had driven yet another human being into the wire and that he now lay there, dressed only in rags, a lifeless bundle within the so-called neutral zone. This was a strip of gravel, two metres wide, which ran along the wire obstacle and anyone entering this strip was fired at immediately. Others were found hanging by their belts at their bedside in the morning. In such cases the prisoner responsible for order in the block would report the number of suicides to the commandant. The "identification service" would then hurry to the scene and photograph the corpses from all angles and statements would be taken from the other occupants of the room to ascertain whether the wretched prisoner had, perhaps, been murdered by other camp inmates. The farcical hypocrisy displayed on these occasions was unsurpassed. As if the SS authorities of the camp in which thousands of people were systematically murdered daily were the least interested in the fate of one unfortunate man.

As in all other concentration camps, the junior appointments on the staff were generally held by professional German criminals brought from the civil prisons and specially trained for their work by experienced concentration camp staff. These men were usually serving long sentences for crimes of violence. They were, obviously, most suitable material for carrying out Himmler's criminal plans.

Those who were not due for speedy extermination were registered and given numbers. These numbers were originally sewn on the prisoners' clothing, but, from 1942 onwards, were tattooed on their forearm. There were also special badges for categories of prisoners, a red triangle for political prisoners, green for ordinary criminals, pink for homosexuals, black for prostitutes and female perverts, and purple for the clergy. The Jews bore the Star of David in a triangle and, later, a yellow stripe above it. From the moment of registration they lost all trace of individuality and became mere ciphers. They were not allowed to keep any property, all their belongings being confiscated and stored except what was stolen by the SS staff and guards for themselves or their families.

Punishments were awarded for everything and for nothing. Flogging, transfer to the Penal Company, standing or kneeling for hours on end, and confinement in a dark narrow cell in which there was only just room to stand. This punishment was called "*Stehzelle*," and it was accompanied and enlivened by other forms of torture such as the removal of fingernails, the pouring of water under high pressure into the ears, deprivation of all food for several days except for over-salted vegetables in order to produce an unquenchable thirst. The flogging was usually administered in public, during evening roll-call, on the buttocks with a leather whip. If the person fainted, whether a man or a woman, he or she was revived and the punishment completed.

In one special block lived what was known as the Penal Company. The following is a description of this block given by a former member of the camp staff.

Outwardly, it hardly differed from the other twenty-eight buildings in which the prisoners lived or which were used as kitchens or hospitals. A few innocent stone steps led to the entrance at the front. Unlike the other blocks the door of this block was always shut. When the bell was rung, an SS sentry would appear, his steps already echoing from afar in the apparently deserted building. He regarded every caller suspiciously from the little grille before admitting him. In the semi-darkness of the corridor one could now recognise a massive iron grid gate which seemed to seal off the main part of the building. Even from outside one was struck by the fact that the windows were almost completely walled in, admitting light through only a narrow slit.

In this dark forbidding-looking building lived the members of the Penal Company. They were always out in the open in all weathers, and often in water up to the waist. When they were not at work they lay in freezing rooms on the bare floor. The sick rate in these conditions was very high, and as no member of the Penal Company was ever allowed to be admitted to hospital many of them died. A still greater number, however, died from violence. The block leader, whose name was Krankenmann, killed many of them with his own hands. Lining the prisoners up against a stone wall he would strike their jaws so hard as to fracture them and the back of their heads struck the wall and were smashed in. As the inmates became unfit for work they were weeded out and murdered. The selection was made on special parades. The sick and aged, who knew very well the purpose of these parades, tried to appear healthier and younger. They held themselves upright and threw out their chests. When selected they were put into special blocks which the prisoners called "the blocks of death."

Gassing was not the only means by which the useless were put to death. A method of killing prisoners by giving injections of phenol was devised by one of Eichmann's medical staff. He was assisted by other members of the camp staff and between them they murdered not less than 25,000 prisoners in this way. "The condemned man was seated in a chair similar to a dentist's, and two prisoners seized his hands while a third blindfolded him with a towel and held his head. Then a doctor named Kehr approached him and drove a long needle into his chest. The prisoner did not die immediately, but everything appeared black before his eyes. Other prisoners, who had assisted Dr. Kehr when the injection was given, then led the half-conscious victim into an adjoining room and laid him down on the floor where he died in less than half a minute."

This evidence was obtained by the Central Commission for the investigation of war-crimes in Poland and was produced at the Nuremberg trial of major war-criminals.

Evidence of the appalling conditions in Auschwitz was given by a young man, now living in Jerusalem, who was only fourteen years of age when he was taken to the camp with his father, mother, elder brother and little sister. He described their arrival at the railway station where a group of SS officers was waiting for them. The family were immediately separated. His father, who was in ill-health, and his mother and little sister, were taken off in one direction while he and his brother were sent off with the fit grown-ups to join a labour group. He never saw his parents or sister again for they were all taken to the gas-chambers. He went first to Camp A, which overlooked the town, but later all boys under the age of 16 were moved to another place. Questioned by the Attorney-General as to whether the gas-chambers and crematoria were in Birkenau or Auschwitz the witness answered: "At Birkenau. The first two furnaces were there at either end of the railway station. One was near the gypsy camp and the other was at the opposite end."

Q: You were not allowed to leave the place?

A: This was in Camp D. We were housed in two barracks, numbers 25 and 27. I was in 27 which was for those who were working. All the other people in the barracks were veterans and had their numbers tattooed on their arms. We did not know why we were taken there, but we were locked up.

Q: From time to time did some of the boys go outside the hut?

A: Yes, this was when we went to the *Sonderkommando*, the Jewish group that worked near the gas-chambers. Their two barracks were enclosed by walls and there was a wall round the parade ground and no contact between us and the outside world. We used to break into the *Sonderkommando* unit to get food.

Q: What did the *Sonderkommando* do?

A: They burnt the bodies after they had been taken out of the gas-chambers.

Q: Were all of them Jews?

A: Yes. We would smuggle ourselves in there and speak to them, but not too much. It was always deadly quiet there and they never smiled, although they had all they needed unlike the others. They had food.

Q: Do you remember an incident when a boy was whipped?

A: Yes.

Q: Please tell the Court about it.

A: One day in Camp D I saw the Assistant Commander walking over to beat someone with a rubber hose. I got out of my bunk (when we were not working we sat around all day on the bunks), because I wanted to see whom they were going to beat. I went after him and saw him go up to one of the bunks and order a boy of about fourteen years of age to get down and then he began to whip him. There were several of us watching for this was a frequent occurrence, but this time something special happened. The boy did not scream, nor weep, nor sigh, he was completely silent, and we stood around and counted the lashes, ten, twenty, thirty, we had never seen anything like it. After the fortieth stroke he threw the boy to the ground and continued beating him, on the soles of the feet, on the back, on his face and the boy never uttered a sound. He gave him fifty lashes and left him. Some of us went up to the boy and helped him to get up and we asked him, "What did you do? Why were you beaten?" And he said, "It was well worth it. I brought a few prayer books for my friends so that they could pray. . . ."

Q: Do you remember the Jewish New Year?

A: Yes, I do.

Q: Please tell the Court what you remember.

A: It was the Friday before the Jewish New Year. Dr. Mengele [6] appeared with his deputy, Dr. Tilo, and went into the children's block (*Kinderblock*) to make a selection. He ordered us to undress down to the waist. Almost all were under the age of sixteen.

Q: What happened then?

A: After ordering us to strip to the waist he walked between the lines. The little thin boys were sent on to the road and the bigger ones were sent to the back gate of the barracks. I was sent with the little ones to the road, and when I got there and was waiting for something to happen, I thought to myself, "I wonder whether I could possibly escape?" I then left the ranks very slowly and quietly, trying not to be noticed, and went in the direction of the barracks where my brother was.

Q: In the meantime there were still some 1,000 children on the road?

A: Yes. They were taken into other huts and locked in there until the New Year.

Q: What did they do with them on New Year's day?

A: On New Year's day they ordered a block curfew and all the Kapos [7] were given instructions that anyone who tried to

[6] Dr. Mengele was responsible for carrying out many kinds of brutal so-called medical experiments in Auschwitz. One of these consisted of the painful injection of various dyes into the eyes of babies to investigate whether, by this method, the colour of the iris could be permanently changed.

Until the summer of 1960 he was thought to be living in Buenos Aires, and Germany applied for his extradition. He is now supposed to have moved to Brazil. If extradited he will be tried in Germany together with other members of the Auschwitz camp-staff already under arrest.

[7] In all the concentration camps the Kapo system was in force. A Kapo was generally a German criminal brought from one of the other

leave the barracks would be killed. When it became dark they
began driving trucks into the camp and they loaded the boys on
to the trucks.

Q: Who did this?

A: I was not outside, but the SS people did it. Most of them
were German criminals.

Q: And what did they do then?

A: They began loading them on to the trucks and the screams
were terrible. This took several hours. I had never heard anything like it at Auschwitz before. Although, usually, during the
summer, victims were taken to the gas-chambers in hundreds
and thousands, they did not know where they were being led, but
we, who had been in the camp for quite a long time, we knew
what was going on.

Q: What happened on the Day of Atonement that year?

A: Well, 2,000 of us boys remained. We thought perhaps that
this would be the end of the matter, but on the eve of the Day
of Atonement the news began to spread that we would get an
additional ration of bread. We were very happy about this and
we all spoke about this sudden generosity. During the afternoon
orders suddenly arrived about curfew. We had barely entered the
barracks when new orders arrived. "All boys out to the football
field." When we got there we were arranged in groups of 100.
A rumour was spread around that we were being taken to collect
the potato harvest. There were 2,000 of us altogether. All of a
sudden, however, a shudder passed through the parade ground
like an electric current. The "angel of death" had appeared on
the scene, Dr. Mengele on his bicycle. Someone took his bicycle
and, with his hands behind his back and his lips, as always,
tightly closed, he walked to the centre of the parade ground
and scrutinised the whole parade. At last his gaze settled on a
little boy about fifteen years old, standing in the front rank
not far from me. The boy came from the Lodz Ghetto. He
was very freckled. I remember his face very well. He was blond,

---

camps and appointed the superior of the other prisoners. He was put in
charge of a block of huts and in return for the brutal discipline which
he enforced on his subordinates was better treated, did not work, got
more food and was given something to smoke.

very thin and very sunburnt with freckles. He was standing in the first line when Mengele approached him and asked, "How old are you?" The boy trembled and said, "18 years of age." I saw immediately that Dr. Mengele was very annoyed. He started shouting. "I'll show you," he said, "bring me a hammer, nails and a little plank." Somebody immediately ran off to get them and we remained standing stock-still. A deathly silence stole over the parade ground. Mengele was standing in the middle and everyone was watching him. At last the man with the hammer, the nails and the wood arrived. Dr. Mengele then approached another boy. He was also in the front rank but he was tall. His face was round and he looked quite well. Mengele approached him, grabbed him by the shoulder, and led him to the goal post. The man with the piece of wood and the tools was told to follow them. He put the boy near the goal post and gave orders to nail the plank above the boy's head so that it was like the letter L only in reverse. And then he ordered the first group to pass under the board. The first group of boys started going in single file.

Q: Did he tell you what would happen to you after you passed this height measure?

A: No, it was not explained to us. But we understood that anyone who was not tall enough to reach the board would be taken away and put to death.

Q: Was this quite clear to you or could it possibly have meant something else?

A: No, it could have had no other meaning. It was a hundred per cent clear to everyone what the purpose was. We all began stretching. Everyone wanted to gain another half-inch, another centimetre. I also stretched as much as I could, but I was in desperation for I could see that even taller boys than myself did not obtain the necessary height. Even their heads did not touch the piece of wood. Anyone who failed to touch it was put on one side with the smaller boys who had already been selected on the previous Friday.

Q: Did your brother touch the plank?

A: My brother was standing near me. Yes, he did. While he was standing near me waiting for his turn he whispered to me, "If you want to live you had better do something." I woke as from a dream and started looking for a way of escape. All of a sudden I saw some stones near-by. My brain worked quickly. Perhaps these would save me. I managed to bend down without being noticed and picked up a few small stones, opened my shoe-laces and started stuffing the stones into my shoes. Fortunately I had shoes which were a little too big for me. I stuffed the stones under my heel and this added about an inch to my height. I thought this might be just enough. Then when I saw that I could not stand to attention with the stones in my shoes I told my brother that I was going to throw them away. He told me not to throw them away and that he would give me something to help. He gave me a hat which I tore in two and stuffed into the shoes. This made the stones a little softer and I was able to stand up on them.

I stood there for about ten minutes with my shoes full of stones and rags and thought, "Perhaps I can make it." While I was standing there for another ten minutes several boys passed under the board. Two would make it and two would not. Finally my brother who had kept looking at me said, "No, you have not got enough yet." He asked another boy in the row to estimate my height. They both looked at me and said I had not a chance of making the required height, so I started looking for another way of escaping. I thought that I might possibly slip away and hide in the group of tall boys who had already passed under the plank and made the grade. They were standing in groups of a hundred or more on the other side of the football ground, and the little ones, who were too short, were on the other side. I tried to worm my way into one of the groups of big boys. I very nearly succeeded in doing so, but another boy also tried and Dr. Mengele then noticed me. He started shouting at the Kapos and the guards and then ordered the entire group to be taken back and passed under the plank a second time. As we were being taken back I managed to escape back into my former place in the front rank. I stayed there for a short time and afterwards managed to get back into the group of large boys once again. Altogether 1,000 out of 2,000 did not make the grade.

Q: What eventually happened to the boys who did not pass the test?

A: They were exterminated in the gas-chambers.

Q: And only a thousand survived?
A: Yes, only a thousand survived.

In addition to getting rid of as many Jews as possible in
Auschwitz by these means, Eichmann was also interested in
what was to him an intriguing side-line, namely the formation
of a collection of Jewish skeletons for the University of Strasbourg and he specifically ordered the murder of 112 Jews for
this very purpose.

It all began in this way. In response to a request by Dr.
Brandt, who was the chief accused in the "Medical Case," tried
by one of the American Military Tribunals at Nuremberg in
April 1949, a report was drawn up by a Dr. Hirt of Strasbourg
University on the desirability of securing a collection of Jewish skeletons. In this report Dr. Hirt advocated the murder of
"Jewish Bolshevik Commissars." "By procuring the skeletons
of Jewish Bolshevik Commissars," he wrote, "who personi-
fied a repulsive yet characteristic sub-humanity, we have the
opportunity of obtaining tangible scientific evidence. The actual obtaining and collecting of these skulls without difficulty
could best be accomplished by issuing a directive to the *Wehrmacht*, for the future, to hand over to the police, all Jewish
Bolshevik Commissars who are captured." The Field Police
were then to report to a special office which would send out
specialists to have photographs and anthropological measurements taken, and ascertain the origin, birth, date and other
personal data of the victims. Hirt's report went on to say, "Following *the subsequently induced death* of the Jew, whose head
must not be damaged, the head must be separated from the
torso and forwarded immediately in a well-sealed tin containing preserving fluid specially made for the purpose. On the
basis of the photographs, the measurements of the head and,
finally, the skull itself, comparative anatomical research of
racial classification, pathological views on the skull formation,
form and size of the brain, and many other things could be
determined. The new Reich University of Strasbourg would

be a most appropriate place for the collection of and research upon the skeletons thus acquired."

On 27 February 1942 Dr. Brandt informed Dr. Hirt that Himmler would give instructions to Eichmann's department to provide the necessary material. Hirt's murderous inhuman plans were carried out in a way that differed slightly from the suggestion made in his preliminary report. It was eventually decided to preserve the whole skeletons of the victims rather than the skull alone. On 2 November 1942 Brandt got in touch with RSHA and asked them to provide 150 Jewish inmates from Auschwitz to carry out this plan and on 6 November he wrote to Eichmann and asked him, in view of Himmler's agreement, to put everything at Dr. Hirt's disposal necessary to complete the collection of skeletons. Dr. Brandt's assistant, whose name was Sievers, also wrote to Eichmann on the same subject on 21 June 1943:

RSHA. Office IV B 4, for the attention of SS *Obersturmbannführer* Eichmann, Berlin, Prinz Albrecht Strasse 8, Assembly of Skeleton Collection.

With reference to your letter of 20 September 1942. IV B 4/ 3576/42 G 1488, and the personal talks which have taken place between us in the meantime on the above matter. You are informed that the colleague in this office who was responsible for this subject, SS *Hauptsturmführer* Dr. Bruno Bager, finished his work in the Auschwitz concentration camp on 15 June 1943 because of the existing danger of infectious diseases. A total of 115 persons were worked on, 79 of whom were Jews, 2 Poles, 4 Asiatics, and 30 Jewesses. At present these persons are separated according to sex, and each group is accommodated in a hospital building in Auschwitz concentration camp where they are in quarantine. In order to carry on with the processing of these selected persons an immediate transfer to Natzweiler concentration camp is now imperative. This must be accelerated in view of the danger of infectious diseases in Auschwitz. Enclosed is a list containing the names of the selected persons. It is requested that the necessary directions should be issued. As, with the transfer of the persons to Natzweiler, the danger of spreading disease exists, it is requested that an immediate shipment of disease-free, clean, personal clothing for 80 men and 30 women should be sent from Natzweiler to Auschwitz. At the same time accommodation for the 30 women in the Natzweiler concentration camp must be provided *for a short period.*[8]

According to a statement made by the commandant of Natzweiler, 80 inmates from Auschwitz, including a number of females, were transferred to Natzweiler and there killed by gas on Eichmann's directions. A special gas-chamber was built for the purpose. The corpses of the victims were then sent in three lots to the Anatomical Institute at Strasbourg University. The above evidence, given by the commandant of Natzweiler, was corroborated at the Medical Case Trial by a French witness named Henri Pierre who testified that at the beginning of August 1943 the principal autopsy technician of the Anatomical Institute, whose name was Bong, received an order from Hirt to prepare tanks in the cellar of the Institute for approximately 120 corpses. At intervals of two days three loads of corpses, 30 female and 56 male, arrived by lorry from an unknown place. All of these victims were Jewish. The corpses were then preserved in the cellar of the Institute in tanks which had been prepared by Bong.

Early in September 1944, when the Allied armies were approaching Strasbourg, Sievers approached Dr. Brandt with a request for instructions as to what should be done with the Jewish bodies still lying in the tanks in the cellar of the Institute. He informed Brandt that Hirt would be able to remove all the flesh from the corpses and thus render them unrecognisable. But in that event, part of the research already done would have been in vain, "and it would be a great scientific loss for this was a *unique collection.*" A telephone call to Eichmann, however, settled the matter. He did not want his precious collection discovered by the Allies and he gave orders for its immediate disposal.

[8] The italics are mine. For obvious reasons they would not be making a long stay.

IV

The *Einsatzgruppen*[1] in Russia

I
T WAS NOT, however, only in the extermination and concentration camps that this murderous work was done. All
Jews were destined for extermination in one way or another,
and it was only the method of implementing this policy that
varied from country to country.

As the Attorney-General told the Court:

It was different in Norway and Denmark, for instance, where
the Germans showed a certain consideration for the sensitivity
of the population, than in Poland, which was regarded as nothing
more than a reservoir for slave labour, or in the Soviet Union,
Hitler's most hated rival, against which he only succeeded in
quenching his wrath for a while because of his wish not to become involved in a war on two fronts. When he had completed
his conquests in the West, and it became apparent that it would
take time to subdue England, Hitler decided to execute his
long-standing plan to launch an onslaught on the Soviet Union,
which now embraced the Baltic States, Eastern Poland and part
of Bessarabia. "Operation Barbarossa" was made ready in the
spring of 1941. Germany wanted a savage lightning campaign
which would deal the Soviet Union a fatal blow with the maximum speed. Detailed preparations were made, incorporating
the most drastic measures to ensure that the intended blows

[1] *Einsatzgruppen* were special SS groups established for the purpose
of massacring human beings because they were Jews.

would prove effective, and that the rear of the German Army would be secured. With this in mind, the SS organised new operational units (*Einsatzgruppen*) in May–June 1941. Heydrich and Streckenbach of the RSHA dealt with the matter personally. Eichmann was a party to everything concerning Jews. He took part in the secret meeting at the Prinz Albrecht Palace in Berlin, at which Heydrich explained to the Commander of the *Einsatzkommandos*, of which the *Einsatzgruppen* were composed, the nature of their mission to exterminate all the Jews. It was agreed with the Army that the handling of the Jews would be left to the Security Police and the SD, which would operate independently, though in co-operation with the Army. Von Brauchitsch, Commander of the invasion force, agreed to grant the widest powers to the Security Police. The instructions issued by the RSHA to the operational units were to kill the Jews, including women and children, in addition to all Communists leaders and functionaries.

While the German armies were invading Russia and the Baltic States the infamous *Einsatzkommandos* followed in their wake, giving the Jews what, in one of Eichmann's directives, was euphemistically called "special treatment," in other words the massacre of many thousands by shooting, hanging, gassing and drowning. The Nazis were experts in the use of euphemism, and when it came to killing they never called a spade a spade. Special treatment, extermination, liquidation, elimination, resettlement, and final solution were all synonyms for murder.

The reports of the atrocities committed by the *Einsatzkommando* were received in Eichmann's office in Berlin, and he was thus able to keep a continuous check on the progress of extermination in the East.

Many of these reports were produced in evidence by the Prosecution, and the Attorney-General had this to say about them:

They are blood-curdling and hair-raising documents. One reads dozens of these reports . . . and one asks oneself again and again: "How could it ever have happened?" It is almost impossible to believe that for many months, thousands of people daily, in cold blood, deliberately and of set purpose, murdered multitudes of human beings with their own hands, the number rising steadily until they totalled three-quarters of a million. It is difficult to accustom oneself to the idea that such beasts ever walked the face of this earth.

Murder was committed as a matter of daily routine. After every such blood-bath, the murderers would eat a hearty meal, have a smoke and a chat about this and that, and then they were ready for the next group of victims, who had meanwhile been formed up in line . . . And so the victims arrived, in endless columns. Rabbis in long, velvet coats, young children, babies, old men. They were all brought to the edge of the open grave, shot and buried, and the next in turn laid down on top of them. So, in a routine office-report, together with general information on affairs in the occupied areas and the attitude of the local populations, we read of the massacre of 55,000 Jews in White Russia, 54,696 in the Simferopol region, 10,000 in Dnieprope-trovsk, some 10,000 in Czernigov, 45,467 put to death in the centre of the front, 16,964 in the Minsk and Moscow districts, 5,000 in Nicolaiev, and many more in other cities. Together they combine to create a picture of wholesale slaughter of hundreds of thousands of people along the total length of German-occupied territory in the Soviet Union and annexed areas.

The arrangements, referred to above by the Attorney-General, whereby these SS units were allowed to operate in the Army Areas, were quite revolutionary and very unpopular with many of the senior commanders and staff officers of the *Wehrmacht*, for the *Einsatzgruppen* came directly under the orders of a representative of the SIPO at each Army Head-quarters unless operational necessity made it imperative for orders to be given by the Army. Despite angry denials to the contrary these operations were carried out with the full knowledge of Keitel, Hitler's Chief of Staff, and there can be very few senior staff officers fighting in the East who did not know something about them. The following is an extract from a report written by the C.O. of one of these special units: "Our task was hurriedly to establish personal contact with the Commanding-Generals of the Armies and with the Commanding-General of the Rear Army. Cooperation with the armed forces was generally good, in some cases it was very close, almost cordial." In many other reports rendered by the *Einsatzkommando* stress is laid on the excellent cooperation with the Armed Forces. After describing how thousands of Lithuanian Jews had been "rendered harmless," another euphemism for killing, during a particular pogrom in June 1941, one report stated that the operations "went smoothly because the Army authorities showed full understanding, for the procedure had been explained to them."

The greatest care is usually taken by most criminals not to leave any clues behind which will lead to their detection. Not so the Nazis, who always provided unchallengeable evidence of all their misdeeds in the records, returns, orders and other documents, all carefully preserved, which fell into Allied hands after the unconditional surrender of the German Forces in Europe. When they employed prisoners of war on prohibited work, the Nazis rendered reports to the appropriate army formation; when they gassed Jews they sent detailed reports to Eichmann in Berlin; when they shot hostages they posted up lists on public buildings, as a warning to others; when they conducted painful and disgusting experiments on unwilling inmates of their concentration camps they made careful case-notes. As fast as they committed these crimes so, with characteristic German thoroughness, they collected and tabulated documentary evidence of them. In the famous *Einsatzgruppen* case, tried before an American Military Tribunal at Nuremberg in September 1947, the prosecution evidence was founded entirely on official reports prepared by the criminals themselves. As the Court stated in its judgment, "the story of the *Einsatzgruppen* is not something pieced together years after their crimson deeds were accomplished. The story was written as the events it narrates occurred, and it was authored by the doers of the deeds. It was written in the terse, exact way which military discipline requires and precision of reporting dictates. . . . It is only by quoting from these reports, because of the very language of the actual performers, that a shocked world can be led to believe that these things could come to pass in the twentieth century."

"A special action was executed, during which 1,013 Jews and Jewesses were shot. . . . During the period covered by the report, 2,010 people were shot, mostly Jews. . . . In Riga, on 30 November 1941, 10,600 Jews were shot. . . . Of the remaining 30,000 approximately 10,000 were shot." These were some of the quotations from the *Einsatzgruppen* reports.

Before long the authors of these reports began to get tired of the word "shot" and wrote, 4,000 Jews were disposed of, but so that no one could be in doubt as to what that meant, for it was not yet in general use, the word "killed" was added in brackets. Eventually even the expressions "execute" and "liquidate" became monotonous and new terms were brought into use: "rendered harmless," "done away with," "taken care of," and even "properly treated"—but they all meant the same thing. Later it became unnecessary in some cases to give any figures, and it was concisely announced that the area "has been cleared of Jews" (*Judenrein*), or that in a certain place "the Jewish question was solved."

An eye-witness account of one of these massacres was given in evidence by Mrs. Yosselevska who miraculously survived it. When the Germans invaded Russia, Mrs. Yosselevska was living near Pinsk in a town where there were about 500 Jewish families. She was examined in Court by the Attorney-General.

Q: When the Germans entered your home-town in 1941 what happened to the synagogue?
A: They turned it into a stable and put all their horses into it.
Q: When you say "they" do you know to what units these Germans belonged?
A: Most of them were SS men.
Q: Will you tell the Court what happened on 15 July 1941.

A: It was a Saturday afternoon and the non-Jewish workers from the near-by villages came to tell us that the Germans were killing the Jews and it might be better if we ran away and hid.

Q: What did your grandfather say to this?

A: We asked our grandfather what to do. He consulted the Rabbi and the other elders of our village, and they decided that we were not to run because that would be no use. Perhaps a few of the young men would be taken for work by the Germans but we would not be killed.

Q: And what happened next day?

A: There was great excitement in the village. A Jew came running in from a near-by village. His name was Ziedl and he ran through the village shouting, "Jews, run for your lives. The Germans are out to kill us."

Q: And what did your grandfather say then?

A: Grandfather said, "You children run and hide. I will stay behind. They will do no harm to me." And to my father he said, "Stay with me. I will hide. But they will do no harm to me." We saw the Germans entering the village and they caught this young Jew, Ziedl, and shot him dead. Then all the Jews started running. A number of them got away but not all because the Germans were already in the village. We hid in a small wood. During the day we heard a lot of shouting and screaming. We thought perhaps the Germans were leaving the village.

Q: Did you then return?

A: Yes, we started to go back. On the way we met some non-Jews from the vicinity and they said, "It is all right, you can go back now, the Germans killed everybody who was left behind."

Q: And when you returned did you find out that about 150 Jews had been rounded up, including the Rabbi and the local elders of the community? Do you know what happened to them?

A: The Rabbi's wife told us. She refused to leave, for she had ten children. She told us that when they came for the Rabbi they ordered him to take his prayer-shawl with him. They then collected all the Jews into the centre of the village. The Rabbi was ordered to put on his praying-shawl and to preach a sermon. When he began to preach he was beaten. The Germans then ordered him to sing and dance, but he refused.

Q: What happened to the other people?

A: They were also beaten up, and driven to the old cemetery where there was a shallow grave all ready.

Q: Do you know what happened to them when they got there?

A: Yes, the same people who told us all this said that they were ordered to lie down in the grave in fours and they were then shot.

Q: Were there some who still remained alive who had remained in the village?

A: Yes.

Q: Your father was registered as a shoe-maker, was he not?

A: Yes, my father survived the first operation, and continued to carry out his trade.

Q: Were you allowed to go and work outside the ghetto?

A: Not every day, but we were allowed on some days.

Q: On one occasion when you returned you had hidden some lumps of sugar in your hair?

A: Yes of course, whenever we went out of the ghetto we tried to bring back some sort of food for the children.

Q: And did the sentry discover the sugar?

A: Yes. One of the German sentries searched me and found the lumps of sugar in my hair. He started to beat me. My mother saw that I was being beaten and she started crying, "Beat me instead of my daughter," and so they started beating her as well as me.

Q: Do you remember the first Sabbath in August 1942?

A: I remember that day very well . . . normally there was much commotion in the ghetto. The Germans were coming and going during all hours of the night. That evening there was obviously something in the air. We tried to prevent father going into the cellar to say his prayers but he would not listen to us. He went down to the cellar and we saw that the place was full of Germans. We asked why there were so many Germans in the ghetto and we were told that there was a partisan woman trying to get into the ghetto to mingle with us. This was not true. Father came up from the cellar after praying. He could not speak to us. He only wished us "a good month," as this was the first day of the month of August, which is the month of prayer before the Jewish New Year. We were told to leave the house and to take with us only the children. We were quite used to leaving the ghetto at short notice because very often they would call us all out for a roll-call. Nevertheless we had a nasty feeling that this was not an ordinary roll-call but something very special, as if the angel of death was in charge. The place was swarming with Germans, four or five Germans to every Jew.

Q: What happened then?

A: We were left standing in the ghetto. The Germans began by saying that if anyone wished to save his life he could do so with money, jewels and other valuables. This would be regarded as ransom and he would be spared.

Q: What happened towards dawn?

A: The gates of the ghetto were opened. A large truck drove in and all of us were put on to the truck, either thrown or we climbed in ourselves.

Q: Did they count the Jews?

A: Yes, they were counted. The Germans again entered the ghetto and searched for every missing person.

Q: When the truck was full what happened to those for whom there was no room?

A: Those for whom there was no room in the truck were ordered to run after it.

Q: And you ran with your daughter?

A: I had my daughter in my arms and ran after the truck. There were some mothers who had two or three children and held them in their arms running after the truck. We ran all the way. Some fell but we were not allowed to help them. They were shot—right there—whenever they fell. All my family were amongst these. When we all reached the destination those who had been in the truck were already on the ground and drawn up in line without any clothes on.

Q: Where was this?

A: This was some three kilometres from our village where there was a kind of hillock. We were ordered to stand at the top of the hillock and the four devils shot us—each one of us separately.

Q: Do you know to which German unit they belonged?

A: They were SS men—all four of them. They were armed to the teeth.

Q: Please go on, what did you see?

A: When I came to the place where the others had alighted from the lorry I saw them all lined up naked. We were still hoping that we were only going to be tortured. There is always hope—the hope of living. One was not allowed to move but I wanted to see what they were doing on the hillock and to see if there was anyone down below. I turned my head and saw that some three or four rows were already lying dead on the ground. There were about twelve of them. When we were lined up in the ghetto before leaving it my child said to me, "Mother, why did you make me wear the Shabbat dress;[2] we are being taken to be shot." And when we stood near the grave, she said, "Why are we waiting? Let us run." Some of the young people started to run, but they were caught immediately and shot where they stood. We were eventually driven up to the grave, already undressed and our clothes taken away. My father refused to undress and remained in his underwear. He was then beaten. We begged him to undress but he refused, he wanted to keep on his underclothes. He did not want to stand naked.

Q: And then they tore them off?

A: Yes, they tore off his clothes and shot him. I saw this with my own eyes. And then they took my mother and shot her too. Then there was my grandmother, my father's mother, standing there. She was eighty years old and she had two children in her arms. And then there was also my aunt. She also had children in her arms and she was shot on the spot still holding them.

Q: And finally it was your turn?

A: Yes, finally my turn came. My younger sister begged the Germans to let her go. She went up to them with one of her friends and they both stood there naked asking for their lives to be spared. He looked into their eyes and shot them both. They fell together, embracing each other, the two young girls, my sister and her young friend. Then my second sister was shot and my turn came.

Q: Were you asked anything?

A: My child and I turned towards the grave and the German turned round and asked, "Whom shall I shoot first?" I did not answer. I felt him take my child from my arms. She cried and was

---

[2] Shabbat = Sabbath. The expression is the equivalent of "Sunday clothes."

shot immediately. Then he aimed at me, first he caught hold of my hair and turned my head round. I remained standing. I heard a shot, I continued to stand, then he turned my head again and he aimed the revolver at me, told me to look and then he shot at me. I fell to the ground into the pit amongst the bodies, but I felt nothing. The first thing that I did feel was a sort of heaviness and then I thought perhaps I am not alive any more and I am feeling this after death. I really thought that I was dead and that this was a feeling which comes after death. Then I felt that I was choking. People kept falling on top of me. I tried to move and then I realised that I was alive but I could not get up. I was suffocating. I heard more shots and prayed for another bullet to put an end to my suffering. However, I kept on struggling to find some air to breathe and then I felt that I was climbing towards the top of the grave above the other bodies. I rose and I felt bodies pulling at me with their hands, biting at my legs, and pulling me down, down, down. And yet with my utmost strength I reached the top of the grave and when at last I did I could not recognise the place, so many dead bodies were lying about. Some of them were dead, some dying, many suffering. Children were crying out, "Mother, Father." I could not stand on my feet.

PRESIDENT OF THE COURT: Were the Germans still around?

A: No, the Germans had gone. There was nobody there.

ATTORNEY-GENERAL: And you were undressed and covered with blood?

A: I was naked, covered with blood, dirty from the other bodies, with the excrement from other bodies all over me.

Q: Were you wounded?

A: I was wounded in the head. I have a scar to this day and yet somehow I did come out of that grave. This was something I thought I would never live to tell. I searched for my little girl and I cried out for her, "Merkele," that was her name. There were children still crying out for their mothers and fathers, but they were all smeared with blood and unrecognisable. In the distance I saw two women standing. I went up to them. They did not know me and I did not know them. I told them who I was and then they said, "So you have survived." There was another woman crying out, "Pull me out from amongst the corpses. I am alive. Help."

Q: Will you please tell the Court what happened afterwards?

A: There we were all night fighting for our lives, listening to the cries and screams and all of a sudden we saw more Germans. We had not noticed them before because of the screaming and the shouting going on all around us.

Q: And did these Germans then round up all the children and others who had managed to get out of the pit and shoot them again?

A: The Germans piled up all the corpses into one big heap including a number of children who were still alive. I still sat in the field with some of the children around me.

Q: Did the Germans come again and round up all the children?

A: Yes, they kept coming and going. We were ordered to collect all the children but they did not approach me and I sat there watching them collect the children and shoot them. It did not take many shots to kill them. Most of them were dead already.

Q: Mrs. Yosselevska, after the Germans left you went back to the grave, did you not?

A: They all left, the Germans and the non-Jews from around the place. They removed the machine-guns and they took away the trucks. I saw that they had all left, and the four of us women who still survived went up to the grave praying that we could be swallowed up in it, even alive, envying those who were dead already and praying for death to come. Blood was spurting from the grave in many places, like a spring of water, and whenever I pass a spring now I remember the blood which spurted out of that grave. I started to dig with my fingers trying to join the dead in the grave. I dug hard but I could not open it. I did not have enough strength. I cried out to my mother and to my father, "Why did they not kill me? What was my sin? I have no one to go to. I saw them all being killed. Why was I not killed?" And I remained there stretched out by the graves for three days and three nights.

Q: And then a shepherd passed by?

A: I saw no one. I heard no one. Not a farmer passed by. After three days a shepherd drove his sheep on to the field and began throwing stones at me but I did not move. He kept on throwing stones at me believing that I was either dead or mad. Eventually I had to move and I hid somewhere else near the grave.

Q: And later did a farmer find you, give you some food, and help you to join a group of Jews in the forest?

A: Yes, he did and I spent the rest of the war with them until the Russians arrived and liberated us.

The organisation of the *Einsatzgruppen* was as follows. Each group consisted of roughly from 800 to 1,200 men and they were under the leadership of Heydrich, then still Chief of the Security Police (SIPO) and SD, who was Eichmann's immediate superior. Under the guise of ensuring the political security of the conquered territories, their job was to liquidate ruthlessly all opposition to National Socialism. Whole categories of people were to be killed without investigation, without pity, tears or remorse. Women were to be slain with the men and the children also because, otherwise, they would grow up in opposition to National Socialism. One of the principal categories was the Jews. There were four *Einsatzgruppen* in all, numbered A, B, C and D.

Between September 1941 and February 1943 *Einsatzgruppe* D, under the command of Otto Ohlendorf, was attached to von Manstein's 11th Army in Russia and operated in the Ukraine. It was responsible for the mass extermination of many thousands of Jews by shooting, hanging, gassing and drowning. Its orders were that all Jews within the Army Area were to be "liquidated" and these orders were repeated verbally by Himmler when he visited the units in Nicolaiev just after their arrival there. He must have realised that what they had to do was terrible, for he told the officers and men, when he addressed them, that they bore no personal responsibility for executing the orders which were Hitler's. The existence of these orders and their execution must have been known to the Army Commander. Indeed instructions were sent out from his headquarters to the effect that no liquidation must take place within 200 kilometres of them.

Nor was that all. At Simperopol, where 10,000 Jews were killed in a mass execution, the Army Command asked Ohlendorf to push on with the liquidations because of the threat of

famine and the acute housing shortage. During the first nine
months of Ohlendorf's period of command, *Einsatzgruppe* D
destroyed more than 90,000 men, women and children, an
average of 340 a day, though the number was frequently
higher. The majority of them were Jews, though the total also
included gypsies, Asiatics, and "undesirables."

By April 1942 Ohlendorf was able to report to Eichmann,
"The Crimea is free of Jews. Only occasionally some small
groups are turning up, especially in the northern area."

The following account of a typical mass execution was
given by Ohlendorf in a statement which was used at the Nuremberg trial and also produced in evidence by the Attorney-
General at the trial of Adolf Eichmann:

> The unit selected for the task would enter a village or city and
> order the leading Jewish citizens to call together all Jews for the
> purpose of resettlement. They were requested to hand over their
> valuables to the leaders of the unit. . . . They were then led to
> the place of execution which was usually an anti-tank ditch.
> There they were shot, kneeling or standing, and the corpses ei-
> ther fell or were thrown into the ditch. Before their bodies were
> finally buried the firing squad commanders had to make sure that
> all were dead, and themselves finished off any who were not.

But the most dramatic and moving account of one of these
mass shootings was given by a man named Hermann Friedrich Gräbe in a statement made under oath on 10 November
1945, which was produced in evidence by the Attorney-
General:

> From September 1941 until January 1944 I was manager and
> engineer in charge of a branch office in Sdolbunow, Ukraine, of
> the Solingen building firm of Josef Jung. In this capacity it was
> my job to visit the building sites of the firm. Under contract to an
> Army Construction Office, the firm had orders to erect grain-
> storage buildings on the former airport of Dubno.
> On 5 October 1942, when I visited the building office at
> Dubno, my foreman, Hubert Mönnikes of 21 Aussenmühlen-
> weg, Hamburg-Haarburg, told me that in the vicinity of the site,

Jews from Dubno had been shot in three large pits, each about
30 metres long and 3 metres deep. About 1,500 persons had been
killed daily. All of the 5,000 Jews, who had still been living in
Dubno before the pogrom, were to be liquidated. As the shootings had taken place in his presence he was still much upset.

Thereupon I drove to the site, accompanied by Mönnikes and
saw near it mounds of earth, about 30 metres long and 2 metres
high. Several trucks stood in front of the mounds. Armed
Ukrainian militia drove the people off the trucks under the supervision of an SS man. The militia men acted as guards on the
trucks and drove them to and from the pit. All these people had
the regulation yellow patches on the front and back of their
clothes, and thus could be recognised as Jews.

Mönnikes and I went directly to the pits. Nobody bothered us.
Now I heard rifle-shots in quick succession, from behind one of
the earth mounds. The people who had got off the trucks—men,
woman and children of all ages—had to undress upon the order
of an SS man, who carried a riding or dog whip. They had to put
down their clothes in fixed places and in separate heaps, shoes,
outer clothing and underclothing. I saw a heap of shoes about
800 to 1,000 pairs, great piles of underlinen and clothing. Without screaming or weeping, these people undressed, stood around
in family groups, kissed each other, said their farewells, and
waited for a sign from another SS man, who stood near the pit,
also with a whip in his hand. During the fifteen minutes that I
stood near the pit I heard no complaint or plea for mercy. I
watched a family of about eight persons, a man and woman, both
about fifty with their children of about one, eight and ten, and
two grown-up daughters of about twenty and twenty-four. An
old woman with snow-white hair was holding the one-year-old
child in her arms, singing to it and tickling it. The child was
cooing with delight, the couple were looking on with tears in
their eyes. The father was holding the hand of a boy about ten
years old and speaking to him softly; the boy was fighting back
his tears. The father pointed toward the sky, stroked the boy's
head, and seemed to explain something to his companion, who
counted off about twenty persons and instructed them to go
behind the earth mound. Among them was the family, which I
have mentioned. I well remember a girl, slim with black hair,

who, as she passed close to me, pointed to herself and said, "23." I walked around the mound, and found myself confronted by an enormous grave. People, closely wedged together, were lying on top of each other so that only their heads were visible. Nearly all had blood running over their shoulders from their heads. Some of the people shot were still moving. Some were lifting their arms and turning their heads to show that they were still alive. The pit was already two-thirds full. I estimated that it already contained about 1,000 people. I looked for the man who did the shooting. He was an SS man, who sat at the edge of the narrow end of the pit, his feet dangling into the pit. He had a tommy-gun on his knees and was smoking a cigarette. The people, completely naked, went down some steps which were cut in the clay wall of the pit and clambered over the heads of the people lying there, to the place to which the SS man directed them. They lay down in front of the dead or injured people; some caressed those who were still alive and spoke to them in a low voice. Then I heard a series of shots. I looked into the pit and saw that the bodies were twitching or the heads lying already motionless on top of the bodies that lay before them. Blood was running from their necks. I was surprised that I was not ordered away, but I saw that there were also two or three postmen in uniform near-by. The next batch was approaching already. They went down into the pit, lined themselves up against the previous victims, and were shot. When I walked back, round the mound I noticed another truck-load of people which had just arrived. This time it included sick and infirm people. An old, very thin woman with terribly scraggy legs was undressed by others who were already naked, while two people held her up. The woman appeared to be paralysed. The naked people carried the woman round the mound. I left with Mönnikes and drove in my car back to Dubno.

On the morning of the next day, when I again visited the site, I saw about 30 naked people lying near the pit, about thirty to fifty metres away from it. Some of them were still alive. They looked straight in front of them with a fixed stare and seemed to notice neither the chilliness of the morning nor the workers of my firm who stood around. A girl of about twenty spoke to me and asked me to hand her her clothes, and help her escape. At that moment we heard a fast car approach and I noticed that it

was a party of SS. I moved away to my site. Ten minutes later
we heard shots from the vicinity of the pit. The Jews still alive
had been ordered to throw the corpses into the pit, then they
had themselves to lie down in it and were shot in the neck.

I make the above statement at Wiesbaden, Germany, on 10 November 1945. I swear before God that this is the absolute truth.

HERMANN FRIEDRICH GRÄBE.

Until the spring of 1942 all Jewish exterminations in the
Ukraine were carried out in that way, but orders were later
received from Eichmann that in future women and children
were not to be shot, but must be put to death in gas-vans. The
reason for this order was given by the Attorney-General:

The SS men themselves began to grumble. Eichmann considered that the method then being used was turning them into
sadists. Others had complained that it was not an "elegant" way
of killing.

A full description of these vans and their operation is contained in a top secret document written by Dr. Becker, an
Untersturmführer in the SS, reporting the final tests and over-
haul of some of them. The report was sent to Eichmann's
office in Prinz Albrechtstrasse, in Berlin, and was produced by
the Prosecution at the Nuremberg trial of major war criminals where it was identified by Ohlendorf when giving evidence.

Becker reported that the tests on two types of vans, Series I
and Series II, had been completed and adjustments and modi-
fications made. Series I could be operated in most weathers.
Series II were useless, even after a little rain, and could only
be used in absolutely dry weather. It was a matter for consideration whether the vans should only be used when sta-
tionary at the place of execution. Many difficulties had been
experienced. First of all, the vans had to be driven to the place
selected for the execution, which was usually some ten miles
away from the main road and inaccessible in wet weather. If
the victims were marched all that distance they immediately

became suspicious and restless. This was "undesirable." The only solution which Becker could suggest was to load them on to the vehicles (he wrote as though they were goods) and drive them to the spot. Becker gave instructions that the vans of *Einsatzgruppe* D should be camouflaged as trailer caravans by putting a set of shuttered windows on each side of the trucks and two sets on the larger type. Nevertheless, they became so well known that they were soon known as the "death vans," not only by the troops but by civilians as well, and in Becker's opinion it was impossible to keep their purpose a secret even by camouflage. The rough ground and bad roads over which the vans had to be driven rapidly made them rattle, and the rivets and caulkings became loosened. This, of course, meant a leakage of gas and it became necessary to have this seen to frequently in the unit workshops. The drivers and operators were also ordered to keep well away when the gassing operation was in progress to avoid any ill-effects from the escaping fumes.

Becker's report ended as follows: "I should like to take this opportunity to bring the following to your attention: several commands, after the gassing is completed, have had the bodies unloaded by their own men. There is great danger that this will lead to their health being affected, if not immediately at least later on. The commanders did not want to countermand these orders, for they feared that if prisoners were employed they would find some opportunity to escape. The application of gas is not always carried out in the correct manner. In order to get the job finished as quickly as possible, the driver presses the accelerator down to the fullest extent. Thereby the victims suffer death by suffocation, and not by dozing off as was intended. By correct adjustment of the levers death comes faster and the prisoners fall asleep peacefully. Previously the victims' faces and other signs showed that they died in agony."

But some of the Germans themselves who were in charge of certain areas in occupied Russia protested that the operations of the *Einsatzgruppen* were more than they could stomach. As early as October 1941, when these murder squads had only been at work for three months, the Commissioner of the Territory of Sluzk wrote to the Reich Commissioner-General for Minsk on the subject. "For Heaven's sake," he wrote, "keep these *Einsatzkommandos* away from me, whatever the cost!"

Such protests, however, were of no avail, and the slaughter continued with unabated ghastliness. In February 1942 Heydrich, who was still Eichmann's chief, reporting on the work of the *Einsatzgruppen* in Russia said: "We are aiming at cleansing the Eastern countries completely of Jews. . . . Estonia has already been cleared of Jews. In Latvia the number of Jews in Riga, which was 29,500, has now been reduced to 2,500." These figures were, doubtless, obtained from Eichmann's office.

Worse than anything else, perhaps, was the Christmas massacre at Simperopol, in the Crimea. Early in December 1941, the H.Q. of *Einsatzgruppe* D had moved from Odessa to Simperopol. Of the 40,000 Jews then in the Western Crimea, approximately one quarter lived in that town. The preparatory registration and segregation was soon carried out, and Ohlendorf was informed by the SS Liaison Officer at 11th Army H.Q. that they wanted the shooting of the Simperopol Jews to be finished by Christmas. The task was entrusted to one of the units commanded by an officer named Braune. As the mission was too big for him to carry out with unit resources, he visited "Q" Branch at Army H.Q. and asked for help. Lorries, cars, motor-cycles, drivers and guards were placed at his disposal on the understanding that the soldiers were not to take any part in the actual shooting.

The execution then began, and was described by one of the witnesses at Field-Marshal von Manstein's trial in Hamburg in December 1949. The Jews were assembled at collecting points, put on lorries, and transported in convoys at suitable intervals to the scene of the execution, an anti-tank ditch a short distance outside the city. There they were shot. It only took three days, and by the end of the third day they were all dead and buried. The usual arrangements were in force for the disposal of the victims' property except that on this occasion about 120 watches were sent by special request to 11th Army H.Q. for the use of the Staff.

The question is often asked, what kind of people were they who could do such things, or order them to be done? Were they criminals, were they savages? This same question puzzled the Court which tried Otto Ohlendorf and his twenty-two associates. They were not, said the Court, as might be imagined, "untutored aborigines incapable of appreciating the finer values of life and living." Nearly all of the twenty-three were well educated. Eight were lawyers, one was a university professor, another was a dental surgeon and another was an art expert. They included an opera singer, a parson, and a descendant of the great composer Franz Schubert. If these men did wrong, said the Court, it was not lack of education that led them astray.

So many of these SS men appear to have had a schizophrenic capacity for sentiment and sadism, but that was, doubtless, largely because the latter was all just part of their job. The stoker, whose duty it was to look after the fires in the concentration camp crematorium, could gather round the Christmas tree with his wife and young children, after lunch on Christmas Day, singing *"Heilige Nacht,"* and a few minutes later glance at his wrist-watch and hurry away to be in time for the evening shift.

Rudolf Höss was a lover of animals as were other Nazi villains. One of the officials in Ravensbrück Concentration Camp, named Ramdohr, carried out the cruellest physical and mental tortures on the women in his charge. After he had been convicted by a British War Crimes Court in 1947, and sentenced to death by hanging, many of Ramdohr's relatives and friends wrote to say that "dear kind Ludwig could never do harm to any animal"; that he was a comrade "who took delight in nature"; that he was a "protector of the poor and oppressed"; that when "walking in the country he sometimes gave queer little jumps to avoid crushing a snail or a lizard under his foot," and that when his mother-in-law's canary died he "tenderly put the birdie in a small box, covered it with a rose and buried it under a rose-bush in the garden."

Having regard to what he was proved to have done at Ravensbrück it is difficult to reconcile the brutal Ramdohr of Ravensbrück, the terror of the camp, with the "dear kind Ludwig" remembered by his friends and family.

At the end of the supply line for all this machinery of death was Eichmann, yet another little man, like Höss, but completely obsessed with his "divine" mission, to rid Europe of the Jews and, by 1943, convinced that there was no time to lose if that mission were to be completed. By then he already entertained doubts, according to Höss, about a German victory and vigorously opposed anything which, in his opinion, endangered the success of his plans for a final solution of the Jewish question.

V

The Final Solution in Northern and Western Europe

THE VICTORY of Hitler in Europe in May and June 1940 meant that almost another half-million Jews came into the clutches of the Nazis. Many of those who previously lived in Holland, Belgium and Luxembourg had fled westwards as the German armies advanced, and when the armistice was signed with France there were not less than 40,000 Jews there who had come from other countries including Germany.

The burning question was what to do with them? Not even Hitler had imagined on 10 May 1940 that by 21 June France would have surrendered and England be standing alone. Moreover, the Germans have never been much good at dealing with the unexpected, witness the Battle of the Marne, and they had worked out no plans for dealing with the Jews in France.

They soon made the suggestion, however, to the Vichy Government that all Jews living in France, but of foreign nationality, should be declared to have forfeited it, and in October 1940, with Pétain's agreement, a *Statut des Juifs* was passed which provided that all the refugee Jews who had been deprived of their German nationality, should lose their civic rights. By the end of 1940, by virtue of this law, 30,000 Jews in the occupied zone, and 20,000 in the free zone, were deprived of their liberty by being sent to internment camps like that at Drancy. At the same time all sorts of petty restrictions and indignities were imposed upon them, the yellow star was introduced, and all books by Jewish authors were withdrawn from sale.

It was about this time that the Madagascar project was first mentioned. The details of much of it had been worked out by Eichmann. At that time the Germans thought that the war would soon be over, and someone had made the curious suggestion that all the Jews in Europe should be deported to Madagascar. According to Wisliceny, whose evidence at the Nuremberg trial was produced at the trial of his former colleague, the Accused, Eichmann was instructed in August 1940 to draw up a plan for this mass emigration, and Dannecker, who was his Paris representative, practically lived at the French Ministry for the Colonies digging out information on Madagascar for Eichmann's use. It was the intention of the Germans to requisition Madagascar from France, and the German Foreign Minister agreed to the scheme being prepared. It soon became out-dated, however, for it was not very long before it became obvious to even the most optimistic German that they were not going to win the war in a few weeks, and that even if they did win it at all it would only be after a prolonged struggle. No one ever heard of the scheme again.

The measures eventually taken against the Jews in France were similar to those in other occupied foreign countries. They all followed precise instructions which emanated from Berlin, and the general principles were laid down from time to time at periodic conferences held at Amt IV B 4 under Eichmann's directions. Eichmann visited France on several occasions to confer with his representatives who ran the Jewish section of the SIPO headquarters in Paris. Dannecker was succeeded by Röthke and then by Brunner. Pierre Laval and Darnard cooperated with them all.

Most of the documents sent out from Eichmann's office referred to the final solution of the Jewish question. Whatever that may have meant a few years earlier, there can be no doubt that by the summer of 1942 it meant only one thing to people like Eichmann and his subordinates, namely the deportation of all Jews to the extermination camps in Eastern Poland and their annihilation.

Wisliceny put this beyond doubt in his evidence. There were three phases in the anti-Jewish programme, he told the Court. Until 1940 the general policy was understood in Eichmann's department to be settling the Jewish question in Germany and areas occupied by Germany. The second phase was the concentration of all Jews in those countries into ghettos. The third was the so-called "final solution," namely the planned extermination and destruction of the Jewish race. This period lasted until October 1944 when Himmler gave the order to stop their destruction.

Wisliceny first heard of the order to exterminate the Jews when he was shown it by Eichmann. It was signed by Himmler and dated April 1942.

In March of that same year at a conference called by him in Berlin, Eichmann gave certain directions following the suggestions of his representatives in Paris and Brussels. A note of this conference was afterwards made by Dannecker: "Paris, 10 March 1942. Subject: The Deportation from France of 5,000 Jews. Memorandum: At the conference at RSHA IV B 4 on 4 March, I explained briefly the difficulties we were experiencing in France, and I stressed the necessity of making some definite proposals to the French Government regarding the deportation of several thousand Jews.

"Subject to the final decision being reserved to the Chief of the SIPO and SD (who was still Heydrich) it was decided by Eichmann that negotiations should be opened with the French authorities for deportation to the East of 5,000 Jews. The first to go should all be males, under fifty years of age and fit for work. French Jews should be deprived of their nationality before deportation or, at the latest, on the day of it. At the same time steps would have to be taken to dispose of their personal effects. Other deportations more important are imminent. The Slovakian Government has already agreed to pay 500 reichmarks for each Jew who is allowed to get away, the sum calculated by a percentage of their total wealth. Some similar arrangement must be brought into force for all the Jews in France before the deportations begin, and an assessment of the total Jewish wealth in both zones must be made forthwith. Signed: Dannecker."

It was always Eichmann's intention from 1942 onwards eventually to deport all the Jews from France for the purpose of extermination, and it was only the pace of the programme, due to obstacles put up by the Vichy Government, which differed from that in other countries. They were first hunted down, rounded up and taken to collection camps such as Drancy, Compiègne, Pithiviers and Beaune-la-Rolande.

Very soon after Eichmann's conference in March 1942 the first deportations of Jews began and all were deprived of their nationality before leaving. By June more than 10,000 had been evacuated. The usual deception was used to conceal the purpose of these dreadful train loads of unhappy Jews being taken off to forced labour until no longer fit, and then the gas-chamber. The operation was called "Jewish resettlement." Later, after another conference with Eichmann, new orders were issued and the wretched deportees were merely referred to as "Jewish livestock."

The figures gradually rose, however, despite the difficulties caused by Vichy, and by the end of October 1942, more than 50,000 had been deported from the Occupied Zone.

The whole business of sending so many people to their death continually throughout the year took on the nature of a routine. Eichmann never gave a thought to the horror or wickedness of it. The only thing that was important to him was whether the job was carried out well or badly, for that brought either praise or blame. Deporting large numbers of

Jews to the gas-chambers became a matter of prestige and advancement, and success as a mass-murderer was a matter for congratulation. The following document reveals the contempt in which human life was held by these people, and shows that nothing mattered so long as they carried out their orders to the letter.

One day in France a train had to be cancelled because there were not enough Jews available to load it fully. This infuriated Eichmann, who telephoned through to his new representative in Paris, whose name was Röthke, asking for an explanation. Röthke thought it wise to make a note of the telephone conversation for his files and a copy of the note was produced in evidence at the trial:

Subject: *The Deportation of Jews to Auschwitz.* On 14 July 1942 towards 7 p.m. SS *Obersturmbannführer* Dr. Eichmann telephoned us from Berlin to find out why the train scheduled for the following day had been cancelled. I replied that it had originally been intended that all those who wore the Jewish star would be arrested, but in accordance with a new agreement recently concluded with the French Government this could no longer be done and only stateless Jews could be arrested. The convoy of 15 July, therefore, had to be cancelled because information had been received from the SD Commandant in Bordeaux that they had only 150 stateless Jews there, and at such short notice I could not get enough Jews to complete the convoy. *Obersturmbannführer* Eichmann said that this was a question of prestige. It was only after a very complicated negotiation with the Reich Minister of Transport that the necessary rolling stock had been made available, and here was Paris cancelling a train! Never had such a thing happened to him before! The incident was a matter for censure. He did not want to have to report it to SS *Gruppenführer* Müller, for the blame would only recoil on himself, but he wondered whether, because of it, he ought not to give up France as an evacuation country. I begged him to do nothing of the sort and explained that the cancellation of the train was not the fault of my office for we did not know until it was too late that there were only 150 stateless Jews in Bordeaux, and as soon as this information had come to hand we immediately got in touch by telephone with RSHA. I assured him that the other convoys would be leaving on time.

RÖTHKE, Obersturmführer.

But the pace was much too slow for Adolf Eichmann, and at a further conference the French were told that most other countries were much nearer to the final solution of the Jewish problem and that they must do something about it.

Eichmann was also having a lot of trouble with the Italians who were doing all they could to hold up the deportation of Jews from that part of France which was under Italian occupation.

He did, however, succeed in one direction: not even the children were to be spared and train-loads of them would in future be dispatched. Eichmann tried hard to create the impression that the children were, in fact, travelling with their families, and whenever they were deported a number of adults were always made to travel with them. One of the "Deportation Instructions" read as follows: "The Jews arriving from the Unoccupied Zone will be mingled at Drancy with the Jewish children now at Pithiviers and Beaune-le-Rolande so that out of a total of 700 only 300 will be children. According to instructions from RSHA [that meant Eichmann's office] no trains containing Jewish children only are to leave."

A pathetic account of one of these journeys was given by Dr. Georges Wellers, in a book entitled *De Drancy À Auschwitz*. He repeated it during the evidence which he gave at the trial of the Accused:

MASSACRE OF THE INNOCENTS

In the second half of August 1942, 4,000 Jewish children were taken to Drancy with their parents. They had been arrested with their parents a month earlier, and two days later were all sent from Paris to the camp at Pithiviers. There the Germans separated the children from their parents and deported the latter direct from Pithiviers and then sent the children on to Drancy in groups of a thousand, mingled with 200 grown-ups who were total strangers to them. The children were between two and twelve years old. They were turned out of the bus into the middle of the parade ground like cattle. The bus had arrived with policemen on the platform and the barbed-wire was guarded by a detachment of gendarmes. Most of the gendarmes were unable to hide their emotion at such a spectacle and their distaste for the work which they had to do. Many of the tiny children did not know their own names, so their companions had to be asked to give what information they could. Their surnames and Christian names having being obtained, these were put on a wooden label round the neck of each child, but sometimes a small boy would be seen wearing one bearing the Christian name of a girl, for the children played with the labels and exchanged them. Each night, from our camp, we could hear these unhappy children crying ceaselessly, and from time to time some of them screamed when they lost their self-control.

They did not remain long at Drancy. Two or three days after their arrival half of the children left the camp for deportation, again mingled with 500 strange grown-ups. Two days later it was the turn of the second half to go. The night before their deportation all the children were searched and each one entered the hut where the searching took place with his small parcel where the inspectors of the P.Q.J. (*Police aux Questions Juives*) would carefully search all the luggage and then push the children outside with their bundles still undone. Little brooches, ear-rings and bracelets belonging to the girls were confiscated by the P.Q.J. One day I saw a little girl of ten leaving the hut with a bleeding ear, because a searcher had torn off one of her ear-rings which in her fear she was unable to remove quickly enough. On the day of the deportation the children were woken up at five o'clock in the morning and dressed in the half-light. It was very often chilly at that time of the morning, and most of the children had to go down on to the parade ground lightly clad. Woken up in the dark, dead with sleep, the little ones began to cry, and one after the other they all joined in. They did not want to go on the parade ground, they struggled and refused to be dressed. Eventually, however, they went.

It sometimes happened that a whole roomful of children, as

though seized by an ungovernable panic and frenzy, no longer listened to the cajoling of the grown-ups who could not get them downstairs. Then the gendarmes would be called and they carried the children under their arms screaming with terror. On the parade ground they waited their turn to answer their names, but often gave the wrong answer. The older ones held the hands of the little ones. In each convoy there was a certain number of children who were only included at the last moment. These were those whose names were unknown. They were distinguished on the list by a question mark, not that that was of any importance, because it was very doubtful whether half of these unhappy kids would ever stand the journey and the survivors would, without doubt, be put to death the moment they arrived, for it has been established that before the end of August all of the 4,000 children who arrived at their destination were gassed.

After the German surrender a document was found in a file belonging to Röthke regarding the train-load of children described above. It contained a report that the railway wagons used for transporting these children were inspected by Belgian railwaymen on their return empty from Auschwitz. The bodies of twenty-five children, aged between two and four, were found lying in them. They, and they alone, had never reached the gas-chamber.

In 1943, and during the first half of 1944, before the Germans were driven out of France, the deportations mounted in intensity but, despite this, the final solution there was not achieved. Nevertheless, many more thousands were sent off in train-loads like cattle to the slaughter-house. The following is an account of one of these nightmare journeys given by someone who took part in it and miraculously survived:

The heat became suffocating, as the sun's rays hit the sides of our wagon until it became red-hot. At each stop the temperature rose, I saw my companions one after the other take off their vests, shirts and trousers until only their underpants were left, some of them, despite my advice, even took all their clothes off. Their bodies were dripping with sweat, their breath came in short gasps. A terrible silence fell upon everyone, no one joked, everyone was dozing off. Gradually some of them began to get excited and one could scent the coming storm as their nerves got near to breaking point; my anxiety gradually mounted. At one end of the wagon one of the men became ill and then fainted, his neighbours passed him from arm to arm and hoisted him towards the air vents and fanned him with a handkerchief. Eventually he came to, and asked for water. One of them offered him his water-bottle which he had been preciously guarding. He drank greedily while all the others regarded him jealously, save for the one who had given up the little water he had. Later another one fainted and the procedure was repeated.

It was barely an hour since we had left Compiègne and the situation was getting critical. Moving the sick ones about disturbed the others, and in the end we had to stop doing so in order to prevent further disorder and the disturbance which it caused. As conditions got worse people began to lose their tempers, shouting at each other and calling each other by filthy names. A fight suddenly broke out and N. tried to intervene. He approached the fighting couple, a punch hurled him back upon those who were seated behind him. They held him up to stop the fight. At last the two were calmed down. Another man, B, who a short time ago had been humming a tune to himself, suddenly stopped, suffering from the lack of air and with a look of anguish on his face. At his side another man, his head dropped down on to his chest, seemed to be asleep.

We had just passed Soissons. The train was always changing over from one track to the other because the recent bombing had caused a lot of damage to the permanent way. The sun was merciless, and one knew that it would be like that for the whole of the day, and one's thirst was terrible. To try and assuage it, some ate a bit of their sausage, but this was seasoned and only made their thirst more intense. Despite all our entreaties the guards refused to let us have water. Occasionally the engine-drivers, at the risk of their lives, succeeded in passing us along a bottle of water. Suddenly there was a terrible frightening cry, "L. is dead. I thought he was asleep but when I shook him to wake him up he just slumped down." X, who had just made this discovery, looked at him aghast, he could hardly realise what had happened. The dead man's eyes were half open, his face was a reddish-purple, and he was dribbling from the mouth. He must have been dead for some time but no one had noticed.

We would not have to wait long for the next death, nor did we. It was the man next to M, the one who had been mixed up in the first fight. Suddenly he cried out and attacked one of his neighbours. They exchanged blows and he fell back exhausted. A few minutes later he stopped breathing. Tragedy followed tragedy, increasing every minute. In two or three hours, sixty-four of our companions had died of heat, suffocation or thirst. As the air got thinner and thinner signs of asphyxia became more evident. Our bodies were soaked and the atmosphere was laden with sweat, and then scenes of madness and delirium began. Some, crying out desperately for help, threw themselves violently against the sides of the wagon.

However, our little group from Clermont remained calm. P. leaning up against the door seemed lost in a dream. More than sixty years old he knew that in order to stand the journey he must save his strength. In one of the inevitable struggles I found myself at his side. R. and Professor Vles were next to us. We were all leaning against the door through which a little air was moving. Each one was looking at his neighbour fearing the worst. Suddenly, one of the prisoners from Riom in a mad fury threw himself on M, struck him full in the face making it run with blood. The madness spread through half of the wagon, some throwing themselves on the others, hitting them with their bodies or shoes. One after the other they fell exhausted and died on top of one another, not having the strength to disentangle themselves.

An irresistible feeling of sleepiness seized me and I dropped off only to be woken by Professor Vles. "I cannot go on any longer," he said, "my pulse at one moment goes faster and at another almost stops. I can hardly breathe, what must I do?" After I had dabbed the back of his neck once or twice with cold water he seemed somewhat relieved, but shortly afterwards it was my turn to feel terrible. My fingers began to tingle and my hands doubled up with cramp, first one and then the other. I tried to speak but I could not because my throat was dried up. I realised that I had tetanus of the hands and that only a change of

my breathing rhythm could relieve the cramp. I slowed down
my breathing and gradually the cramp relaxed. I had only one
fear, however, and that was that some madman might throw
himself on me, for in that case I would be quite unable to resist.
Gradually the atmosphere got slightly calmer as more and more
people died. Once more the train stopped. Staring at me was a
young man who had told me, just before we left, that he was a
member of the maquis in the Haute Savoie. His breathing was
very very slow. I suddenly looked at his pupils and asked myself, why is the right one dilating so when we are not moving
and the light remains the same? The left one also got bigger and
bigger. Eventually his pupils became as large as the irises, his
breathing stopped and he doubled up in the middle just like a
deflated balloon, fell forward and lay there. I shook him but it
was in vain. He was dead. One more of them.

Suddenly the scenes of delirium started again and the whole of
the wagon was just like a hut filled with madmen, strangling
themselves, trying to hang themselves, striking themselves on
the head, opening their veins and falling down, worn out or
moribund, on those who were sleeping. To make it worse some
of them cried out the whole time that they were dying. "Help,
help, I do not want to die." By this time half of the people were
dead and the cries of anguish echoed in my head. I dozed off
while I thought of those at home I loved; how long I dozed I
have no idea. The sun shone obliquely through the air-vent and
lit up a frightening picture of piled up corpses. There was complete silence again, except for one delirious man repeating in a
low voice, "I do not want to die. God have pity on me. I do not
want to die. God have pity on me. I do not want to die. God have
pity on me." Gradually his voice got lower and lower, and slower
and slower, until it stopped just like a gramophone record which
had run down, "*Je-ne-veux-pas-mourir—Je-ne.*" I started to look
for Professor Vles. Before I had fallen asleep he had been next to
me. Eventually I found him. "My son," he said, "I am done for."
Then after a long silence, "I must talk to you about my research.
I have not spoken of it to anyone. Five years of work." I leant
over towards him but he had a faraway look in his eyes. I heard
him say a few words, "My laboratory, my wife, and B, my assistant." He then became unconscious. Gathering all my strength

I dragged him towards the air-vent and managed to hoist him up as far as the barbed-wire. How long could I hold him there? The train jolted and I had to let him go. The little air seemed to help him, but he was breathing very feebly all the time. Slower and slower, and then his features relaxed and he looked calm and serene. He was no more.

Rohmer! Who was that calling me? I expected it was my brave R. and felt better. One must not die: one must struggle to the end. If they want to do us in we must make them pay the price. I got on to my feet, very groggy, and tried to reach my friends. My feet were embedded in the corpses. I stumbled over a head and then fell with my nose in a crack in the floor, lying on whom I knew not, but he was still breathing slightly. I fell into a coma. When I came round the heat was less intense, the sun had almost set, and the train was going more quickly. P. shook me. They were calling the roll. Only twenty-four answered. Then we laid down. I could do no more and went to sleep at once. During the the night R. prevented me from sliding in between the dead bodies and suffocating myself.

During this terrible journey 984 of those Jews died, and later 1,416 of them lost their lives at Dachau and other concentration camps. Only 121 of the total number returned from captivity at the end of the war. This was, however, happening all over Europe without cessation as the Nazi's anti-Jewish policy developed in its intensity. It was always the same story. Registration, segregation, humiliation, degradation, exploitation and extermination. These were the milestones on the road of suffering along which these unfortunate Jews made their last journey.

Georges Wellers, when giving evidence at the trial of the Accused, was examined by Mr. Gabriel Bach. He stated that he was born in Russia but went to live in France in 1929. He became a naturalised Frenchman shortly before the war and at its outbreak volunteered for the French Army. At the time of the armistice he was stationed in the Bordeaux area but was soon demobilised and returned to his civilian employment in the medical faculty at the Sorbonne. He was then asked:

Q: When was the first round-up operation against the Jews carried out by the Germans in France?

A: The first important action took place in May 1941.

Q: What Jews were arrested then?

A: Mostly Poles, Czechs and Russians. It took place in Paris. They were asked to go to the police stations to have their papers examined and when they reported all male adults were arrested.

Q: Where were they taken?

A: To Beaune-la-Rolande and Pithiviers. These were the first two camps established by the Germans.

Q: When was the next round-up?

A: On 20 August 1941 in Paris. They surrounded the Onzième Arrondissement, where a large number of Jews lived, and went from house to house and from shop to shop rounding up all adults who were fit for work. In the round-up in May about 4,000 men were apprehended and in the round-up in August more than 6,000. They included a number of prominent French citizens.

Q: To what camp were those arrested on the second round-up taken?

A: They were taken to the Château Rancy. This was situated in one of the Faubourgs of Paris.

Q: When were the Jews required to register themselves in Paris?

A: I think that the order for registration was issued by the military commander in France on 27 September 1940. Some two or three days later the decree was published in the French papers. My turn to register came on 19 October 1940.

Q: How did you register your wife and yourself?

A: One had to give details about one's family. I stated that I was a Jew and declared my two children to be Jewish but I did not say anything about my wife. That was as though I had declared her to be non-Jewish.

Q: When were you yourself arrested?

A: On 12 December 1941 by a German policeman who arrived about 5.00 in the morning. I was first taken to the Military Academy in Paris.

Q: Were you and the others with you given any explanation for your arrest?

A: We were told by the SS men that on the previous day, 11 December, Hitler had made a speech and declared war on the U.S.A. He had promised, in a speech made sometime earlier, that if such a war broke out the Jews would be called upon to pay for it. . . .

Q: Were you then taken with 750 other Jews to the camp at Compiègne?

A: Yes.

Q: Who guarded that camp?

A: This camp was guarded by the German *Wehrmacht*. It was divided into three parts, with barbed-wire fences. In the first part were Russians taken in June 1941 when Germany declared war on the Soviet Union. In the second part were Frenchmen, mostly Communists, Socialists, and Masons. And the third part, which was still empty, was earmarked for the French Jews.

Q: You have just said that there were three separate camps and one of these was earmarked for the Jews. What was the attitude towards the prisoners in the Jewish part of the camp in comparison with the attitude to those interned in the other parts of the camp?

A: Those who were non-Jews were permitted to write letters and receive them, and visitors were also allowed. As for us, we were strictly guarded; no correspondence, no parcels, no visits. Nevertheless, although they tried hard to keep our families in ignorance of our fate we were able, because of the friendly contacts between ourselves and the other inmates of the camp, to organise ways and means to get in touch with our families. Nevertheless, the whole thing remained an official secret until 12 March 1942. . . .

Q: Mr. Wellers, when did you first see Dannecker?

A: On 12 December 1941 in the riding-school of the Military Academy in Paris. This was the day of my arrest. At 4 p.m. a small group of German officers in uniform arrived, headed by Dannecker. They walked up and down the hall, and all of a sudden they saw two Jews in army uniform. One was an army Doctor who had been arrested while still on duty. The other was a sapper. Dannecker marched up to them and as he did so a number of other Jews surrounded him. He pulled out his revolver and said that anyone who approached nearer would be shot. He ordered the two men in uniform to be removed. After an hour they came back wearing civilian clothes. He did not want internees to be in uniform, so he had sent them home to change their clothes.

Q: Did you see Dannecker on other occasions?

A: Yes, frequently. He had a violent temper and was always very quick on the draw, and was always shouting at the top of his voice. He used to walk round the camp when it was still forbidden to go out into the courtyard or even to look out of the windows. He would wait there until he saw a face at one of the windows and then he would draw his revolver and threaten the man concerned. He frequently selected individuals to be sent away and I saw, on many occasions, individuals suddenly added to a convoy by the special order of Dannecker. He was cruel and heartless. . . .

Q: Mr. Wellers, would it be correct to state that although you were transferred from Compiègne to Drancy you were not deported with the first convoy because you were registered as the husband of an Aryan woman?

A: Yes.

Q: In the first transport on 27 March 1942 how many people were included?

A: Altogether about 1,000.

Q: From the time when you arrived at Drancy, in June 1942, until you were eventually sent to Auschwitz, and excluding a short period when you were working somewhere else, how many deportations did you witness with your own eyes?

A: I should think something between 40 and 50.

Q: And how many people were deported each time?

A: Between 1,000 and 1,200.

Q: At that time had you any idea where these Jews were being taken?

A: No, we had no idea.

Q: Did you ever receive postcards from them?

A: Yes, I think I saw one or two postcards which had been addressed to people in Drancy camp. The postmark was Birkenau, but at that time the name meant nothing to us. The writers of the postcards said that they were in good health and contented.

Dr. Wellers was then asked about the first large convoy of children which has already been described above under the title of *Massacre of the Innocents*. He was also questioned about the changes that were brought in after Röthke was relieved by Brunner who was a much more prominent figure than Röthke who stayed more in the background. Röthke never spoke to any of the prisoners himself. When the deportations were being carried out he stood quietly near the gate and watched the Jews being put into the railway trucks, but he never intervened personally. Brunner was very different. The first time Wellers saw him was in June 1943 when he personally interviewed every one of the 3,000 prisoners. He interrogated each of them separately. This was when he first arrived at the camp. Counsel for the Prosecution then continued his examination.

Q: When Brunner took over did he introduce any administrative changes?

A: There was a complete transformation when Brunner arrived at the camp on 2 July 1943. He dismissed all the members of the staff who were officials of the Vichy Government. All the Vichy officials beginning with the commandant, the policemen, the doctors. From that day the *milice* [1] were not allowed to enter the camps and could only be on duty outside. He even sent away the two Red Cross nurses who had been there for over eighteen months. He brought in three new SS men, junior officers.

Q: How did Brunner behave towards the inmates of the camp?

A: For the first fortnight or so he tried to terrorise us. Many of us were beaten, and he invented a kind of torture which we called "going-around-in-circles."

Q: Why was it called that?

A: They used to place a stick in the ground, only a few inches high, and the man who was being tortured would have to touch the stick with his right hand, put his left hand behind his back and walk quickly round the stick. They called it the spinning-top torture. This meant that the man's head was bowed down be-

[1] The Vichy special police.

cause the stick was quite low. Two of Brunner's assistants used to beat the men as they were spinning round the stick. I was not tortured in this way but I believe that it is very difficult to do it more than three or four times. The Germans forced people to go round in circles at least ten times until eventually many of them fainted.

They had another special kind of amusement. If they saw a group of camp inmates in the distance they would suddenly draw their revolvers and shoot in their direction. Apparently they can only have been shooting into the air because I never saw anyone hit. Nobody was hurt but when large stones were thrown at the internees they received wounds on the face, hands and legs. One of Brunner's friends named Bruckler was particularly brutal.

Q: When this spinning-top torture took place where was Brunner?

A: He was frequently present.

Wellers was not himself deported to Auschwitz until June 1944, when he was personally selected by Brunner to join a convoy. Like nearly all the others, the train on which he travelled was made up of freight wagons each of which contained about eighty passengers. The journey took four days during which they received no food and only once did they obtain something to drink. His convoy consisted of about 1,000 men and women of whom only three or four were still alive when the war ended. He was eventually transferred to Buchenwald on 18 January 1945, when Auschwitz was evacuated as the Russian Army approached, and it was from Buchenwald that he was finally released when the Americans liberated it.

Less than 65,000 out of an estimated total of 300,000 Jews were deported from France during the German occupation. This was principally due to the attitude of the Vichy Government to the anti-Jewish policy of Hitler. Every obstacle was raised to prevent or delay the deportation of French-born or naturalised Jews, but in order to achieve this Vichy did not protect stateless or refugee German Jews to the same extent. This is proved by the fact that nearly all in the latter category became victims of the final solution whereas ninety per cent of the French Jews managed to survive. With the exception of Italy and Denmark, no other Jewish community in the whole of occupied Europe suffered less than the French. This was due in large measure to the inherent sense of justice of the French people.

HOLLAND

The Dutch Jews had a much worse time than those in France, for out of 140,000 Jews living there when Holland was invaded on 10 May 1940 110,000 were deported to Poland where the ultimate fate of the majority of them was never in doubt. About 2,000 more were sent to Buchenwald and Mauthausen. Many of these were later transferred to Auschwitz where they were gassed and their ashes were sent, after cremation of the bodies, to their families against a payment of 75 guilders.

The large number deported from Holland was largely due to the attitude of Seyss-Inquart, who was Reich-Commissioner there, for he co-operated to the full with Eichmann's representative at The Hague, *Sturmbannführer* Zoepf. Speaking in Amsterdam early in 1944, Seyss-Inquart said: "The Jews to us are not Dutch. They are enemies with whom we can come to neither an armistice nor a peace. . . . The *Führer* has declared that the Jews have played their final act in Europe and they have therefore, played their final act."

Seyss-Inquart admitted at the Nuremberg trial that he knew the destination of all the deportees, but expected the Tribunal to believe that he had no idea that they would come to any harm. It is not surprising that his judges refused to do so.

In his opening speech the Attorney-General dealt at great length with what he called "the tragedy of Dutch Jewry."

When the German Army turned westward in May 1940, the Netherlands was defeated and occupied within a very few days. A Gauleiter was appointed with full legislative and executive authority. In the office of the Chief of SIPO, there was a special department for Jewish affairs which was eventually known by the same name as Adolf Eichmann's department in RSHA, namely IV B 4. At the head of this department was Zoepf, already referred to above. In Amsterdam an Emigration Centre was set up, the true purpose of which was to register the names and addresses of the Jews for future deportation.

The anti-Jewish campaign began immediately after the occupation, following the pattern already laid down in September 1939, when the Master Plan for the extermination programme was revealed; anti-Jewish legislation depriving the Jews of human and civil rights; identification by compelling them to wear the badge of shame; theft of Jewish property; and finally, deportation for extermination.

The decrees depriving the Jews of their civil and human rights were soon brought into force and implemented in co-operation with Eichmann's department. By them the Jews were ousted from all economic life, Jewish officials were dismissed, their movement was either forbidden or restricted, and they were not allowed to attend the theatres or other places of entertainment. They were issued with special identity-cards and all Jewish children were expelled from the schools.

It was not long before further restrictions were imposed. The Jews were later forbidden to use the telephone or any public means of transport, they were not allowed to enter non-Jewish shops or stores, an evening curfew was imposed, and they were forbidden to enter Gentile homes. Perhaps one of the most aggravating of all these measures was the prohibiting of the Jews from riding bicycles, which they were made to hand in to the occupation authorities.

That the Germans were able to adopt, from the very commencement of the occupation, a much more hostile policy towards the Jews in Holland than they were doing in France was mainly due to two factors. Firstly, unlike France where the Vichy Government was never totally supplanted, even after the landing in North Africa, the German occupation authorities in Holland were in full control from the moment of the Dutch defeat. Secondly, sixty per cent of the Jews in Holland lived in Amsterdam. This made the task of rounding them up much easier.

The man chiefly responsible in Holland for carrying out this task, in accordance with general instructions issued from Eichmann's office, was SS *Obergruppenführer* Hans Rauter who was tried by a special court at The Hague in January 1949 and sentenced to death. The first charge in the Indictment dealt with his crimes against the Jews. "The accused intentionally, within the framework of the German policy of the persecution of the Jews, the object of which was to eliminate the Jews from Europe and exterminate them . . . took measures, the general object of which was the segregation and arrest of the Jews as part of their deportation across the German frontier which, as the accused must have foreseen, resulted for many in their death." The discriminatory measures referred to above were quickly followed by the establishment of concentration camps in Holland where Jews, who had been rounded up, were temporarily detained pending transfer to the concentration camps in eastern Poland.

Reporting progress to RSHA on 10 September 1944 Rauter wrote: "The rounding up of Jews is making us rack our brains to the uttermost. I will on no account fail to make use of any influence I may have, for what is gone is lost. The mixed marriages have been classified and so have the munition workers, diamond cutters and so on, so that this great purge can begin in Holland. By that time the big Jewish camps at Westerbork and Vught will be ready and I can accommodate 40,000 in them."

A few days later, in another letter to RSHA, he wrote to say that there would shortly be an increase in the number of Jews arrested, and he would like to be supplied with three trains a week instead of only two. "30,000 Jews," he wrote, "will have been got away by Christmas, so that a total of 50,-000 will then have been evacuated from this country."

By 2 March 1944 he was able to report to IV B 4 that the Jewish problem in Holland "to all intents and purposes" could be considered solved, for within the next ten days the last "full Jews" would be deported from Westerbork "to the East."

Rauter made no bones about the necessity of applying ruthless and pitiless measures. "This is not a nice job," he wrote, "it is dirty work, but it is a measure which, seen historically, will have great significance. There is no room for tenderness or weakness. Anyone who does not understand this, or who is full of pity or silly talk about humanitarianism and ideals, is not fit to lead in such times as these. And this is what is going to happen. Not one Jew will remain in Europe."

Judging from his general attitude in the witness-box during his trial, the accused Eichmann would, at one time, have agreed with those sentences and, like Eichmann, Rauter in his defence regarding the deportation of the Jews to the East protested that he had no idea of the fate which awaited them when they reached their destination.

It was in Holland that the Germans first met with active resistance, on the part of the local non-Jewish population, to the measures taken against their Jewish neighbours. After the first big round-up of Jews in Amsterdam a general strike broke out in the city which quickly spread to Utrecht, Hilversum and other places. Gas and electricity installations were put out of action and passengers were taken off trains. The strike developed into a revolt against which strong measures were at once taken. SS *Totenkopf* units from Germany were soon on the scene, the police were reinforced, and orders were given to fire on the crowds. The leaders of the Dutch resistance were arrested, some were executed and others imprisoned. Jewish children of mixed marriages were sent to concentration camps where they were done to death. The revolt was crushed and the deportations continued.

But there were still other difficulties as Zoepf reported to Eichmann on 8 June 1942. Things had not gone too smoothly regarding the introduction of the Jewish badge. As a demonstration of solidarity with the persecuted, non-Jews in their thousands had also begun to wear the yellow Star of David, "but we have taken energetic steps to prevent this," he wrote. At first the Jews, to his surprise, were proud of their badge of shame but later, he stated, the fear of what lay ahead became stronger.

There were other minor difficulties. For a time the Germans did not know what to do with the Spanish and Portuguese Jews, of whom there was a large community, especially in Amsterdam. Were they to be included with the others? A ruling was issued by Eichmann's office to the effect that they were to be regarded as "full Jews" in all respects and were to suffer the same fate as the rest of their brethren.

As the manhunt increased in intensity, more and more Jews went into hiding, like the family of Anne Frank now known throughout the world. To cope with this, Eichmann gave instructions that the reward given to informers should be increased and a monthly quota for deportation fixed.

As the Jews were arrested, so was their property misappropriated. This came within the purview of Eichmann's department. In May 1941 all Jews were ordered to register their movable property for sale and deposit it with a German firm. According to the report of the Netherlands Commission on war crimes, all Jewish organisations were abolished and their funds and other property deposited in specified banks, and in May 1942 the Jews were ordered to hand over all their money, gold, jewellery and other valuables.

Every man has his price, however, and some Jews were allowed to get away provided they could pay sufficient ransom. Eichmann's office issued instructions that the emigration of old Jews might be allowed on payment of 100,000 Swiss francs. There were not many who could raise such a sum, but sometimes payment in kind was accepted in lieu of cash. The owner of one large industrial plant was allowed to buy his freedom by handing it over to the Reich.

Those who were arrested were put into camps to await the

fate that was to come to nearly all of them. Some, however, still contrived to get passports and emigration papers smuggled into the camps, but they were few in number. When Eichmann heard of this he ordered an inquiry to be held, and made it known to prevent the repetition of "such undesirable occurrences" he alone would, in future, determine the fate of all the Jews still in Holland. After 5 November 1943 those interned in these camps were completely cut off from all contact with the outside world. The Jews imprisoned there were only allowed to send one postcard each month; it had to be written in German and contain nothing but personal greetings and family matters. All this mail had to be sent to Eichmann's office in Berlin whence it was forwarded to its destination.

There still remained the question of what was to be done with the property of foreign nationals, and Eichmann pressed the Foreign Office to make a decision regarding the property of Jews who were not of Dutch nationality. He summoned a conference which was attended by representatives from all the Ministries directly concerned. It was decided that in future the following principle should be followed in all occupied territories. In return for Germany waiving her right to receive the property of German Jews residing in such territories, when they were sent to one of the extermination camps, she would not hand over to the Governments of foreign countries the property of their Jewish citizens who were deported from Germany. In other words the property of Jews deported for extermination would remain in the country from which they were deported.

All was now ready for the final stages of the operation. In the words of the Attorney-General:

The Jews had been segregated, labelled, assembled, robbed of their property, squeezed dry to the last drop, and now came the phase of their shipment to camps in the East where their bodies would be further exploited by forced labour, their hair would be shorn off for various uses, and finally they would be sent to the gas-chambers. After death, their gold teeth would be extracted from their mouths and their wedding rings removed from their fingers—these were valuable—and when this was done their corpses would be piled into furnaces and of all these human beings only a pile of ashes would remain.

Eichmann, as he has freely admitted, made all the arrangements for transporting the Jews to the East, and some of the relevant documents which emanated from his office were produced as exhibits at the trial; letters arranging for conferences in his office to discuss these matters, the minutes of such conferences, and the instructions which were issued as a result of them. When corresponding with the Foreign Office on the subject of these deportations it was always emphasised that these Jews were only being deported "to work" in Auschwitz and other camps, and that only those fit for work were involved.

The Attorney-General told the Court that the deportations from Holland began in the middle of July 1942 and that Eichmann gave July 1943 as the completion date. He undertook to provide at least one train a day, and emphasised that a special effort should be made during the summer months as the railway authorities would not be able to provide transport during November, December and January.

Nevertheless, although Zoepf did all he could to keep the programme up to schedule, he was obliged to inform Eichmann towards the end of April 1943 that only 68,000 Jews had, so far, been deported, and that over 70,000 still remained. Eichmann was not satisfied with this. He insisted that 8,000 should be deported in May and 15,000 in June and he told Zoepf that Holland should be *Judenrein* by the end of the year. He also ordered the compulsory sterilisation of all children of mixed marriages and again increased the rewards to be paid to anyone who gave information which led to the apprehension of Jews still in hiding.

Eichmann's orders were faithfully carried out, and by 1944

only a few special groups still remained, including a number of diamond cutters and other skilled artisans of whom the Reich still had need. Altogether about 120,000 Jews were sent to the Polish extermination camps, of whom a mere 5,000 survived. Evidence of all this was given by a Dr. Melkman, who possessed a double qualification for so doing. He had personal experience of what happened to the Jews in Holland during the war, and from 1957 to 1960 he was the Director of Yad Washem in Jerusalem where the archives of the holocaust are kept. While holding that appointment he carried out a comprehensive research into the whole subject. When the Germans invaded Holland on 10 May 1940 he was classical master at a non-Jewish private school in Amsterdam, and the editor of a Jewish weekly. He was also Chairman of all the youth organisations in Holland and an ardent Zionist. After the unconditional surrender of the Dutch armed forces, the Germans began to pass discriminatory measures against the Jews and every civil servant was made to sign a declaration that he was not of Jewish origin, otherwise he was dismissed. This included teachers. Dr. Melkman's headmaster opposed this vigorously, but he was eventually forced to give way and he closed the school. The Germans then tried to incite the Dutch population against the Jews and instigate anti-Jewish riots, but they met with no success. The first major round-up of Jews took place early in 1941 when 400 young men were arrested on the Sabbath while many of them were in the synagogues. They were temporarily imprisoned in a camp in Amsterdam and then deported, first to Buchenwald and afterwards transferred to Mauthausen. Only one of them was alive at the end of the war. The reaction of the inhabitants of Amsterdam to this first *Aktion* was extremely hostile. A general strike was declared in the city and soon spread to a number of other towns in the vicinity.

Dr. Melkman, who was examined by Mr. Gabriel Bach, was then asked:

Q: When did the deportations from Holland start?

A: On 14 July 1942.

Q: Who were the first Jews to be deported?

A: The Jews first affected by the regulations were stateless Jews or, to be more exact, German Jews who had been deprived of German citizenship. They were usually young people. I know that in the first convoy most of the deportees were German Jews. They were, first of all, sent to Westerbork but later a sort of transit camp was established in Amsterdam itself and all the Jews who were rounded up were detained there temporarily until there were enough of them to send in one convoy to another camp. . . .

Q: When the deportations of German Jews were being carried out, what was the reaction of Dutch Jews? Had they then begun to realise that it would, in due course, be their turn?

A: Although the early deportations mainly concerned Jews of foreign nationality, a number of Dutch Jews went with them so that by that time they knew quite well that the intention was to deport Dutch Jews as well as the others.

Q: How were these arrests carried out?

A: The German police, who were in possession of lists of registered Jews, sometimes came to the houses where they lived and arrested them there. Sometimes they would be summoned by letter to report to their local police stations. The arrests were usually carried out systematically, district by district. The first round-up took place during one of the Jewish festivals when it was known that all the Jews would be at home. The second round-up took place in May 1943 when the old Jewish residential quarter in Amsterdam was surrounded. On that occasion trucks fitted with loud-speakers were driven along the streets blaring out that all Jews were to go out of their houses and give themselves up. . . .

Q: You were eventually taken to Westerbork in a goods train, were you not? How long did you stay there?

A: I was there for eight months, until 15 February 1944, and then I was sent to Bergen-Belsen.

Q: How many people on the average were kept in Westerbork at that time?

A: It was difficult to say because when I arrived there one of

the largest transports of Amsterdam Jews had just arrived and there were thousands pouring in. At the same time large convoys of about three to four thousand people were constantly leaving for the East, so that there was a constant turn-over. . . .

Q: Dr. Melkman, what other camps existed in Holland for the detention of Jews?

A: There was one big camp in the south, and a Phillips' factory was also used for the purpose. Another camp was used as a training camp.

Not all the Jews in Holland went to Auschwitz and the other extermination camps in East Poland. Melkman and a large number of other Dutch Jews were sent to Belsen. This camp was situated near the village of Bergen on the road from Celle to Hamburg. It was originally quite a small camp but it was later enlarged and in November 1944 Joseph Kramer, who had previously been on the staff of Auschwitz, was sent there for the avowed purpose of running it as a convalescent depot for sick persons from the concentration camps, factories and farms and for displaced persons in the whole of north-west Europe.

There were no gas-chambers in Belsen but thousands were, nevertheless, exterminated by disease and starvation. During the last few months of the camp's existence, the shortage of food was so acute that the prisoners resorted to cannibalism. The camp staff, however, were still well fed.

Dr. Melkman stated in his evidence that Belsen was split up into a number of different camps, and he had the opportunity of visiting them all as he was employed on permanent coal fatigue. In the course of this duty he visited the section of the camp which was reserved for women who had arrived there from Auschwitz in November 1944. There he saw women searching in the refuse bins for scraps of food, and being beaten by some of the women guards for so doing. He even heard of cases of cannibalism. This was confirmed by a witness at the trial of Kramer and the camp staff of Belsen by a British Military Court in Luneberg.

A former British inmate of the camp gave evidence that, when engaged in clearing away dead bodies, as many as one in ten had a piece cut from the thigh or other part of the body, which had been taken and eaten, and that he had seen people in the act of doing it. To such lengths had they been brought by the pangs of hunger. This witness said:

I noticed on many occasions a very strange wound at the back of the thigh of many of the dead. First of all I dismissed it as a gunshot wound at close quarters, but after seeing a few more I asked a friend and he told me that many of the prisoners were cutting chunks off the bodies to eat. On my very next visit to the mortuary I actually saw a prisoner whip out a knife, cut a portion out of the leg of a body and put it quickly into his mouth, naturally frightened of being seen in the act of doing so. I leave it to your imagination to realise to what state the prisoners were reduced to risk eating bits of flesh from black corpses.

Belsen camp differed little from most of the others. A graphic description of the sight which met the gaze of the first British officers to enter after its capitulation will convey a vivid picture of what went on within those barbed-wire fences.

With the first troops to enter the camp was Captain Derek Sington, then in command of No. 14 Amplifying Unit, in order to make any announcements which were thought necessary or desirable and to act as interpreter to the officer in command of the Regiment of Artillery which moved in to occupy the camp.

At the gate Captain Sington was met by the commandant, Joseph Kramer, who said there were 40,000 in number one camp and a further 15,000 in number two camp, mostly habitual criminals, felons and homosexuals but that there were also *Schutzhaftlinge*.[2] These comprised, of course, ninety-nine per cent of the inmates and they came from every country the Germans had invaded since the beginning of the war.

When Brigadier Glyn Hughes, the Deputy-Director of Medical Services, British Army of the Rhine, entered the camp

[2] *Schutzhaftlinge*—literally those in protective custody.

a few hours after Captain Sington, the conditions he found were indescribable. "No description, no photograph," he said, "could really bring home the horrors that were there outside the huts and the frightful scenes inside were much worse."

Piles of corpses were lying all over the camp, outside and inside, some of them in the same bunks as the living. Near the crematorium were massed graves which had been filled in, and there was one open pit full of corpses. The huts were filled to overflowing with prisoners in every stage of emaciation and disease; in some, which were only suitable to accommodate a hundred people, there were as many as a thousand.

There was no sanitation, and the conditions inside the huts were revolting because most of the prisoners were suffering from some form of gastro-enteritis and were too weak to go outside to relieve themselves. In any event, the hut lavatories had long been out of use. In the women's compound there was a deep trench with a pole over it but no screening or form of privacy at all. Those who were strong enough could reach the compound: others performed their natural actions where they lay. The compounds were covered with human excreta.

In one compound there were 8,000 male prisoners and typhus was rife. In one of the women's compounds there were 23,000 women and many corpses were still lying about.

Seventy per cent of the inmates needed to go to hospital and it was more than probable that 10,000 of these would die before they could be admitted.

Every form of disease was prevalent. But those most responsible for the hopeless condition of the patients were typhus, tuberculosis and starvation. The conditions in the camp must have been bad for several months to produce death in persons who were fit and well.

The morning after his inspection, Brigadier Hughes made a further tour of the camp with Kramer who took him to one of the open graves. The commandant appeared quite callous and indifferent. "I have been a doctor for thirty years," said the Brigadier, "and have seen all the horrors of war, but I have never seen anything to touch it." He also stated that there appeared to have been no attempt made at all to preserve the lives and health of the inmates.

BELGIUM

In Belgium the measures adopted to get rid of the Jews were very similar to those used in Holland. Discriminatory anti-Jewish laws, compulsory registration, the wearing of the Star of David badge, curfews, and the round-up of Jews in Antwerp, Brussels, Liège and Charleroi whence they were taken to the famous Breendonck camp. It was in this camp that whenever one of their number was executed the Jews had to march up and down in front of the corpses singing *"Wir werden nie Breendonck Vergessen das Paradies der Juden"*— "Never shall we forget Breendonck, the Jewish paradise."

Nevertheless the Nazis' methods were less successful than in Holland, and in a way the pattern of deportation resembled that in France. When the registration of Belgian Jews began, more than fifty per cent failed to register and, after the war had ended, it was found that about 60,000 out of 85,000 had survived. This was to a great extent due to the German Military Governor, General von Falkenhausen, who did all he could to put obstacles in the way of the Security Police whose responsibility it was to round up the Belgian Jews and send them to the extermination camps in the East.

As in France, Jews living in Belgium, not of Belgian nationality, and Jewish refugees from other countries, were not protected in the same way. Many of them had fled across the border to France when Belgium was invaded and were arrested there. Those who remained, and they were not many in number, were soon hunted down and sent to their death.

Eichmann himself certainly intended that all the Jews in Belgium, irrespective of nationality, should be put on the trains which took them from the camp at Malines to Auschwitz and he must have made representations to the German Foreign Office when he discovered that this was not being done. In any event Rademacker addressed a firm protest to von Falkenhausen's headquarters on the subject, and complained that during the first three months since the commencement of these convoys not a single Belgian-born Jew had been deported. Later the position changed slightly, but the number was never considerable.

NORWAY AND DENMARK

There were not more than 1,750 Jews living in Norway at the time of the Nazi invasion. About half of them fled at once to Sweden. The remainder were deported to the extermination camps in Poland. Of these only twenty-one survived. The Norwegian resistance forces did what they could to smuggle Jews out of the country and the whole population did a great deal to sabotage the deportation programme. They were rewarded by the Germans with brutal reprisals which will not be forgotten.

The handling of the Jewish question in Norway was the responsibility of the Chief of the Security Police (SIPO) of whom Eichmann said, according to the Attorney-General, "This was my office." He also did his best to thwart the Swedish Government's efforts to rescue the Jews of Norway from their fate. A letter was sent from Amt IV B 4 to the German Foreign Minister in Stockholm complaining that the Swedish Government was granting Swedish nationality to Norwegian Jews and protesting that this should not be allowed to continue.

In another letter he accused the Swedes of attempting to frustrate the measures being taken against these Jews.

The story of Denmark's Jews is very different. Until a state of emergency was proclaimed by the Germans in September 1943 the occupation differed from that of every other country which they had invaded. They intended to establish Denmark as a model protectorate, and for the first three years after the invasion there was little or no interference with the government of the country. King Christian and his Government continued to function. No discriminatory measures were introduced, no registration took place nor was the Jewish badge worn. Later the position changed. As the Attorney-General told the Court:

> The Germans themselves were hesitant and the Foreign Office doubted the advisability of imposing the extermination programme on Denmark. But where Jews were concerned a man like Eichmann would never give way. As early as April 1943, he told von Thadden, of the Foreign Office: "They will shortly persuade you to change your attitude." Eichmann eventually got his own way. An outbreak of strikes and the intensification of the anti-German underground operations provided a convenient opportunity. A state of emergency was declared by the occupation authorities in September 1943 and the SS angel of death, the Chief of the SIPO, appeared in Copenhagen and immediate plans were made for rounding up the Jews.

Eichmann immediately sent his second in command, Rolf Günther, to Denmark with a special unit from Amt IV B 4, but it was found impossible, at first, to obtain the co-operation of the army of occupation under General von Hannecken. The Foreign Minister then asked Eichmann, as the head of the Jewish Office of the Gestapo, to try and persuade the military to assist.

On 1 October the blow was due to fall. The Germans swooped down on all Jewish houses on the first two days of the month, but they found very few Jews in them. There had been a leak somewhere, and the Danes had got wind of the operation. At very great risk to themselves, and in the nick of time, they organised a miniature Dunkirk. Fishing-boats, yachts, pleasure boats, and any other small seaworthy vessel that they could lay their hands on, were assembled at the little fishing ports along the coast of Denmark nearest to Sweden. The Jews were escorted to various points by guides, consisting mostly of students, put on board and secretly transported to Sweden.

More than 6,000 full Jews, and more than 1,000 half Jews, were smuggled into Sweden in this way between 26 September and 12 October. Only about 500 fell into German hands, most of whom were sent to Theresienstadt. Less than 100 lost their lives.

SOUTHERN FRANCE AND ITALY

When the Free Zone of France was entered by the Germans on 11 November 1942, after the Allied landing in North Africa, the Italian Army occupied Nice, Grenoble and the Alpes Maritimes. But the Italians, despite Mussolini who was not unwilling to cooperate with the Germans in their extermination programme, put every obstacle in the way of Eichmann's staff. East of the Rhone they intervened continually in favour of the Jews. This must have occasioned some surprise at the time, for in 1938 anti-Jewish legislation, similar to that in Germany, had been brought into force by Mussolini. Genocide, however, was another matter. The Italian people would never support that.

With regard to the solution of the Jewish question in Italy itself the Nazis decided to call on Himmler personally to conduct negotiations with the Duce. Eichmann and his associates complained bitterly about the "sabotage" of the Italian authorities in Southern France, Greece and Yugoslavia. A letter on the subject was written by the Gestapo Chief, *Gruppenführer* Müller, to the German Foreign Office and he mentioned in it that his source of information was Eichmann's Amt IV B 4. The letter complained of the Italian authorities' attitude and their constant habit of taking the side of the Jews. This greatly interfered with the final solution, wrote Müller, and set a bad example to other countries who made the excuse that if one of the Axis Powers took this view it could hardly be wondered at if a country under Nazi occupation did the same.

After the fall of Mussolini and the surrender of Badoglio, Dannecker was transferred from France to become Eichmann's representative in Italian territory under Nazi occupation. Now that the Germans were in control they expected to meet with fewer obstacles from their former allies, but when a general round-up of Jews took place in Rome, on 16 October 1943, it met with little success, for the Italians, at great risk to themselves, hid most of the Jews and saved them from arrest. The Pope also intervened on their behalf. When similar operations were attempted all over Northern Italy, the clergy rescued Jews and hid them in monasteries. All this angered the Germans intensely. After his rescue by Skorzeny, Mussolini re-established the Fascist Republic in Northern Italy and continued to maintain an embassy in Berlin. On one occasion the Ambassador asked the German Foreign Office for information on the fate of a certain Jew.

Günther, Eichmann's deputy, replied to the Foreign Office in the following terms:

We are refraining from fulfilling the request of the Italian Embassy regarding the holding of an investigation to obtain the requested information regarding the domicile of the above-mentioned Jew. It would be advisable to recommend to the Ambassador that he should desist from making such unnecessary requests in order to further the implementation of our extermination programme. In the fifth year of the War the German authorities have other and more important duties to perform than investigate the fate of a deported Jew. It is a matter for regret that the Italian Ambassador should still consider it his duty to interfere in Jewish matters.

Considered in this context, Eichmann's insistence that he felt keenly for the Jews, and had no opportunity to make decisions regarding any of them, does not sound very convincing.

VI

The Extermination of Hungarian Jewry

APART FROM Poland, Russia and Rumania, Eichmann's greatest successes were in Czechoslovakia and Hungary, but in both these countries the final solution was preceded by suggestions that perhaps Jewish lives could be bought.

Himmler, for a long time, had been interested in what is generally known as the Europa plan which proposed "a rational exportation of the Jews," this being a euphemism for selling them to the highest bidder. This idea was the lineal descendant of a practice which had been permitted in the very early days of the war, namely to allow rich Jews to emigrate in exchange for hard currency. In Holland, for instance, fifty wealthy Dutch Jews had been able to purchase their safety for a ransom of between five and ten thousand dollars a head. Towards the end of 1942 Himmler and his immediate colleagues were thinking of extending the idea to other countries, beginning with Slovakia where deportations had just been temporarily suspended. Eichmann, however, was always strongly opposed to any such weakness. He wanted no compromise. He had a sacred mission, to destroy the Jews, and he was convinced that their extermination was necessary for the survival of the German race. If he could succeed in destroying the "biological basis" of Jewry in the East by complete extermination, Jewry as a whole would never recover from the blow.

By the beginning of 1944, however, Hungary was the only country in Europe, within the sphere of influence of the Third Reich, which still had a considerable Jewish population. After the annexation of Southern Slovakia, Northern Transylvania and Carpatho-Russia, there were about 800,000 Jews living in Hungary.

Ever since 1942, when the German Foreign Office tried to get the Hungarian Ambassador in Berlin to persuade the Regent of Hungary, Admiral Horthy, to carry out the *Führer's* wishes and take an active part in the "solution of the Jewish problem," there had been constant pressure upon the Hungarian Government to come into line with Germany over the Jewish question. A promise was made that all Jewish property would be turned over to the Hungarians, in return for which the Hungarian Government would be expected to remove the Jews from all positions of influence in the cultural and economic life of the country, introduce the Jewish badge, and deport them all to the East.

Nevertheless, this pressure was resisted for a long time. Nicholas Kallay succeeded Laszlo Bardossy as Prime Minister of Hungary in March 1942, after which there were no more pogroms or deportations. Although Kallay was not pro-Jewish he would still not agree to the Jews being deported to the East, for he did not feel happy about what would happen to them when they got there. The persistent rumours of what was going on in Poland disturbed him, and he made it clear that he did not want to be accused of having exposed the Hungarian Jews, after their deportation, to misery or worse. In reply to a question put in the Hungarian Parliament by a member of the Arrow Cross party as late as December 1942 Kallay had stated that the time was "not appropriate" for imprisoning the Jews in labour camps and ghettos.

A full report of this was, in due course, sent to Eichmann whose views had already been stated in September of that year when the German Foreign Office proposed that action should be taken against Jews from other countries who had taken refuge in Hungary. He was not in favour of only partial action being taken and wrote, "In my view, it would be necessary for this purpose to set the whole deportation machine in motion . . . without bringing us any closer to the solution of the Jewish question in Hungary. It would be better to wait until Hungary is ready to include her own Jews in the scope of this operation."

Meanwhile the Germans were getting very restive, and the question was raised by Hitler directly with Horthy at a meeting between them at Klessheim Castle on 17 April at which Ribbentrop was also present. A note of the meeting was kept by Dr. Schmidt,[1] and it is still in existence. The subject of the Jews came up during a discussion between the two statesmen regarding the black-market which, Hitler said, was negligible in Germany. When Admiral Horthy said that he had, so far, been unable to keep the black-market under control, Hitler replied that this was the fault of the Jews who considered hoarding and profiteering as their main sphere of activity even during a world war, in exactly the same way as in England sentences for rationing offences and the like now chiefly concerned Jews. Horthy then asked, what should he do now that he had deprived them of almost all the possibilities of living? He could not just kill them off. Ribbentrop said that the Jews must either be exterminated or sent to concentration camps. There was no other possibility. To Horthy's remark that it was easier for Germany to do this, for she did not possess so many Jews, Hitler quoted figures to show how predominant Jews were in certain professions, and mentioned the fact that whereas the town of Furth admitted Jews, Nuremberg had not tolerated Jews within its walls for four hundred years. The result was that Nuremberg flourished greatly while Furth had degenerated.

The Admiral was then treated to one of Hitler's stock

[1] Hitler's official interpreter.

tirades against Jews in general which did not reflect great credit on the *Führer's* knowledge of history. It was recorded by Dr. Schmidt in these words:

The Jews did not even possess organisational value. In spite of the fears which I have heard repeatedly in Germany, everything has continued to go its normal way without Jews. Where the Jews have been left to themselves, as for instance in Poland, the most terrible misery and decay prevailed. They are just poor parasites. In Poland this state of affairs has been fundamentally cleared up. If the Jews there did not want to work, they were shot. If they could not work, they had to succumb. They had to be treated like T.B. bacilli with which a healthy body may become infected. This is not cruel if one remembers that even innocent creatures of nature such as hares and deer have to be killed so that no harm is caused by them. Why should the beasts who wanted to bring us Bolshevism be spared more? Nations which did not rid themselves of Jews perished. One of the most famous examples of this was the downfall of a people who were once so proud, the Persians, who now lead a pitiful existence as Armenians.

Horthy listened politely to this harangue but it had no effect on Hungarian policy *vis-à-vis* the Jews. Perhaps Hitler overestimated the extent of the Hungarian political leaders' anti-Semitism, otherwise he would hardly have openly admitted his knowledge of the Jewish extermination in Poland.

Nine months passed, and the Germans had still failed to persuade Horthy to adopt a "realistic" policy in regard to the Jewish question. At the end of 1943 Edmund Veesenmayer, who was later to be German Ambassador in Budapest, reported to Hitler that the only thing which bound the Admiral to Germany was his fear of Bolshevism, and Prime Minister Kallay regarded all measures taken against the Jews as crimes against the Hungarians. He also suggested to Ribbentrop that Germany should no longer rest content with the fact that independent Hungary was her ally, and that the country should be occupied in order that Hitler's policy for the extermination of the Jews could be forced on the Hungarian Government. The advice was taken, and when the German troops occupied the country in March 1944, a special *Kommando* came with them, under Adolf Eichmann, whose task was to liquidate the Jews. As the Attorney-General said:

> Eichmann brought into Hungary his whole group of accomplices, the entire gang of murderers, who together with him had carried out the extermination programme in the various conquered lands: Krumey, Wisliceny, Dannecker, Hünsche, Novak, Brunner and others,[2] all of whom had already sent millions of Jews to the slaughter and had gained experience throughout Europe in methods of persuading and inciting the local populations. All of these, who had already proved their efficiency and talent, now swooped down upon Hungarian Jewry. Here they could not wait. The Soviet Army had already re-occupied the Ukraine and advanced into the Carpathian mountains. There was serious ground for fearing that if they did not carry out their evil work quickly, they would never be able to get it done. The leading lights of IV B 4 were, therefore, assembled in Hungary after being released from their duties in other countries where the extermination programme had been completed or could continue in their absence. Here there was an apparent sense of urgency in all their activities, a desire to finish the job at all costs, a need to concentrate all stages of the preparatory work, at times to

[2] Dannecker disappeared after the war and has never been seen or heard of since; Hünsche was last seen in 1945 in Alt Aussee; Wisliceny was sentenced to death and hanged in Bratislava in July 1948; Brunner was hanged by sentence of the Vienna People's Court in the Russian Sector in May 1946. Towards the end of 1960 the Public Prosecutor's Office in Frankfurt offered a reward of the equivalent of £900 for clues leading to the arrest of Franz Novak and within a few days he was arrested. He is now awaiting trial which will take place in Vienna. Krumey, who was previously released through lack of evidence by the Frankfurt Council of Appeal when accused of murdering eighty-eight children from Lidice, has, since the capture of Eichmann, been re-arrested and he is now awaiting trial at the War Crime Investigation Centre in Ludwigsburg.

skip some of them, to take short cuts with the sole purpose of achieving results as quickly as possible.

The gang had at their disposal all the power of the German Army as well as the Hungarian civil service when Sztojay, a puppet of the Germans, was appointed Prime Minister. It is doubtful whether the Nazis any longer believed at that time that they could win the war, but they wanted at least to complete the destruction of the Jews. On this front, come what may, they wanted to guarantee themselves a victory.

Whereas formerly Eichmann had directed the extermination programme from behind a desk, here in Budapest he was on the spot and in immediate control. He did not merely make the plans and issue directions; in Budapest he also implemented them.

The lesson of the Warsaw Ghetto had not been forgotten, and Eichmann was determined that there should be no repetition of it in Hungary. As the Attorney-General said:

Particular attention was devoted to ensuring that it would never occur to the Jews to revolt or attempt to escape and save their property. Eichmann's aim here was to murder and inherit at one and the same time. The illusion was spread that no harm would come to those Jews who were prepared to work.

As soon as Eichmann arrived he arrested most of the leading personalities in Jewish political and business circles in Hungary, together with journalists and "anti-Fascist" politicians.

Before he could put the final solution into operation, however, much had to be done in Auschwitz which, by then, had almost closed down as an extermination centre. Höss was sent for by Eichmann and told to get everything ready to prepare the gas-chambers for another influx of victims. He told Eichmann, however, that he could not "accommodate" them in such large numbers as before, and a compromise was reached. There would only be two train-loads on one day and three the next. Nevertheless there had never been such a period of fever-ish activity in Auschwitz as in the summer and autumn of 1944. The gas-chambers and furnaces worked day and night, but many bodies had to be burned in the open. At one time the daily gassings, according to Höss's own evidence, reached the fantastic number of 10,000.

Meanwhile, Eichmann, with his two assistants Wisliceny and Krumey, summoned all the Jewish leaders to a meeting where, at the point of a revolver, they were informed that all the existing institutions and organisations of the Jewish com-munity would be forthwith dissolved, and a Central Jewish Council set up as the only body recognised by the occupying forces. In future, they were told, all Jewish affairs in Hungary would be supervised by the *Sondereinsatzkommando Eich-mann*, but the Jews were not to worry. Nothing would hap-pen to them so long as they behaved themselves.

If any of them really believed this promise they did not have to wait long for disillusionment. As the Attorney-General told the Court:

> From then on, the flood of the all too familiar laws and decrees was let loose: the prohibition to leave one's place of residence, the prohibition to use transport, the disconnection of telephones, the freezing of bank-accounts, house-curfews, the closure of shops, the registration of all property, and the like. When the community representatives lodged complaints, the Accused re-torted that all orders must be carried out without delay.

At the beginning of April all Hungarian Jews from six years of age and over were obliged to wear the yellow badge. An air attack on Budapest provided the command with a pretext to com-mandeer 500 Jewish apartments, which were turned over, com-plete with furnishing and equipment, to Hungarians, and when the Jewish representatives protested the number demanded was raised to 2,000.

Jews were arrested on the trains and in the streets. Those ap-prehended were assembled in camps, of which Kistarcsa Camp was the worst. A round-up of Jews was started in the provincial towns, according to prepared zones marked out in advance. In a number of towns ghettos were set up where conditions were so appalling that they almost defy description.

To carry out the round-up in Budapest in one sweep was no easy task, as its quarter of a million Jews were scattered throughout the city. It was thus found necessary to operate in stages, the houses in which Jews were ordered to live being marked with a large yellow sign.

Here too, Hungarians and Jews were informed by Eichmann that the latter were only wanted for work. The Hungarian Government agreed to put 50,000 Jews at the disposal of the Reich "for work in Germany." But the official German correspondence, all in the name of the Accused, clearly indicates the true objective —Auschwitz.

Nevertheless, for a time, most of the leading Jews in Budapest were inclined to believe that, perhaps, after all the worst might not happen. One of these was Yoel Brand who has stated that the precedent of Gisi Fleischmann's activities [3] encouraged him and the other leaders of Waada [4] to hope that they could "buy" Wisliceny if only they could get into direct touch with him. Brand even promised the *Abwehr* [5] agents 20,000 dollars if they could arrange an interview with him. This they refused to do, for they feared that they would lose the profit they themselves were already making out of the Hungarian Jews if the Jewish leaders were able to deal directly with SS headquarters. The *Abwehr* were prepared to take the 20,000 dollars, but all they would promise in return was to tell Wisliceny that a Jewish deputation would like to meet him.

Another leading Budapest Jew who had considerable dealings with Eichmann about this time was Pinchas Freudiger, formerly Philip von Freudiger who, with Brand, gave evidence at Eichmann's trial. He was examined by Mr. Gabriel

---

[3] See pages 197–198.

[4] This was a Hungarian Jewish relief and rescue organisation, and the other two Budapest leaders were Dr. Kastner and Samuel Springmann.

[5] The German Intelligence Bureau.

Bach, one of the Counsel for the prosecution, and described the meeting with Krumey and Wisliceny already mentioned.

MR. BACH: Mr. Freudiger, you told the Court yesterday that you went to Wisliceny in order to obtain the release of your brother. You began telling the Court about your conversation with Wisliceny. Will you please tell the Court what took place at this conversation and what you were told by Wisliceny?

FREUDIGER: As I said yesterday, Wisliceny promised me that nothing would happen to my brother and he told me to come to a meeting that afternoon and said that after the meeting he would speak to me.

Q: Did you go to the meeting?

A: Yes.

Q: And what took place?

A: About forty to fifty people were present at the meeting representing all the Jewish institutes of Budapest. Krumey and Wisliceny were also there. Krumey opened the meeting and later on asked Wisliceny to speak. Wisliceny repeated exactly what we had heard the day before, though in greater detail, and the tenor of his speech was that nothing would happen to the Jews apart from certain regulations and ordinances. He told us that we would be able to live in peace and quiet. He obviously wanted to calm us down.

Q: Did he demand anything from you in regard to other Jews?

A: He told us to calm down the other Jews so that order should be preserved. Then we asked him a few rather delicate questions. First of all we asked him why people were being arrested at the railway stations and rounded up overnight, because hundreds of Jews had already been arrested and were shut up in the Rabbinal Seminar, in so-called protective custody. Wisliceny then said, "Well, after all, we are taking hostages. This is done everywhere. But nothing is going to happen to them. They are merely kept there as hostages so as to ensure law and order. You must, however, understand that no Jews may leave their homes and that they are forbidden to travel unless in possession of a special permit.

Q: Special permit from whom?

A: He said that the Jews needed a special permit in order to travel, but he did not specify what kind of permit or from whom it could be obtained. He simply said that no Jew could change his place of residence. . . .

Q: . . . Mr. Freudiger, did you meet Adolf Eichmann in Budapest?

A: Yes.

Q: You see the Accused here in Court—can you identify him?

A: I remember *Obersturmbannführer* Eichmann in uniform, high boots and a pistol in his hand, shouting at me in the tone of voice so typical of the Master Race, nevertheless, in spite of all this, I recognise him.

Q: Will you tell the Court in what circumstances you first met him?

A: The first time I met him I did not know that it was Eichmann. I went to Schwannenburg to see either Wisliceny or Krumey, as they had impounded the synagogue and I wanted to ask them to give back for use the volumes of the Torah which were there. I was met by an officer who asked me what I was doing there and I told him. He replied: "All right. I'll see to it. The matter will be arranged."

Q: Did you, in fact, recover the scrolls?

A: Yes, the matter was arranged and we did get them back. Meanwhile, about 15,000 people had already been deported, people who had been arrested at the railway stations. They were sent to Kistarcsa Camp where the conditions were terrible. I also wanted to speak to Krumey and Wisliceny on this subject. I wanted to ask them what the meaning of it all was. On this occasion again I met an officer. I did not know him from Adam and he asked me what I was doing there. He told me after I had spoken to him that there was nothing to be done. Then I asked him what crime had these people committed. After all they were doing nothing except travelling by the train at a time when there was yet no ban on railway travel. He said, "Quite out of the question, please do not bother me any more." That ended the interview. A day or two later I met Wisliceny and resumed my plea. I told him that I had met an officer who had told me that it was quite impossible to help these people. Wisliceny said, "You have been speaking to Eichmann. If Eichmann said 'No,' it means 'No.' "

Q: Do you remember the exact words used by Eichmann when you met him?

A: Yes. He told me that it was absolutely out of the question. The Jews would have to stay where they were. I argued with him and then he started shouting at me. He said, "I will teach you what discipline means. I will deal with you!"

Q: Mr. Freudiger, did you ever meet Eichmann again?

A: Yes, but this was a very different meeting, much more important. I think that it was on 16 April. We had just got news that Hungarian Jews were being rounded up in a town called Nyiregyhaza and concentrated in towns near the Eastern borders of Hungary. . . . All the Jews had to leave their homes and take with them only 30 kilos of baggage. They were arrested by the gendarmerie, concentrated in one place, but we did not then know what was going to happen to them. All this took place shortly after we had handed over some 250,000 dollars to Krumey as a kind of ransom for our brother Jews. We called a meeting of the Central Committee, but we were at a loss to know what to do. One of our number, Dr. Reiner, whose family lived in Nyiregyhaza, including his parents who were both over eighty years of age, was the most excited of us and he suggested that we should immediately go to see Wisliceny and Krumey and ask them to explain what was going on. I eventually agreed to accompany Dr. Reiner, and later that afternoon we went to Schwannenburg to try and see Krumey. I felt that I could speak frankly to him as it was only a week earlier that he had taken a quarter of a million dollars from us. While we were waiting to see Krumey, Eichmann arrived. "What are you doing here, my dear boys?" he asked. "We are waiting for *Obersturmbannführer* Krumey." He said, "All right, kindly step into my office." We went into his office which was next to Krumey's office. There we saw a large map of Hungary on the wall. We stood in front of the map on which the districts near the Eastern frontier were clearly marked. Eichmann said that he had given orders for all Jews living in these frontier areas to be concentrated in ghettos. This would affect 310,000 Jews. He then went on to tell us that the Russians were in force on the other side of the Carpathians and it was absolutely impossible to leave 300,000 hostile Jews to move about freely in areas so close to the frontier. It was 300 miles away. Eichmann then said, "You'd better ask your Hungarians! The whole of this area is under the supervision of the third brigade of the Hungarian Army. The whole area is treated as a frontier district. . . ." I could find no answer, and Eichmann then continued, saying: "The Hungarian Army has to be there because we must keep peace and order, and see to it that there are no epidemics." One of our colleagues said, "How can we possibly look after hygiene if the means at our disposal are so limited?" Eichmann then began shouting again. "There you go again," he said, "starting this horror propaganda. Who told you all that?" I said, "Yes, I know." Because it was quite obvious what the conditions were, and Krumey then chipped in and said, "All right, if you have parents let them come to Budapest." The meeting then ended.

Another witness who was called by the prosecution and who had much contact with the Accused was Yoel Brand. He was brought up in Germany and had intended in 1934 to emigrate to Palestine but changed his mind and went, instead, to Budapest where he became an active Zionist.

In 1941 the first deportations of Jews from Hungary to Poland took place, amongst whom were his sister-in-law and her husband, and it was in this way that he first learned about the mass shootings that were taking place in Poland. The Zionist party then decided to set up a rescue Committee with the object of preventing further deportations. The Committee had three directors, Kastner, Springmann and himself.

On 19 March, when the Germans entered Hungary, Brand was at the Majestic Hotel in Budapest. Three Hungarian officers approached him and said that the Nazis were occupying Budapest and that his name was on the list of persons to be arrested. The list, they said, had been prepared by Eichmann and the officers then proceeded to take Brand into "protective custody" but released him three days later.

In the witness-box he was asked by the Attorney-General whether he knew by that time that Wisliceny was in Budapest. He answered, "Yes."

Q: Were you trying to establish contact with him?
A: Yes, we wanted to get in touch with him at all costs. We

knew about the negotiations which had taken place between Gisi Fleischmann and Wisliceny in Slovakia and we knew that they had met with some success as a number of Slovakian Jews had been saved from deportation. We also knew of the second transaction, the so-called Europa Plan, according to which Wisliceny was prepared to save all the Jews in Europe for two or three million dollars.

Q: And eventually you established contact with Wisliceny through the mediation of the Schmidt group? [6]

A: Yes, we bribed the Schmidt group with dollars in order to establish contact with Wisliceny and they managed to arrange this for us.

Q: Who took part in the meeting?

A: Two officers came to represent the SS, Wisliceny and a captain named Lausnitzer. The Army counter-intelligence was represented by Schmidt himself and a man named Wieringer. Our group was represented by Kastner and myself.

Q: You paid a certain sum of money just to obtain their consent for the meeting you are speaking about?

A: Yes.

Q: How much?

A: We paid the Schmidt group officially 20,000 dollars and to the individual agents an additional bribe for themselves of 1,000 dollars each, the total amounting to some 24,000 dollars.

Q: At the meeting what did you ask of the Germans?

A: As my German was better than Dr. Kastner's I put the questions and these were our demands: first, that there should be no concentration of the Jews and no setting up of ghettos for the Jews in Hungary, second, that there should be no pogroms, no Jewish blood should be spilled in Hungary, third, that no Jews should be deported from Hungary and fourth, that permission should be granted for Jewish emigration to Palestine. Until then there had been legal emigration of about fifty Jewish children a month to Palestine, although it was occasionally possible, clandestinely, to include adults among them.

Q: What was the proposal that you put to the Germans for this purpose?

A: Precisely what Wisliceny had already demanded in Czecho-

[6] Dr. Schmidt was head of the *Abwehr* in Budapest.

slovakia, i.e. that 2,000,000 dollars should be paid in ten monthly instalments of 200,000 dollars each. We assumed that the war would be over within ten months.

Q: What was Wisliceny's reply?

A: He gave us a long lecture. I remember he was so fat that he could not sit on a single chair. He said that they would not force the Jews to settle in the ghettos, but that it would be to their own advantage to leave the small villages and provincial towns because, as he said, the SS could not act as bodyguards to the Jews and it would be safer for them if they were transferred to the larger towns.

On the second point, he said, the Germans are here, but it is not in their interests that there should be unrest and there will be neither pogroms nor bloodshed. Nevertheless, the SS could not be bodyguards for the Jews. As he put it, "When wood is cut, chips must fall."

Regarding the third point his reaction was quite positive and he said, "There will be no deportations." He said, "For deportations you need two sides, the deported and the receiver, i.e. the one who is prepared to accept the deportees. Here in Hungary there was no one who was prepared to accept deportees or to deport them.

Q: And what about the fourth condition, that is to say emigration?

A: His reply on this point was strange. He was against the emigration of small groups from Hungary, because, he said, in such cases it would mean taking out the rich and the leaders and he would be left holding the ordinary people. Nevertheless he suggested that a plan should be worked out for the emigration of the entire Hungarian Jewry and that such a plan would have a chance of being accepted by his superiors.

Q: What about the question of emigration to Palestine?

A: He gave us a long talk about this and said that it was quite out of the question because there was an agreement between the Germans and the Mufti of Jerusalem. The Jews, he said, should look to other countries, North Africa, North America, Australia perhaps, and Latin America. If the Jews emigrated to any of those countries and then were able to get to Palestine, he would, of course, not interfere as it would not be his affair.

Q: Did Kastner mention a number of pioneers who were already preparing for emigration?

A: Yes, Kastner said that it would be much easier for us to obtain help from abroad if we could point to positive results and he said that there was a certain ship which was about to set sail from Constanza to Turkey, and that we possessed some 600 to 700 certificates for emigration to Palestine and it would have been a token of good-will on the part of the Germans if they would allow the departure of those who held such certificates.

Q: Did Wisliceny then suggest that a list of these persons should be brought to him?

A: Yes. He asked for a list of names and then said that he could not, as he put it, "Sell the Jews of Hungary f.o.b." He said that they would have to become "German merchandise." They had to be transferred to Germany, then they would become German merchandise and then they could be sold as such. This sounded to us very peculiar. His proposition was that these Jews should first be taken to Germany by steamer along the Danube, and that as soon as they were on German soil they would be re-embarked on another ship going down the Danube and would then reach Constanza as "German merchandise." This use of the expression "German merchandise" was quite frightening.

Q: Did you pay money to Wisliceny?

A: Yes. Wisliceny said that he could not yet meet our demands because after all, 2,000,000 dollars was not very much, but he was going to ask for instructions from his superiors and meanwhile the best thing to do would be to pay him a first instalment of 200,000 as a token of good faith.

Q: Did you pay anything and if so how much?

A: We paid a few instalments but not all at once. Most of the money we paid in pengos and sixty per cent of it we received direct from the Jewish community.

Q: Did you have contact with any other members of the group, for instance Krumey and Hünsche?

A: Yes.

Q: Who was Krumey?

A: Krumey was Eichmann's deputy in Budapest.

Q: How many meetings did you have with them?

A: At least four, perhaps even five.

Q: How did the negotiations proceed?

A: Nothing really came out of them. Each time we brought money to pay the instalment due, but it really made no impression. They seemed to be almost more annoyed with the Hungarians than with the Jews. Krumey and Wisliceny, by what they said, made it quite clear that there was competition between the Germans and the Hungarians so far as the looting of Jewish property was concerned. We did, however, obtain a few minor concessions. For example we would make a number of requests for the release of arrested colleagues, such as the secretaries of the Palestine office, and our requests were usually granted. We also obtained permission to visit all concentration camps. Krumey agreed to our being issued permits for this purpose but he said that he could not understand the importance of it.

PRESIDENT OF THE COURT: What didn't he understand?

A: He did not understand how important it was for us to see the camps and to see whether the people had got enough food. Although to start with Krumey granted us permits, he later found a very simple way of nullifying their usefulness. He did this by issuing permits only for visiting camps in Budapest, and not for camps situated outside the city. Nearly all the camps were situated outside Budapest and we were, therefore, able to visit very few of them. . . .

Q: In your talks with Krumey did the question arise as to where the Jews would go?

A: Yes, I think that I have already answered this question in part. They mentioned Spain, and North Africa, but not Palestine because they said that this would run counter to the agreement with the Mufti of Jerusalem. . . .

After asking him formally to identify Eichmann as the prisoner in the dock the Attorney-General then put the following questions to the witness.

Q: On what day did you first establish contact with Eichmann?

A: I think that it was on 25 April but I am not absolutely certain. I used to have a meeting every morning with members of the *Abwehr* in a little café in Budapest in order to find out what could still be done to save the Jews. On that particular morning I was told to wait in another café on the other side of the road and in about half an hour a car would come and take me to the Majestic Hotel where I would be able to have an interview with Eichmann.

Q: What happened when you arrived at the Hotel?

A: I was taken to his room which was on the ground floor.

Q: Was he wearing uniform?

A: Yes, he was extremely smartly dressed in the uniform of an SS officer. There was one other man present, who was wearing civilian clothes. I did not know at the time who he was, but I know now that it was Kurt Alexander Becher.

Q: What happened at the meeting?

A: As soon as I entered the room and approached Eichmann, who was standing in front of the table with his arms akimbo, he barked at me, "Do you know who I am? I am in charge of the *Aktion* here. You know what happened in Poland and Czechoslovakia; now it is Hungary's turn."

Q: What else did he say to you?

A: He said that he had sent for me to talk business. He was ready to sell me one million Jews. He said, "Goods against money, money against goods."

Q: What was your reply to this proposition?

A: I was so dazed by the proposal that all I could find to say was, "I have no right whatsoever to determine who is going to remain alive or not. I want everyone to be saved."

Q: What did Eichmann say then?

A: He said, "Which *do* you want, merchandise or blood? More than a million we cannot give you now—perhaps later."

Q: Did he describe himself as being swayed by certain idealistic motives when proposing this transaction?

A: Yes, he called himself an "idealistic German" and bestowed on me the title of "idealistic Jew." I was, therefore, worthy to sit at the same table with him, so that some arrangement could be concluded. "Tomorrow, however, we may again be on the battlefield," he said.

Q: Yes, go on.

A: I said, hesitatingly, that I had no merchandise to offer. It had all been already confiscated by the Nazis, therefore they did not need me. Nevertheless, I told him that I could offer him quite a large sum in foreign currency. He said that he was not interested in money, not even interested in Hungarian goods, only foreign manufactured goods. He told me to go abroad and establish direct contact with my people. When he asked me where I wanted to go first to establish contacts I hesitated in my mind between Switzerland and Turkey, but eventually I decided in favour of Turkey because I knew there were in that country a number of delegates representing Jewish organisations who had been sent there by the Jewish Agency.

Q: So you said you wanted to go to Turkey?

A: He said, certainly you can, but I am not yet quite certain what kind of goods we need most. I will have to go to Berlin in order to get final instructions regarding the kind of goods we want. He asked me to think it over and to find out what kind of goods we could possibly offer. He then said, "You have a mother, wife and children. They will remain here as hostages. Nothing will happen to them. I will look after them and see that nothing goes wrong with them. But it will give me a guarantee that you will return."

Q: Did he say anything about the Hungarian authorities?

A: Yes, he forbade me to speak about this conversation to anyone, but I told him that such a condition would make it impossible for me as I could not take any concrete steps without having some consultation with my closest friends, and with those who were already cooperating with me. It may well be, I told him, that they will decide that I am not the one who is most suited to carry out this particular mission, and some other name may be suggested. Eichmann then told me that I had his permission to divulge the contents of the conversation to my close friends and colleagues, but I must not breathe a word of it to anybody else because it was a top-secret matter within Germany and it must not, on any account whatever, be divulged to the Hungarians.

Q: Did you then discuss the matter with your colleagues and was it finally decided that you should proceed with the suggestion?

A: Yes. As soon as I left the Majestic Hotel I joined the Committee which was already waiting for me and I told them everything that Eichmann had said. After a long discussion we decided that the proposal should be accepted because it was the last straw to which we could cling regarding the possibility of saving hundreds and thousands of Jews. After alternative proposals had been put forward by Kastner, it was unanimously decided by all the members of the Committee that I should be entrusted with this mission.

Q: Did you have anything to do with a man named Bandi Grosz in connection with this affair?

A: Yes.

Q: Who was Bandi Grosz?

A: He began his career as a smuggler. Later on he was an agent of the Hungarian counter-espionage. But it was not only the Hungarians whom he served for he was, also, a double agent. He served the English, the Americans and ourselves. He helped us quite a lot.

Q: In what way was he connected with the "business" transaction between yourself and Eichmann?

A: He established contact with the counter-espionage section of the SS, known as Amt VI, and with the representative of that office in Budapest who was named Klages. . . .

Q: Did Grosz have any direct contacts with you?

A: Yes, he did. We were almost in daily contact with him as well as with the German *Abwehr*.

Q: Was Himmler's name mentioned?

A: Yes. At one of these meetings I was told that Himmler was very much in favour of Eichmann's proposal. Himmler, I was told, was in fact a good man and did not want the extermination of the Jews to continue. I was told that it was only in this way that the remnants of European Jewry could be saved from destruction.

Q: And after that you had your second meeting with Eichmann?

A: Yes. Eichmann was, of course, present, but I cannot now say with certainty whether Becher also attended the meeting.

Q: Did something surprising happen when you entered the room?

A: Yes. Eichmann and Klages were already sitting at a table and in front of them was a large bag full of money. Eichmann said, "You see here between fifty and fifty-seven thousand dollars and seventy-two thousand Swiss francs. This money has come here to aid the rescue of children. I have no objection to helping children. Here is the money and here are the letters which were sent with the money. Most of them are written in Yiddish, Hebrew or Polish. There is no time to pass them through the censorship, so you can take them away and if there is anything else in them report it to me." I took the money and the letters but I was feeling very uncomfortable.

Q: Why?

A: I was not used to receiving money from a Nazi officer or being given illegal mail so that I should check it.

Q: Who did you think gave it in the first place to Eichmann?

A: The money came from Switzerland. It was a large sum and our agent was, in fact, a relative of the Pope. He was to have brought the money and correspondence to us but apparently Bandi Grosz turned our agent over to Klages in order to please him. Klages appeared very anxious to complete these negotiations. I shall speak about this later. So he had, obviously, suggested to Eichmann that these letters and the money should be given to me so that I could send a receipt for them to our people in Switzerland in order not to endanger the present negotiations.

Q: After you had accepted the letters and the money did the conversation return to the suggestion made by Eichmann at the previous meeting?

A: Yes. Eichmann asked me whether I had been thinking over the question of what goods I could offer them. He did not, however, wait for me to give an answer, even had I got one, which I had not, but he immediately went on to say that he had obtained full consent from Berlin to carry out negotiations with me and he could now tell me exactly what he was interested in. "Trucks!" he barked. He then gave me a long explanation about the urgent need he had for vehicles. The front-line units had good vehicles but those at his disposal were no good. He coveted the vehicles which the front-line units had, but he could only get some of them if he were able to let them have replacements.

Q: Was any specific number of trucks mentioned?

A: He said, "You want a million Jews, don't you?" I said, "I want all of them." He said, "Well, for the time being we are only speaking about one million." And again he barked, "10,000 trucks, 100 Jews for one truck, and that is a pretty good price for you." He added that the trucks would have to be modern ones with all accessories. . . . He also said that he would appreciate it if, in addition to the trucks, we added a few tons of coffee, chocolate, tea, soap and so forth.

Q: Did he say anything about the destination of the new trucks?

A: Yes, he said that he would give his word of honour that they would never be used against "your allies," as he put it, on the Western Front, but only against the Russians on the Eastern Front.

Q: What was your reply to that?

A: I was surprised, amazed, happy and confused, all at the same time. I said to myself, who would believe it possible . . . who would believe that I could have been made such a fantastic offer.

Q: Did you express your feelings and misgivings to Eichmann?

A: Yes.

Q: And what did he say?

A: He said that no doubt we all thought he was a crook but, and again he bawled out, "A German officer keeps his word!" He then went on to say that he would prove that he placed more confidence in me than I in him, but only if I returned from Turkey with a favourable reply. Then, he promised he would blow up the Auschwitz installations and would be prepared to let us have ten per cent of the one million Jews, in advance, that is to say he would give us a hundred thousand Jews and concentrate them on any frontier we liked to name and only then would we have to give, in return, the first ten per cent of the trucks, namely 1,000. I was still embarrassed and confused. I said to him, "Who will believe me if I bring such an offer from Eichmann?" He shouted at me and said, "I have already agreed to those six to eight hundred Jews who emigrated. I even added two hundred to their number," he said, but we had not given him the proper lists. At that moment the thought flashed through my mind that perhaps this was a real possibility, perhaps we would get these 100,000 Jews in advance, perhaps they would really blow up the gas-chambers in Auschwitz. I was naïve enough to have some trust in him. If that was so, I thought, it would take a few months and in the meantime, perhaps, the war would be over.

PRESIDENT OF THE COURT: Which six or eight hundred people was he talking about?

A: The six hundred Jews about whom I spoke earlier.

ATTORNEY-GENERAL: And then you decided to meet again?

A: Yes. He said, "Very soon you will be told how you should go about it."

Q: A few days later were you again sent for by Eichmann?

A: I cannot remember whether I was summoned or whether I went there on my own. This was at a time when the Jews were being concentrated on a large scale and we had been receiving terrible news and the Committee was interested in concrete achievements and not vague promises for future years. They wanted to prevent these atrocities and the concentration of Jews in ghettos. We also wanted to try and get a few of the local Jews released from so-called "protective custody."

Q: So you went to his office: were you kept waiting for a long time before you were allowed to go in and see him?

A: Yes, there were a lot of other officers with him.

Q: Did you know their names?

A: Not all but I knew some of them: Becher, Klages, Novak, Hünsche and Dannecker.

Q: When you gained admittance to his room what did he say?

A: He was very annoyed and shouted at me, "What are you doing here?" The others appeared amazed to see me here. I said, "I have not yet received my travel papers." He said, "You will receive them very soon. Go over to Krumey's office." I cannot remember whether the next thing I said was at this meeting or a subsequent meeting, but I told him that I had received terrible news from the ghettos. He replied, "I have just been travelling all over the country and I have sent wagons full of bread for the Jews." He then told me to bring my wife to his office so that he could see her. He also said that he did not want to have contact with anyone else in my absence. He said that I must come back quickly and contact should be maintained with him through my wife. She would be the liaison.

Q: And did you bring your wife to Eichmann's office?

A: Yes. . . .

Q: When was your last meeting with Eichmann?

A: My last meeting with him was on 15 May 1944. On that day Eichmann told me that I must delay no further and leave immediately and that from that very day he would begin deporting 12,000 Jews a day. He said he could not wait any longer and waste time. He could, perhaps, delay sending them to Auschwitz by sending them first to Austria or Slovakia, but he could not keep them there for more than a fortnight or so and I would have to hurry up and bring back the answer.

Q: What else did he say?

A: He said that the young and the strong would be able to work, but the old people and the children would have to be taken away. It was up to me, he said, to prevent this.

Q: But he told you where you could go?

A: This had already been agreed and he said that *Obersturmbannführer* Krumey would escort me to the aircraft and he repeated once again that I must get the job done quickly and hurry back. He said once again that if I came back with an affirmative answer he would blow up Auschwitz and I could have the first ten per cent of the Jews.

Q: Before you left did you receive a letter from the Central Office for the Jews of Hungary signed by Freudiger and Stern confirming their decision that you were authorised to carry out this mission?

A: Yes, and I also got a letter from the Jewish Council. . . .

Q: Mr. Brand, I would like to refer back to the meeting which took place with Eichmann when your wife was present. I have not yet asked you what took place at that meeting.

A: Eichmann told my wife that she would not be allowed to leave Budapest nor would the children. She must remain there under his supervision. I am not sure whether he actually used the word "hostages" or not, but that was obviously the meaning of what he said. He also said that she must report to him daily and bring any news of me which she had.

Brand then said, in answer to a number of questions by the Attorney-General, that Krumey took him to the airport and before seeing him on the aircraft told him that he should tell people abroad whom he met that all officers of the SS were not like Eichmann. There were decent officers like Wisliceny and himself, and a number of others whom he mentioned. These officers would do everything they could to carry out this transaction and rescue the Jews.

ATTORNEY-GENERAL: Did Bandi Grosz accompany you on the journey to Constantinople?

BRAND: Yes, he did.

Q: At whose request?

A: I asked Eichmann to let me go with him although I knew that his main contact was with the intelligence section of the SS, with Klages.

Q: Did Eichmann tell you why he wanted Bandi Grosz to travel with you?

A: Yes. He said that Grosz would be able to keep an eye on what I and my friends were "cooking up" in Constantinople and would be able to report it to him when we returned.

Q: Did you know whether this was the only duty which Bandi Grosz had on this journey?

A: I think his job was both to keep an eye on me and to establish contact with the British and American authorities.

Q: While you were in Turkey were you arrested?

A: Yes.

Q: Afterwards you travelled to Aleppo to meet Moshe Sharett? [7]

A: I was on my way to Jerusalem in order to meet Sharett because he had been able to get a visa to enter Turkey.

Q: Were you later arrested by the British authorities?

A: Yes. When I got to Aleppo after crossing the frontier I was arrested by the British Military authorities.

Q: Did you see Moshe Sharett in Aleppo?

A: Yes.

Q: And you explained your mission to him?

A: Yes.

Q: Were you released from arrest?

[7] His name was then Moshe Shertok, and he was Head of the Political Department of the Jewish Agency in Palestine. After the formation of the State of Israel in 1948 he became the Minister for Foreign Affairs.

A: No.

Q: Where were you taken afterwards?

A: To Cairo.

Q: How long were you kept there?

A: Four and a half months.

Brand's mission failed to accomplish anything. The story of what happened afterwards, and why, has been told in a book written by Alexander Weissberg entitled *Advocate for the Dead*. Brand stated in his evidence that although it was actually written by Weissberg, he regarded it as his own book. Asked by the President of the Court to explain what he meant by that the witness answered:

I wrote the book here in Tel Aviv for a publishing firm named Ayanoth, but I had difficulties with them because they had the exclusive world rights. I travelled, therefore, to London where I met Alex Weissberg and the book was published under his name. This was easier. Weissberg improved the style considerably, but the contents and the structure of the book are entirely mine. They were taken from my own manuscript. That is why I regard it as my book. Later, it was published here in Israel under my own name.

Brand's wife, Hansi, was also called by the Prosecution and examined by Mr. Gabriel Bach. Before the occupation of Hungary by the Germans, Mrs. Brand had been actively concerned with the same Rescue Committee as her husband. The function of this Committee, she told the Court, was to see that the stream of refugees reaching Hungary from Nazi-occupied territories received aid and shelter. Her special duty was to get in touch with the refugees who could not speak Hungarian and see that they obtained clothing, personal documents such as ration cards and living accommodation. The refugees for whom she worked came, first of all, from Germany but later they were from Austria, Poland, Slovakia and Yugoslavia.

Mrs. Brand described how the whole situation changed in Hungary after the entry of the German forces in March 1944.

Mr. Bach: And you dealt with the refugees who came in? After March 1944 were there any further duties imposed on this Committee?

Mrs. Brand: It would be right to say that after 19 March the situation completely changed and our Committee was faced with an entirely different situation. At first we had been dealing with refugees only from outside Hungary and we tried to help them with money and find them jobs. But when Hungary was occupied by the Germans an entirely different problem arose. Not only did the danger facing these refugees increase, it now faced the Hungarian Jews also. After we discovered that it was of great help to possess a foreign passport it was decided that I should continue to obtain forged papers for them. These papers purported to have been issued to Christians as, with Christian identity papers, it was easier for the Jews to "go underground." . . .

Q: Will you please tell us when you first saw Eichmann?

A: I think the first time I saw Eichmann was the day before my husband left for Constantinople.

Q: What was the purpose of your visit to Eichmann?

A: Well, theoretically, it was for the purpose of keeping contact with Eichmann during my husband's absence. I reported regularly to his office and gave what information I had received, but I soon realised that the real reason for my having to report to him regularly was to ensure that I and my family remained in Budapest as hostages. Later Eichmann himself told me that this was the reason.

Q: Where did this interview take place?

A: Schwannenburg, in the Jewish department.

Q: Will you tell the Court more about the interview.

A: It took about an hour or three-quarters of an hour because he asked me whether I knew what the purpose of my husband's trip was. He told me that it was top secret and on no account was I to tell anyone about it. If I did so, he said, the consequences would be indescribable. . . .

Q: Did Eichmann tell you what the secret was, what was involved?

A: Yes, he told me that it concerned the releasing of 1,000,000 Jews in exchange for 10,000 trucks. My husband had been given a passport so that he could go abroad and try and bring off the transaction.

Q: During the interview was there some discussion of the fate of about six hundred Jews?

A: Yes. He talked about six hundred Jews who were in possession of certificates of immigration to Palestine for whom there was a ship waiting in Constanza. . . .

Q: Was there a sign outside his office?

A: Yes. *Sondereinsatzkommando* IV B Jewish Department.

Q: What was his attitude towards you at this first meeting?

A: I got the impression that he wanted to keep the conversation strictly on business lines.

Q: Shortly after your husband left did you learn that deportations were already taking place?

A: Yes, we were all shocked to hear that Jews were being concentrated in the Great Synagogue and put into wagons, I remembered that Eichmann, in my presence, had promised that they would be sent to Austria but I did not know, at that time, where my husband was. . . .

Mrs. Brand then persuaded Dr. Kastner to go with her and obtain an interview with Eichmann. They told him that they were very upset to hear of the conditions in which these deportations were being transported, namely ninety to a hundred people in one wagon. Eichmann told them not to worry. These were all Jews from the Carpathians and as they had large families the children did not need so much room. There was plenty of air for them to breathe. He explained that it had become necessary to carry out these deportations, for the Russians were advancing rapidly. The front was getting nearer the border and it was important that in the districts near the frontier there should not be any "undesirable elements." "It was a necessity of war," he said, "to purge this area and to make it clean of Jews" (*Judenrein*). Before her husband left for Turkey the Germans had issued special permits to certain members of the Jewish Committee and its employees. These permits entitled them to use trams and other public vehicles and excused them from wearing the yellow star. Later, when

Mrs. Brand was arrested, these privileges were withdrawn. The circumstances of Mrs. Brand's arrest were as follows. One Saturday afternoon members of the Hungarian Gestapo came to her department and, after making a thorough search, they arrested everyone who was on the premises. Next day they summoned Mrs. Brand to the SD headquarters where she was confronted by a man who had owned the printing shop which had been making the forged documents for her. If she had not been told his name she would not have recognised him. He had been beaten and mutilated beyond recognition. On the following day Mrs. Brand was herself interrogated. She was shown certain photographs and asked whether she identified the people in them. When she was unable to do this she was severely beaten. Later on she was released but not before she had admitted that she had been responsible for having these forged documents printed.

Only three days after the first interview between Brand and Eichmann the first deportation had taken place, 1,500 Jews suitable for work being sent to Auschwitz. There they were forced to write postcards to their relatives telling them what a wonderful time they were all having. The text of these postcards was dictated by the camp staff and an Austrian resort, Waldsee, was given as the place of despatch. But by the time they reached their destination the writers had already met their death in the gas-chambers of Auschwitz.

Meanwhile, information of a more sinister character was beginning to come through from Poland. One message said that there was feverish activity going on in Auschwitz to renovate and modernise the gas-chambers and crematoria which had not been used for some months, and an SS NCO was heard to remark, "Soon we shall get fine Hungarian sausages."

On 15 May the wholesale deportations began. On the day before the first evacuation, all mental cases and prisoners of Jewish origin in Hungary were transferred to the ghettos. About eighty to a hundred Jews were crowded into one cattle truck with one bucket of water. The wagon was then sealed up. At a certain stage of the journey the trains were taken over from the escorting Hungarian gendarmes by the SS. While searching the convoy for hidden valuables they tortured the occupants of the trucks with electric wires and beat them mercilessly. Hundreds of them committed suicide during the trip.

On 27 June the Pope and the King of Sweden both tried to intervene with Admiral Horthy, and about the same time an appeal was made by President Roosevelt to stop the brutal anti-Jewish persecutions. For a time Horthy was able to prevent any more Jews being sent away from Budapest because the police in the capital were still on his side. But he was unable to prevent their deportation from the provinces, and Eichmann managed to send several thousand more Jews to Auschwitz without information reaching Horthy in time for him to try and stop it.

On 15 October a German *coup* ended the Horthy régime and Szalasy took over power. Two days later Eichmann returned by air from Berlin to Budapest. Immediately after his arrival the deportations recommenced, and about 25,000 Jews, mostly women, were forced to march over a hundred miles in rain and snow, and without food, to the Austrian border. Hundreds of them died on the way, and many more hundreds died in Austria from dysentery and exhaustion. The Attorney-General described this march in these words:

And now, with the infamous operation known as "The Death March," came the finale of Eichmann's campaign of murder. There were no longer any trains available, so he organised, with the help of his Hungarian fascist allies, a march of Jews in the direction of Austria, ostensibly to provide labour for fortifications, but actually to murder them. Eichmann's calculation was simple: the weak would fall by the way, the strong would reach their destination to build the fortifications, and would afterwards be destroyed. The march began in November in rain, snow and cold, along a two-hundred kilometre route. The marchers spent each night in the open or in pig-sties. Thus were these women, children and old people deported. Anyone who found the walking difficult was shot by the guards who beat and tormented their victims every step of the way. Those who had no strength left, collapsed and died. Hundreds committed suicide or died of typhus. All that was issued to them, once every two days, to eat and drink, was hot water and a little bread. They died like flies and the whole route was strewn with corpses.[8] The number of those who fell by the way is estimated between six and ten thousand. The horrors obtained such proportions that even the escorting Hungarian officers and soldiers began to mutiny and requested that they be sent to the front. Szalasy, the Hungarian Prime Minister, intervened unsuccessfully to put an end to the march, and then an astonishing thing happened. Himmler himself reprimanded Eichmann for organising this operation, and only then did the terrible march end.

On 8 December the deportations temporarily stopped, but Eichmann refused to carry out the verbal orders which Himmler had given him over the telephone to cease deporting Jews altogether, until he received confirmation in writing. Before that happened all the Jews in hiding with forged papers were hunted down and during those last few months not less than 10,500 Jews were shot in the streets of Budapest or on the banks of the Danube.

That many more Hungarian Jews were not deported to Auschwitz was largely due to the efforts of the Swedish and Swiss embassies who, during the whole of 1944, were providing Jews in Budapest with papers to enable them to leave Hungary. Eichmann complained bitterly about this.

The main target of his venom (the Attorney-General said) was a young Swedish diplomat, Raoul Wallenberg, an architect by profession and a man of sterling qualities who had made the rescue of Jews his life's vocation. Wallenberg gathered around him a team of workers, issued passports giving their holders the right to live in Sweden and, at the risk of his diplomatic status and even his life, instituted rescue operations. He rented houses

[8] Despite the efforts of Raoul Wallenberg. See below.

and other buildings in which he kept the Jews under the protection of the Swedish flag and at one period was housing 4,000 of them. When the "Death March" began Wallenberg accompanied the marchers with trucks laden with food, medical supplies and clothing . . . all this was the work of one courageous man who had the strength to act according to his conceptions and beliefs. His deeds, like those of King Christian of Denmark, again give rise to the sombre thought: how many could have been saved, even in the countries where extermination was being carried out, had there only been others like him among those who had power to act whether openly or in secret.

It is not surprising that Eichmann released a flood of anger against this liberator. The Swedish Embassy in Berlin lodged a complaint that Eichmann had told the Red Cross in Budapest that he had it in mind to shoot "the Jewish dog" Wallenberg. The Foreign Minister apologised to the Ambassador, stating that, doubtless, the words were not seriously meant. In written exchanges it was explained that Eichmann's reaction had to be understood against the background of Wallenberg's illegal activities to rescue Hungarian Jewry, and were meant to restrain him from persisting in his efforts.

The total number of Hungarian Jews who lost their lives is not accurately known, but it was between 180,000 and 200,000.

Although the Prosecution were able to bring ample evidence to support the particulars of offence in respect of the First Count of the Indictment which alleged that Eichmann, together with others, caused the killing of millions of Jews, there is only one murder which he is alleged to have committed with his own hands. This was committed while he was stationed in Budapest.

Evidence of it was given by a witness named Abraham Gordon, a Hungarian by birth now living in Israel, who was still at school in Budapest when the Germans occupied it in March 1944. Gordon was examined by Mr. Gabriel Bach.

BACH: Do you remember 19 March 1944?

GORDON: Yes. It was a Sunday, the day when the German Army occupied Hungary, and entered Budapest. . . .

Q: Were you, shortly after the German occupation, taken away from school with a lot of other young Jews and made to work?

A: Yes, we were arranged in groups for various types of work. Tunnels were being dug, one across the street from the Majestic Hotel to the Eden Hotel. We did not know what the purpose of these tunnels was; we thought that perhaps they were being made as air-raid shelters or munition dumps for the German Army.

Q: How long did you work on these tunnels?

A: I was employed there for about one month.

Q: And during that time did you work in the same place?

A: We went to other jobs as well. Once or twice I was sent to work at the headquarters of the Hungarian police.

Q: During your work did you ever see Adolf Eichmann?

A: Yes . . . after we had finished work on the tunnels we were taken to a villa which, I found out later, was Adolf Eichmann's private residence. Before the war it belonged to a Jewish industrialist by the name of Asher.

Q: What work were you supposed to do?

A: When we arrived we were met by a German who led us to a tool-shed, issued us with tools and told us to go into the back-yard and dig some trenches.

Q: When you say "told us," how many were you?

A: There were fifteen of us.

Q: Who was this German?

A: We did not know who he was but we thought that he was Eichmann's bodyguard.

Q: How did you know that the villa was Eichmann's residence?

A: In the first place the engineer in charge told us that a Gestapo Commander by the name of Adolf Eichmann lived there.

Q: Did you ever see Eichmann himself?

A: I saw him a few times.

Q: You see the Accused in Court? Can you say with certainty that this is the man?

A: I must say that he has changed. I saw his picture in the press.

(Witness was handed some photographs.)

Q: Look at these photographs.

A: I am sure, without a shadow of doubt, that this is Eichmann. (The photograph which the witness identified was a photograph of Eichmann which had previously been shown to Eichmann and he had acknowledged it as being a photograph of him by signing it.)

Q: When you first saw Eichmann where was he?

A: The first time I saw him he was sitting on the balcony sipping a drink. The second time I saw him was during an air-raid and he was then walking about the courtyard. We went on working and he screamed at us and said, "Get into the trenches."

Q: How many times in all did you see Eichmann?

A: The next time I saw him was when I was in one of the trenches and, all of a sudden, I heard screams. Eichmann's chauffeur, whose name was Teitl, went up to one of the Jewish boys who was working with me, whom I knew as Solomon, and who was not more than seventeen years old.

Q: Will you tell the Court in your own words what happened then.

A: I saw Teitl walk up to the boy and shout at him. Then Eichmann's bodyguard, whose name was Slavic, joined them and I heard them shout at the boy, "You stole cherries from the tree." I then saw that Eichmann was standing on the balcony having some kind of conversation with Slavic who was down below. The boy began screaming, "I didn't do it, I am innocent." I then saw Slavic and Teitl leading the boy away in the direction of the tool-shed. He resisted and had to be forced. They pushed him into the tool-shed and locked the door and then I saw the driver, Teitl, walk away and I never saw him again that day. Then I saw Slavic return. He went round the back of the tool-shed and shortly afterwards he re-appeared with Eichmann. Both entered the tool-shed.

Q: What did you see or hear after that?

A: I saw Slavic and Eichmann enter the tool-shed and the door was closed behind them. Then I heard frightful screams and beatings, thuds and weeping.

Q: Could you identify the voice?

A: It was the voice of the boy Solomon. The screams lasted for about ten or fifteen minutes, and then for the first time they stopped. The door then opened and Eichmann came out of the tool-shed. He was rather dishevelled. His shirt was sticking out. I saw stains which I thought were blood-stains. When he had entered the shed he was dressed properly. When he came out, as I have said, he was dishevelled and looked exhausted. A few minutes after Eichmann had left the tool-shed Slavic came out and shouted for the driver. Teitl arrived and together they entered the tool-shed and dragged out the body of the boy. They dragged him by his feet and he gave no signs of life.

Q: Can you describe what you saw?

A: Well, I could not see his eyes but his face was swollen and bleeding. It is very difficult for me to describe what I saw. The driver went away and came back with a car.

Q: Did the car belong to Eichmann?

A: We saw it every day. It was always parked at the villa.

Q: What happened then?

A: After the car arrived I saw the body of the boy being placed in the back seat. I could not see exactly but I thought that they put it under the back seat. Then the car was driven off but returned about half an hour later. In the meantime we had been ordered to carry on with our work. The driver of the car was a Hungarian, but he also spoke German. He said, "I threw the stinking corpse into the Danube and your fate will be the same as that of the boy, so beware."

The cross-examination of this witness by Dr. Servatius failed to shake his testimony, but when he was asked whether this was the only case of bloodshed that he had witnessed in Hungary he answered:

This was the first murder I had ever witnessed in my life. Later I saw many more murders, especially during the last three months.

VII

The Final Solution in Central and South-Eastern Europe

THE EXTERMINATION of the Jews in Yugoslavia followed much the same pattern as elsewhere, including the burning down of all the synagogues and the imposition of heavy collective fines.

The Serbian and Croatian Jews were concentrated in camps and in one of these, situated in Jasenovac, 20,000 were executed. The women and children were mostly taken to other camps where many died of disease and starvation and the survivors exterminated by direct means. Large numbers of Jews from Germany, Czechoslovakia and Austria who were trying to make their way to Palestine were captured on the Danube. About 1,100 of them were taken to Sabac camp and there exterminated. This was done on the advice of Eichmann himself contained in a letter which was produced in evidence at the trial.

Evidence to support the above was given by three Jews, now citizens of Israel, who were living in Yugoslavia when the Germans invaded it in 1941.

In Croatia the Accused was represented by a man named

Abromeit and it was he who carried out the usual preliminaries of registering and segregating all the Jews after anti-Jewish legislation had been passed by the Croatian Government itself. They were later deported to the extermination camps, but in April 1944 Eichmann's department complained that the final solution had still not been completed. The excuse made by the Croatian Foreign Minister was that this presented great difficulties owing to the large number of mixed marriages.

In that part of Yugoslavia which was known as Slovenia, Eichmann had an additional assignment, the deportation of the non-Jewish Slovenian population to Serbia. This was stated to be necessary in order "to resolve national problems in accordance with the *Führer's* decision."

The Attorney-General produced the deportation orders in evidence together with a number of reports on the operation which were rendered by Eichmann's local representative to Amt IV B 4. This was a brutal and callous operation whereby 14,000 Slovenes were forcibly uprooted from their homes, where their families had lived for many years, and were deported to Serbia and Croatia.

SLOVAKIA

The final solution in Slovakia, which was a separate political unity, was conducted in much the same way. The territorial principle, mentioned in a previous chapter, was followed in regard to such matters as looting. Before leaving on their last journey to the extermination camps the Jews were made to sign a sworn declaration that they had "voluntarily relinquished" their property, and in this way they were fleeced of property valued at more than seven billion krone.

Wisliceny was Eichmann's representative in Bratislava. He had been the Accused's colleague for many years, but he was a very different type of man. He was well educated and not a fanatical anti-Semite. Furthermore he was not above doing a profitable business deal, should the occasion arise, over Jewish lives.

As has already been mentioned, Himmler had, for a long time, been interested in the "Europa plan," namely selling Jews to the highest bidder. Toward the end of 1942, he and his immediate colleagues were already thinking of putting this plan into operation on a large scale, beginning in Slovakia, where deportations had recently been suspended.

Eichmann, however, was always strongly opposed to any such weakness. He wanted no compromise. He was determined to fulfill his sacred mission of destroying the Jews.

Nevertheless, after a promising start, Wisliceny met with a severe setback, and out of a total Jewish population of 136,739 probably about 50,000 escaped the final solution. In the early days, when Eichmann paid frequent visits to his branch office in Bratislava, the Slovakian Premier Dr. Tuka and Mach, the Minister for the Interior, had been most cooperative. According to Wisliceny's own estimate 52,000 Jews were deported before an attempt was made to ransom the remainder. Wisliceny himself received a large sum in dollars variously estimated as between twenty and fifty thousand dollars. Pressure was exerted by the Roman Catholic Church and the deportations ceased.

But, as the Attorney-General told the Court:

Eichmann immediately applied counter-pressure. He commissioned Fritz Fialla, a Slovakian journalist, to write articles in the Slovakian Press describing how he had visited labour camps in the East and seen "with his own eyes" the good living conditions that the Jews enjoyed there. Strong pressure was also applied by the German Foreign Ministry and, later, Alois Brunner returned to Bratislava. The round-ups recommenced in September 1944, and once again more than 12,000 Jews were deported while many more thousands were killed in Slovakia itself.

Eichmann decided to try and extort more money from the Slovakian Jews. He demanded from the Government a payment of 300 marks "transfer money" for every Jew deported to the labour camps. Important matters were handled personally by him with the Premier and the Minister for the Interior.

While Wisliceny was planning how to put Himmler's Europa Plan into operation in Slovakia, the same idea, only in reverse, had occurred to a young Jewess, living in Bratislava, named Gisi Fleischmann, who was head of the local branch of the Women's International Zionist Organisation, known all over the world as WIZO. Mrs. Fleischmann had had the foresight to send her two children to Palestine before the outbreak of war, but herself stayed behind to supervise the rescue of other Jewish children and organise a smuggling system to get them out of the country before it was too late. This female Scarlet Pimpernel got in touch with Wisliceny towards the end of 1942 and was told by him that if she could raise £ 50,000 sterling in cash he would stop all Slovakian deportations, and not a single Jew would be harmed in any way. She was given three weeks in which to raise the money with a further extension of two weeks. She managed to collect it, but not before the time limit had expired. Meanwhile Wisliceny had sent another 3,000 Jews to the gas-chambers. When the money was paid to him, however, he promised, "on the word of a German officer," that nothing more would happen to the Jews in Slovakia, a promise which, indeed, he did keep for about six months. He then sent for her and suggested a much more comprehensive deal. "For 2,000,000 dollars," he told her, "we will stop all deportations throughout Europe." Gisi Fleischmann managed to raise 57,000 dollars, but no more, and it was not long before the trains began, once again, their almost daily journeys of death to Auschwitz, Treblinka and Maidanek.

In the autumn of 1944 the Slovak partisans rose in armed revolt. Many young Jews took part and, with the approval of the Allies, Jewish paratroops from Palestine were flown over to aid them. Meanwhile Eichmann, dissatisfied with Wisliceny, had relieved him by Brunner who proceeded to wreak a terrible vengeance on the remaining Jews in Slovakia. He tried to deceive Gisi Fleischmann by telling her that all the Jews left behind would be sent to a camp where they would be kept safely until after the war was over, and asked for her co-operation in transporting them there quietly without resistance.

She was not the kind of woman to be taken in by a story of that kind, and she tried to warn all the Jews of their impending fate. Before she could do so, however, Brunner saw the red light and ordered her arrest and, within a few days, this heroic young woman had left for Auschwitz and the gas-chamber. Dr. Kastner who was, of course, in Budapest heard about her deportation by Brunner and tried to intercede on her behalf with Becher.[1] Becher insisted that Eichmann should send a signal to Brunner, ordering him not to deport her. The signal was sent, in accordance with Becher's instructions, but immediately afterwards Eichmann sent a second message cancelling the first.

RUMANIA

The final solution was at first accepted by Rumania only to be rejected later. The country had the second largest Jewish community in the whole of Europe. Only Poland possessed a larger number. And in no other country in Europe were Jews more ill-treated before the war than in Rumania.

Eichmann's representative there was *Hauptsturmführer* Richter, and under his influence and persuasion anti-Jewish laws were enacted and the looting of property began early in 1941. In the same year the Germans began deporting Jews across the River Bug to Poland but they were not yet ready to "absorb" them. A report written by Richter to Eichmann,

---

[1] Colonel Kurt Becher was, at that time, in Budapest and held the appointment of Chief of the Economic Staff of the Field SS. It was he who in November 1944 passed on a message from Himmler to Pohl and Kaltenbrunner ordering them to stop the liquidation of the Jews. Pohl, who was Chief of the SS Economic Administration, and Kaltenbrunner who was Chief of the SIPO and SS in succession to Heydrich, were both tried by different courts in Nuremberg, sentenced to death and hanged.

which was produced in evidence at the trial, informed him that the 28,000 Jews who had been sent to Poland were duly exterminated in accordance with Eichmann's instructions.

It was, however, agreed between the Rumanian Government and the German occupation authorities that the Jews who still remained in Rumania would be kept temporarily in concentration camps in that country until they could be removed to the East. This agreement was probably regretted by Eichmann because, by the time he had completed all his plans for their deportation, the Rumanian Jews had managed to persuade their Government to change its mind.

The deportations were to have started on 10 September 1942. All the plans had been prepared in Eichmann's office, the German railway administration had made all the necessary transport arrangements, and Eichmann had obtained the consent of the Deputy Prime Minister of Rumania to a wholesale deportation of Jews.

On 26 July 1942, in a letter to Himmler, which was produced in evidence at the trial, Eichmann reported that the Rumanian Jews would be sent to Lublin. Those fit for work would be employed, the remainder would be handed over for "special treatment."

On the very same day he rather carelessly informed the German Ministry for Foreign Affairs that "*only those fit for work*" would be deported. When this came to the notice of the German Ambassador in Bucharest, Freiherr von Killinger, he was extremely angry to discover that Eichmann was going over his head to bring about the extermination of the Jews. Eichmann's behaviour did not surprise him, however, because, as he wrote in a telegram which he sent to the *Deutschland* department of the German Foreign Office, "the operational methods of the gentlemen of the SS are only too well known to me."

When it became obvious that the Rumanian authorities had changed their minds, Richter used every possible means to get them to relent and agree to the deportations taking place, but he was unsuccessful. However, they concentrated the Jews in camps in Transdniestria where many tens of thousands of them were killed or died, but the wholesale deportations to extermination camps in Poland never took place. Nevertheless it is reliably estimated that about 200,000 Rumanian Jews lost their lives, although about 120,000 of these lived in Northern Transylvania which had been ceded to Hungary in August 1940.

Evidence was called by the Prosecution to prove the stubborn efforts made by the Accused to exterminate the entire community of Rumanian Jews and to foil attempts which were made to save some of them by emigration to Palestine.

Some of this evidence consisted of statements made by Wisliceny, between 27 October and 18 November 1946, while he was in prison in Bratislava. The Attorney-General based his application to the Court to admit this evidence upon Section 15 of the Nazi and Nazi Collaborators (Punishment) Act of 1950. "In the case of an offence under this law the Court may deviate from the customary rules of evidence if it believes that this is necessary for a just and proper trial."

Dr. Servatius objected to this evidence being given on the grounds that it was nothing more than an attempt by Wisliceny to shift the responsibility over to the Accused.

A similar provision was contained in the London Charter which governed the proceedings of the Nuremberg Tribunal which tried the major German war criminals.

Article 9 provided that the Tribunal should not be bound by technical rules of evidence. It should adopt and apply to the greatest possible extent expeditious and non-technical procedure, and should admit any evidence which it deemed to have probative value. Similar rules were in force at all war-crime trials before British and American military courts.

These rules were, undoubtedly, less technical than those governing the proceedings of courts conducting trials in accordance with the ordinary criminal law.

It does not follow, however, that any injustice was, thereby, done to the accused. The sole aim was to ensure that no guilty person would escape punishment by exploiting technical rules. The circumstances in which war-crime trials were often held made it necessary to dispense with the ordinary rules of evidence. Many eye-witnesses whose evidence was needed in trials held in Europe had, in the meantime, returned to their homes overseas and been demobilised. To transport them to the scene of the trial would not have been practical. Some were no longer alive. It was for these reasons that affidavits were permitted and widely used.

The Presiding Judge gave the Court's reasons for allowing Wisliceny's affidavits to be produced in evidence. "Between him and the Accused," Judge Landau said, "there were very close ties regarding the subject matter of this trial. The affidavits in question were made not very long after the incidents to which they referred had taken place, and it was very difficult to bring more direct evidence from others who worked hand-in-glove with the Accused." Moreover, on his own admission, the files of his Department in RSHA had been destroyed. The question of whether these affidavits had probative value would be for the Court to determine, and the Court would decide what weight should properly be given to such evidence. When deciding this issue the Court would pay due regard to the objections which had been raised by the Defence and to other factors which might reduce the value of such evidence.

Wisliceny gave five reasons for Eichmann's success in his task of implementing the "final solution" policy.

1. He had the full confidence of Himmler, Heydrich and Müller. When Kaltenbrunner succeeded Heydrich, after the latter's assassination at Lidice, he also continued this confidence in Eichmann.

2. As a result of instructions issued by Goering, from the summer of 1941 onwards, Eichmann had full authority to ignore the appeals and objections from local commanders or other authorities.

3. In areas occupied by the Germans or their satellites the German Foreign Office was not allowed to interfere, and invariably obeyed Eichmann's orders in all Jewish matters, even though, on occasions, they did so grudgingly.

4. The Reich Ministry of Transport placed all the necessary means of transport at Eichmann's disposal, and invariably gave him priority regarding the provision of rolling stock whenever Eichmann required it, despite the difficulties.[2] Without this help the extermination programme could not have been kept up to date.

5. Eichmann's staff were taught to obey all orders without question. Wisliceny himself and Krumey, when they were in Slovakia and Hungary, tried to slow down the programme. The others never gave the possibility a thought.

Eichmann's influence on the others who, according to Wisliceny, were not very intelligent was tremendous. In spite of the fact that everything that Eichmann did was covered by orders from Hitler and Himmler, and he took great care to see that this was so, his share in the decimation of European Jewry was decisive, and full responsibility for this crime must be laid at Eichmann's door for there were ways and means of circumventing the *Führer's* orders.

BULGARIA

The German attempt to get rid of all the Jews in Bulgaria met with opposition almost from the very start.

It began in the usual way with the passing of anti-Jewish legislation, the confiscation of property, the wearing of the yellow badge, and the usual restrictions on movement.

Eichmann's representative in Sofia was Theodore Dannecker who had been transferred from Paris where he had gained his experience in the extermination of French Jewry.

---

[2] It was for this reason that Eichmann was so annoyed when a train which he had provided could not be used at Bordeaux because there were not enough Jews to fill it.

Many sections of the Bulgarian population, and King Boris himself, were in strong opposition to the policy, and the German Ambassador in Sofia, Beckerle, wrote plaintively to RSHA: "The mentality of the Bulgarian people lacks the ideological enlightenment which our people enjoy. Having lived all their lives with Armenians, Greeks and gipsies, the Bulgarians see no harm in the Jew to justify special measures against him."

Nevertheless Dannecker succeeded, in spite of all the opposition, in persuading Alexander Beloff, the Bulgarian Commissar for Jewish Affairs, to sign an agreement with him, on 22 February 1943, to deport 20,000 Jews to German occupied territory in the East. They were to be selected irrespective of age or sex, the Germans would provide the transport, and the Bulgarians would pay for it. The Bulgarian Government undertook, once the Jews had been deported, not to ask for their return. The agreement originally stated that these measures "would apply only to Thrace and Macedonia," which had been annexed to Bulgaria from Greece and Yugoslavia. Subsequently, however, as can be seen from the document itself which was produced in evidence at the trial, these words were pencilled out, but in such a way that they were still legible.

The significance of this erasure was explained by Dannecker in a report which he submitted to Eichmann. Bulgaria did not want to deport its own Jews, but they were prepared to hand over "foreign" Jews from the recently annexed territories. It was, therefore, originally stated that deportations would only be carried out in those territories. Both parties to the agreement, however, as Dannecker pointed out, were well aware that not more than 14,000 Jews lived in Thrace and Macedonia. Beloff undertook to provide the remaining 6,000 from Bulgaria proper. This was prevented at the very last moment as the result of intercession by the people of Sofia. In all, therefore, only about 11,000 Jews were deported. None of them came from the old Bulgaria, and no more were sent out of the country, though many were concentrated in forced labour camps. Conditions in these camps were wretched enough, and many broke down under the strain, but they were never handed over to the Germans.

About five-sixths of the Jews in Greece lived in Salonika. For a long time after the German invasion no anti-Jewish measures were taken but the Jews were already in a bad way. Famine was not far off, 20,000 Salonika Jews were near starvation, and an epidemic of typhus had greatly reduced their number.

The first steps towards the final solution were taken in the winter of 1942. Eichmann paid a personal visit to Salonika where he was represented by Wisliceny, Brunner and Burger all of whom worked in close co-operation with Dr. Morten, the military governor.

In March 1943 the deportations at last began, the victims being, as always, crammed into railway trucks like so many cattle. About 54,000 Jews from Salonika were sent to the extermination camps, nearly all of them to Auschwitz. On special instructions from Eichmann the sick were also deported. He also tried to include Jews who were living in that part of Greece, especially in Athens, which was occupied by the Italians but, as usual, they did not co-operate. Wisliceny was, therefore, sent to Athens to see whether he could force the issue. He met with some success and greatly annoyed the Italians, who threatened to arrest him, by placing the Saul family in custody, the head of which was Chief Legal Adviser to the Italian Legation. Eichmann at once complained to the German Foreign Office about this threat and the persistent opposition which he and his staff experienced at the hands of the Italians. "We shall only be satisfied," he wrote, "if they adopt in their territories the same measures as we do in the territories under German occupation, namely the removal of all Jews to the East."

As in the case of almost every other country the exact number of Jews sent to their death by the Germans will never be known, but it is believed, on such evidence as exists, that not more than 10,000 survived out of a pre-war population of 67,000.

THE GREATER REICH

The two countries which formed part of what the Nazis called the Greater Reich and which have not yet been dealt with are Austria and Czechoslovakia.

Hitler's anti-Jewish policy in the Czech Protectorate, formerly known as the Sudetenland, followed the familiar pattern, discriminatory legislation, confiscation of Jewish property and the enclosure of all Jews in ghettos.

The last of these measures included a special invention of the Nazis, Theresienstadt. At a conference of SS Commanders on 10 October 1941 in which Heydrich and Eichmann both took part, the solution of the Jewish problem in the Protectorate was discussed in detail. It was agreed that, as the Czech attitude to Jews differed from that which existed in the Government-General in Poland, due allowances would have to be made and special methods adopted.

According to the minutes of this conference Eichmann suggested that 5,000 Jews should be deported from Prague to Communist prisoner-of-war camps under the command of Nebe and Rasch.

SS *Brigadeführer* [3] Artur Nebe, Head of the KRIPO [4] commanded *Einsatzgruppe B* in Russia until November 1941. SS *Oberführer* Otto Rasch commanded *Einsatzgruppe C* in the Russian campaign, and was responsible for the Kiev massacre on the 29 and 30 September 1941 in which over 33,000 Jews were murdered. At the opening of the *Einsatzgruppe* trial on 5 February 1948 he was found unfit to plead.

[3] See Appendix.
[4] KRIPO was the equivalent of the C.I.D. in Nazi Germany.

It is beyond doubt, therefore, that Eichmann's intention was that these 5,000 Jews should be "liquidated." The operation was, in fact, carried out, but before they finally met their death they were sent to the ghettos in Riga and Minsk.

A large number of those who escaped this immediate fate were deported to the Theresienstadt ghetto which was established by Eichmann and came under his direct control.

Tens of thousands of Jews were concentrated there which served two main purposes. First, it was intended to pacify the Jews themselves since the Theresienstadt deportees were ostensibly to be allowed to remain alive. As the Attorney-General told the Court, "The Jew who sought some consolation was allowed to deceive himself into believing that if he were sent to Theresienstadt he would not be killed."

Secondly, it was a kind of official shop window to satisfy all those who were claiming that the Nazis were only capable of murder.

Swiss and other representatives of the Red Cross and foreign journalists were often taken to visit Theresienstadt, as were the Heads of States from which Jews were being deported, so that they could satisfy themselves as to the fate of its inmates. It was kept as a show-place in which the Jews supposedly lived and worked under their own independent administration and, most important of all, remained alive.

All this, however, was nothing more than a sham and was never, indeed, meant to be anything else, for when it was decided to form the ghetto it was stated that "the best thing would be to place it under the authority of the 'Central Office for Jewish Emigration.' " After their removal to this temporary collection camp it would be possible to deport them all to extermination camps in the East and to transform Theresienstadt into a model German settlement.

This became, therefore, part of the official programme of destruction.

Although the ghetto was supposed to be administered by the inmates themselves it was, in fact, controlled, in all essentials, by Eichmann's Amt IV B 4. Permission had, however, to be obtained from *Reichsführer* Himmler himself before anyone could be transferred to Auschwitz, or one of the other extermination camps. Such permission was never refused.

Owing to the terrible conditions existing in this ghetto the death-rate was very heavy. Those who entered its gates and either died there or were put to death elsewhere included many thousands from Czechoslovakia as well as large numbers from Germany, Austria, and other countries under German occupation.

In Austria, of course, anti-Jewish measures were put into force immediately after the Anschluss in March 1938, and Eichmann was sent to Vienna with an *Einsatzkommando* of the SD which was, for the first few weeks, under Heydrich's command. When Heydrich was appointed Inspector of the SIPO, Eichmann became responsible for all Jewish questions in that office.

It was shortly after their arrival in the Austrian capital that Eichmann suggested to Heydrich that he should form a central bureau for Jewish emigration, the aim then being to force as many Jews as possible to leave the Greater Reich. Heydrich accepted Eichmann's suggestion and the "Central Office for Jewish Emigration" was set up in the Palais Rothschild in Vienna with Eichmann in charge of it. Thanks to his activity more than 100,000 Jews emigrated from Austria during the period from the middle of 1938 to the outbreak of war.

It was in this way that Eichmann attracted Heydrich's attention, and he soon obtained promotion. While stationed in Vienna, Eichmann renewed his relations with Kaltenbrunner who had, since they last met, become Head of the SS and SIPO of the Danube. It was he who sent Eichmann to Bratislava during the Czech crisis in the autumn of 1938, and it was he who organised the transfer of Jews in the regions which, in accordance with the Treaty of Vienna, were ceded to Hungary.

The Attorney-General likened the machinery set up by

Eichmann in Vienna for getting rid of the Jews to an assembly-line. "A Jew came into the office," said Dr. Hausner, "still an Austrian citizen, with a place in society, a job, a home and his other property. After being thoroughly processed, he came out an emigrant. His property was gone, in part confiscated, in part invested by government order in frozen currency of very little value. His house or apartment was registered for confiscation. He no longer had employment and his children could no longer go to school. All he came out with was a travel permit, stamped '*Jude*,' giving him permission to leave Austria by a certain date, never to return."

Foreign and stateless Jews were ordered to leave the country within twenty-four hours. Jews from the provinces were brought destitute to Vienna, and the Viennese Jews were made to house and feed them until the time came for them to leave Austria. Those who refused to do this were arrested. All Jewish hospitals, convalescent homes and schools were taken over by Gentiles. It is not surprising, therefore, that the official representatives of Berlin Jewry, who were sent to Vienna to see what was being done, were greatly impressed by Eichmann's achievements.

The prosecution produced evidence of Eichmann's day to day dealings with the Jews in Prague and Vienna. He threatened, he cursed and he raved; yet at the same time he tried to give the impression that things might not be so bad as they seemed. Vulgar abuse and hypocrisy went side by side. He assaulted Dr. Löwenherz, a leading Viennese Jew, at their first meeting. He called the Head of the Jewish Community in Berlin, "a sack of dung," yet, at the same time he pretended that he was really interested in Jewish problems and that he would be prepared to listen favourably to any requests.

At the time of the Anschluss the Jewish population of Austria was about 185,000 and by December 1939 the number had dropped to about 64,000. Of these, probably not more than 10,000 survived.

GERMANY

The solution of the Jewish problem in Germany itself has already been described in earlier chapters.

The number of Jews living there when Hitler came to power, according to a census taken in June 1933, was just under half a million, and it has been estimated that when war broke out in September 1939 the number had been reduced by emigration to about 215,000. By the spring of 1943 nearly 120,000 of this number had been deported to the Eastern territories. In all, probably 160,000 were exterminated as part of the "final solution."

Dr. Heinrich Grüber, who is now Dean of St. Mary's Cathedral in Berlin, was called as a witness by the Prosecution to give evidence about his efforts to help Jews in distress during the persecution, and his many meetings with Eichmann.

Until 1939 Dr. Grüber was a clergyman in one of the suburbs of Berlin and, ever since Hitler had come to power, he had maintained close contacts with the Association of Jews in Germany (*Reichsvereinigung*). This relationship became more intimate after the events of November 1938.

The Jews were then considered by the State as second-class citizens, and they did not have the same opportunities for free expression of their views as Dr. Grüber. He, therefore, considered it his duty to do all he could to help them. His three principal contacts in the Association were the Chief Rabbi, Dr. Leo Bäck, Otto Hirsch and a Herr Epstein.

Dr. Grüber gave an example of the way these Jewish leaders were treated by Eichmann and his staff. At a meeting in Eichmann's office, when either Eichmann or his assistant Günther was present, Rabbi Bäck, Hirsch and Epstein were also present. There was only one chair and this was offered to Dr. Grüber. He refused to sit down, saying, "If they stand, then I stand."

Whenever the Association of Jews wanted to obtain some relaxation of the restrictions in force regarding food or money, Dr. Grüber volunteered to make the application on their behalf, for it was easier for him to obtain access to the Ministry concerned.

On one occasion, just before Passover in 1940, the import of flour from Hungary had been prohibited. Dr. Grüber succeeded in persuading the Minister for Food to allow sufficient bread to be imported for the baking of unleavened bread.

Dr. Grüber was asked by one of the junior Counsel for the Prosecution, Mr. Baror, how Eichmann used to behave during their interviews.

The impression he made on me was that of a block of ice or marble, completely devoid of human feeling. . . . This was not just my personal opinion, all the Jews in Berlin gained the same impression. In our eyes he was a *Landsknecht*, not a soldier. Perhaps I can explain the difference by saying that the moment a *Landsknecht* puts on his uniform he becomes oblivious of the demands of justice and his own conscience.

MR. BAROR: Did you ever meet with success at any of these interviews?

GRÜBER: As far as my recollection goes I would always leave his office with a definite "no," or sometimes he would put me off by saying that I would have to wait for a decision. I cannot remember the Accused ever having given me the plain answer, "yes." Unless it was "no" I never left his presence with a positive answer. It was either a "no" or some kind of non-committal answer and an injunction on his part for me to wait.

Q: Do you remember whether, at any of these meetings, the Accused ever referred to superior orders which he had received or was about to receive?

A: As far as I can recall he would always answer me in the first person. He would always use the word "I." I should, perhaps, have said "abuse" it. He said, "I can't," "I shall," "I will," or, "I will give orders that . . ."

I don't know whether he used the first person to raise his own prestige or whether he was the deciding authority but I never remember him saying that he must refer the matter to a higher authority.

Q: Dr. Grüber. Did you have any contacts with more junior Gestapo officials whom you used to meet in Eichmann's office?

A: Yes, for I was kept under constant watch by the Gestapo. I also met some of those who held more junior appointments some of whom I found quite helpful within their own limitations. One of these was *Oberregierungsrat* vom Rath, father of the Counsellor at the German Embassy in Paris who was assassinated by the Jewish youth Herszel Grynszpan in November 1938. He had been given his appointment because the authorities thought that he would like to get his own back on the Jews for the killing of his son and would, therefore, be particularly severe with them. But this was not the case. Our relationship was quite friendly and he secretly helped me on several occasions.

The witness went on to say that vom Rath and another Gestapo official, whose name Dr. Grüber asked leave not to mention, helped him unofficially by giving certain information, which he could not otherwise have obtained, and by letting him see draft orders before publication so that he could be prepared to take certain counter-measures in advance.

The witness was also asked if he could recall a conversation which he had with the Accused concerning his birthplace.

Dr. Grüber said that it was rumoured that Eichmann had been born in a Templar settlement near Haifa, at Sarona. That was supposed to explain his knowledge of the Hebrew language and Jewish customs. It could also explain his antisemitism. Dr. Grüber once asked Eichmann about this. He did not deny it, nor did he confirm. Dr. Grüber was inclined to believe the rumour to be true, until later, when he found out where Eichmann had, in fact, been born.

The reason for believing it was because Dr. Grüber and his friends were always trying to find an acceptable explanation of Eichmann's rabid and boundless hatred of the Jews. It was only later, after Dr. Grüber had been in a concentration camp for several months and saw what went on there, that he began to understand.

When Dr. Grüber asked the Court for permission to withhold the name of the other official who worked in the same office as vom Rath there was some surprise in the court-room. Later in his evidence he was questioned on this point by two members of the Court, Judge Raveh and Judge Halévi.

Judge Raveh told Dr. Grüber that he was not interested in the name but could not understand why the Herr Doktor did not want the man's identity to be known.

Dr. Grüber said that large numbers of the Press were present in Court and it was not desirable that this man's name should be headlined next day in all the Berlin papers, for he now held a responsible post.

Judge Halévi then asked, was it not considered an honour in Germany today to have one's name published in the papers as having helped to save Jews during the Nazi régime? "It *is* an honour in Germany today," Dr. Grüber answered, "but I wish it to be understood that I shall not mention a man's name without asking his consent. Moreover, the entire Press is not of the same way of thinking. There are still some people who threaten those who are honoured for that reason. I myself could have produced a number of threatening letters which I received when it became known that I was to come to Israel to give evidence for the Prosecution at this trial."

Dr. Grüber himself had experience of concentration camps as an inmate, and was very badly treated, but when asked about these experiences he said that he would prefer, provided the Court would allow him, to speak of the sufferings of his Jewish comrades rather than of his own. The cruelty of the SS he told the Court was much worse than could be imagined. It was worse than Dante's Inferno, where it was hell, but one could complain and weep. In the hell of the concentration camp there could be no complaining and no weeping. It was a hell much more hideous and terrible.

Asked about the medical experiments in Dachau, he said that many of his friends had been human guinea-pigs. They were infected with disease and fever, blown up with air, filled with cold water and kept in a glass bell into which air was alternately pumped in or extracted.

He himself narrowly missed becoming the subject of an experiment. On one occasion he had a heart attack and was placed in the mortuary. Friends noticed, however, that he was still breathing and took him to the hospital. As he was unfit for work he was earmarked for an experiment by the renowned Dr. Rascher who welcomed him in the usual way by calling him swine and then informed Dr. Grüber that his grandfather had also been a clergyman. Dr. Grüber told Rascher that he did not think that his grandfather, now in heaven, could be enjoying seeing what his grandson was doing in Dachau. This seemed to have some effect on the Herr Doktor who immediately discharged him from hospital. Next day he signed a certificate to the effect that Dr. Grüber was unfit to be kept in custody, and within a few days he was freed.

Dr. Grüber, whose evidence seemed to create a great impression even, at times, upon the Accused, ended his testimony with a moving plea for forgiveness. He hoped that the proceedings would help humanity and contribute to the understanding between Israel and Germany.

VIII

A World
That Has Vanished

Towards the end of his opening speech the Attorney-
General referred again to the tragedy of European
Jewry and the loss which Europe sustained by reason of it.
Speaking of "a world that has vanished" he asked, "On whose
head did this venomous wrath of extermination and murder
fall?"

The Prosecution intended to prove that the Jewish people
lost almost six million of their number. That meant much more
than just a third of its total, it meant the extinction of those
Jewish communities which represented the most important
elements of the race from the point of view of inspiration,
national consciousness, creative power, cultural and spiritual
resources. There were some grounds for the Nazis' belief that
if they could only succeed in wiping out the Jews in Europe
they would have gone a long way in the battle against world
Jewry.

In Europe a Jewish community which had been in existence
there ever since the second century B.C. was almost exterminated. A dispersed race of which the historian H. A. L. Fisher
wrote thus in the introduction to his *History of Europe:*

As the sunshine of religious toleration spread through Central and Western Europe the Jews were admitted to civic rights.

The hospitality of the Christian State was amply repaid in noble contributions to art, science, and literature.

Of 257 Nobel Prize winners in the first half of the twentieth century, thirty-four were Jews of whom twelve were deported by the Nazis. It would have taken too long to list all the outstanding Jews who came from the countries in Europe which suffered under the Hitler régime, but in order to give a glimpse of the Jewish people's contribution to European culture the Attorney-General mentioned a few. Geniuses like Einstein and Freud; Fritz Haber, the chemist; Henri Bergson, the philosopher; Niels Bohr, the physicist; biologists like Ehrlich; physiologists like Warburg and Chain; thinkers like Martin Buber; writers like Emil Ludwig, Stefan Zweig, Jacob Wassermann, and Lion Feuchtwanger; sculptors and painters like Antokolsky, Chagall, Modigliani and Max Liebermann; Max Reinhardt, the famous producer; and renowned musicians like Rubinstein, Kreisler, singers like Richard Tauber.

Anyone familiar with the history of the persecution of the Jews knows that Germany was the country where they suffered most, yet they bestowed great love and devotion on Germany and regarded themselves as good German citizens as were their Gentile brothers and sisters.

The Jews' folk language, Yiddish, had German as its pattern and they carried it with them to Poland, to Russia and across the seas to the Americas.

It was in the German language that Theodor Herzl wrote his classic works on Zionism, and it was in the same tongue that the proceedings of the earlier Zionist congresses were conducted. Most of the standard books on Jewish history and philosophy were also written in German.

Many Jews who settled in other European countries attained positions of honour, but nowhere, since the beginning of this century, did they display the same enthusiasm and devotion as in Germany.

When war broke out in 1914, the German Jewish community flocked to the ranks of the German Army with fervent patriotism. The aged philosopher, Hermann Cohen, stepped down from his university rostrum and called for a supreme effort on behalf of Germany. Fritz Haber devoted himself tirelessly to the scientific war effort and invented synthetic ammonium which was to prove of such assistance to the Germans' conduct of the war.[1]

Many Jewish officers and soldiers in the German Army received decorations and this was a source of great pride and satisfaction to the Jewish community. After Germany had lost the war the Jews devoted themselves to the reconstruction of the country. Walter Rathenau as Minister of Economic Affairs and, later, as Foreign Secretary, achieved much for his country, and Hugo Preuss, the Jewish Minister of the Interior drafted the Weimar Constitution, one of the most progressive in the whole of Europe.

But all this was to no purpose. It only aroused jealousy and envy. Rathenau, in 1921, was shot dead in the street by some of Hitler's early followers, and the Jewish contribution to Germany was represented by the Nazis as a malignant foreign growth which must be cut out of the body politic.

"European Jewry," the Attorney-General told the Court, "was, on the eve of the holocaust, the very heart of the whole nation, the source of its vitality. The great majority of its spiritual guides and leaders either dwelt there or were of European origin."

It was from Europe that all the great Zionist leaders had come, including those who were soon to found the new State of Israel, including Herzl and Nordau, Jabotinsky, Weizmann and Ben Gurion. Millions of those who lost their lives were waiting for the coming of a new Israel but they were never to

[1] By a strange coincidence another famous Jew, Chaim Weizmann, later to become the first President of Israel, and who had been living in England since 1904, greatly helped the British war-effort by discovering a method of manufacturing large quantities of acetone which was needed for explosives.

see it. An entire civilisation, with a characteristic way of life, was destroyed.

"Adolf Eichmann," the Attorney-General said, "knew what he was about. If he should succeed in destroying this Jewry, he would destroy all Jewry. The others, he hoped, would perish or be assimilated. By the mercy of Providence, which preserved a remnant, his design was frustrated and the intention he cherished was never fully implemented."

Exactly how many Jews were killed in various ways by the Nazis, including those for whose death Eichmann's office at RSHA was directly responsible, will never be accurately known. The estimated number given in the Nuremberg indictment drawn up in November 1945 was 5,700,000. In *The Scourge of the Swastika* I wrote, "The murder of over five million European Jews constitutes the greatest crime in world history," and I added the following footnote, "The estimated number given by the chief British Prosecutor at the Nuremberg trial of major war criminals was 6,000,000. Of subsequent estimates one was as low as 4,372,000. The real number will never be known." That estimate was originally given by an expert on population changes, Professor Frumkin, but he has, since then, stated that the figure of over five million is not necessarily exaggerated for when he made his estimate of 4,372,000 he did not include Russia within its present boundaries nor did he take into account some 23,000,000 of the population of the Baltic countries, Lithuania, East Prussia, sub-Carpathia, Bessarabia, Bukovina and the Polish Eastern Provinces.

Whatever the exact number may be, Hitler's final solution of the Jewish question was the most highly organised and systematic mass-murder recorded in history up to the present day. Eichmann played a more important part in implementing it than anyone else and, if his former colleague Wisliceny is to be believed, he gloried in it.

Part 2

THE DEFENCE

IX

Eichmann in
the Witness-Box

O N 29 JUNE, exactly ten weeks after the commencement
of the trial, Dr. Servatius opened the case for the
Defence.

The Defence would show, he said, that the Accused only
became involved in the attempt to exterminate European
Jewry by virtue of his appointment as the Head of Amt IV B 4
and he could not, therefore, escape being implicated.

The Accused, who would himself go into the witness-box,
would be able to satisfy the Court by means of the documentary exhibits already produced by the Prosecution, and other
documents still to be produced, that the real responsibility
rests upon the shoulders of the political leadership of Germany
during those years. If the Accused is guilty, Dr. Servatius told
the Court, then those who initiated the policy are even more
guilty, particularly those in high positions.

With this statement no reasonable person would be prepared to disagree, but it is now well established by the judgments of many other war-crime tribunals that the plea of
superior orders is not a legal defence.[1]

There is not, however, likely to be general agreement with
the further assertion of Dr. Servatius that as Eichmann was
not a member of the Leadership Corps his position on the
ladder of responsibility was on "the lowest rung." There is

[1] This defence is discussed in Appendix II.

ample evidence that, although his SS rank was comparatively low, his role in carrying out the "final solution" was an important one, and that he had authority to make far-reaching decisions on his own responsibility although he took great pains to cover himself by subsequently reporting his action to higher authority.

Dr. Servatius said that for the convenience of the Court, the Defence would follow the lines taken by the Prosecution.

First he would deal with the RSHA and Eichmann's Departments in Prague and Vienna, with particular reference to the steps taken to implement Hitler's anti-Semitic policy before Eichmann took over Amt IV B 4.

He would then deal with the Wannsee conference, sterilisation, the collection of skeletons for Strasbourg University, the fate of the Lidice children, the action taken against Jews of foreign nationality and the implementation of the "final solution" in the various countries of Europe beginning with France and ending with Hungary.

The Defence would prove that the Accused was not responsible for the wholesale extermination of Jews.

Finally, there would be a complete answer to the accusation, made by the witness Gordon, that Eichmann had murdered a young Jew in the garden of his house in Budapest.

The Accused would tell the Court, said Dr. Servatius, that it was not possible for him to refuse to obey his *Führer's* orders, and that the Jews would have been no better off had he done so.

There is some truth in this argument. If Eichmann had died, or become physically incapacitated or had been transferred to another appointment at his own request where he would not have been involved in mass murder as a matter of duty, the "final solution" would have gone on without him. It might have been difficult to find someone with such a wide experience of Jewish affairs to take his place. Nevertheless a successor would have been found and the holocaust would have continued.

Eichmann began his evidence by declaring that the statement made by him in Buenos Aires to the effect that he was going to Israel of his own free will to stand trial for his crimes was not a voluntary statement. Having regard to the circumstances of his capture no one really believed that it was.

His Counsel then asked him why he joined the Nazi Party which had for its ideology the persecution of the Jews.

Eichmann said that the real object of the Party was to fight the Treaty of Versailles. The slogan "War against Versailles" appeared on the banners of the National Socialist German Workers' Party. Versailles was a turning point in the history of Germany, and Versailles was responsible for all the tragedy of the German people, including some seven million unemployed.

When he joined the Party in 1932, he said, "The struggle against the Jews was a secondary problem because through it the Nazis could not possibly have gained power." The Party was, at that time, anti-Weimar rather than anti-Semitic.

In the early days after Hitler had become the undisputed Head of the State, after Hindenburg's death, the Party was supported by many of Germany's industrial leaders and backed by the leading bankers. Later, "after the early victories of the war *which was thrust upon Germany*, the helm of Government was passed on to others and it was only then that unbridled and senseless measures were taken which I was unable to anticipate because of my junior rank and humble status." Asked by his Counsel why, in a document recommending him for promotion in 1941, it was stated that Eichmann had carried out his duties with "the necessary hardness," he replied by saying that strength of will and personal toughness was expected of every SS man. Anyone recommending someone for promotion in the SS, therefore, had to deal with this question, and if the person recommended lacked this quality his promotion would be shelved.

Eichmann was at great pains to establish the fact, early in his testimony, that he was never anything more than an emigration expert, and that his efforts to promote the emigration of Jews to Europe and his practical interest in the Madagascar plan almost made him a second Herzl [2] for even he had been, at one time, willing to accept Madagascar as a sort of half-way house to the eventual formation of a Jewish State in Palestine.

Nor was this all. As chief railway transport officer in charge of Jewish deportation from the occupied territories, for that is how he liked to regard himself, he eased the sufferings of the deportees.

"When Himmler issued his first directives about the deportation of the Jews," Eichmann said, "there was complete chaos particularly in the field of transport. There was no co-ordination; everyone issued his own orders; every Gauleiter acted independently and every SS and SIPO commander went his own way completely disregarding orders from above. To put it briefly, everyone did as he pleased.

"The main victim was the person who was to be deported. Whether he was a Pole or a Jew he was stuck in trains which were left for hours on end in railway stations or sidings. It was for this reason that Heydrich decided to set up a special section, my section, to co-ordinate all these matters, the planning of time-tables and so on."

On 5 February 1940, Eichmann told the Court, his department was incorporated into the establishment of RSHA, as a sub-section B 4 of the Gestapo which was Bureau IV, hence its name IV B 4. He, Eichmann, was only a glorified railway official "concerned strictly with time-tables and technical transport problems."

Originally, he said, his department was not concerned with Jewish matters, except incidentally by reason of the fact that

[2] Theodor Herzl, an Austrian journalist and author of *The Jewish State*, was the founder of political Zionism. An active movement had been in existence for the resettlement of Jews in Palestine since 1882, but it was Herzl who organised the First Zionist Congress in Basle in 1897 which put Zionism on the map.

the majority of the deportees happened to be Jews. "Jewish affairs" were only added to the department's functions at a later date. By "Jewish affairs," Eichmann explained, he meant all Jewish matters "pertaining to the jurisdiction of his office, not all other Jewish questions with which RSHA as a whole was concerned."

Still later, other matters were passed on to his department which had previously been dealt with elsewhere, e.g. the confiscation of the property of "enemies of the people," the abolition of citizenship and other matters affecting the freedom of the individual.

Eichmann insisted, however, that despite the widened scope of his authority, it was quite impossible for him to take any independent action in his official capacity. He could not possibly have carried out illegal emigration. The border control people, who were independent of his department, would immediately have brought it to *Obergruppenführer* Müller's notice and Eichmann would have been taken to task for it.

The Accused then tried to establish the fact that he was not the sole expert for Jewish affairs in RSHA and he produced a number of documents to prove that officers in other departments also organised and carried out measures against the Jews. He was only concerned with questions which came within the purview of the Gestapo Section IV.

This part of his evidence was so involved, and the Accused's replies to his Counsel's questions were so long that he had frequently to be interrupted by the President of the Court who told him that if he wanted his answers to be understood he must speak in shorter sentences. Everyone knew that in German the verb came at the end of a sentence, but if the wait was too long the full meaning of the sentence tended to be obscured by the Accused's verbosity.

The President's advice appears to have had little or no effect, for most of the Accused's evidence, and it lasted for twenty-nine days, consisted of short speeches rather than concise answers. On one occasion he used more than one hundred and eighty words merely to tell the Court the date on which he arrived in Berlin from Vienna to take up his new post.

On the third day of his examination by Dr. Servatius, Eichmann took the credit for originating the so-called Madagascar Plan. Some years before the war he had read a book by Alfred Böhm entitled *Judenstaat* and it had greatly impressed him. When the question of a "territorial final solution" came up again in 1940 he remembered this book. Although about sixteen or eighteen other government departments also had a hand in drafting the Plan, the section which dealt with climate, population, landscape, communications and transport was the work of his own department, IV B 4, and entirely written by himself. He personally visited the Institute of Tropical Hygiene in Hamburg to gather all the material.

His one desire, he told the Court, was to "try and get some solid ground under the feet of the Jews," a remark that was greeted, not unnaturally, by derisive laughter in the gallery, quickly suppressed by the President.

It was not his idea, Eichmann said, that Madagascar should become a Jewish "Police State," and he also opposed a proposal by the Ministry of Foreign Affairs that before emigrating the Jews should be deprived of German nationality. To support this contention, the Accused quoted from a report issued by the Ministry: "The representative of the security police (*Sturmbannführer* Eichmann) declared that he had reasons to disapprove of invalidating the citizenship of masses of Jews because this would influence other countries which were still ready to open the gates to Jewish immigrants."

The Plan, however, was never implemented. "We were not listened to," said Eichmann, "and the ban on emigration was issued."

Many documents which were put to the Accused by his Counsel appeared to concern matters germane to his Department of RSHA, but whenever their contents were extremely embarrassing to his case Eichmann invariably stated that the documents had only been sent to him for information and that neither he nor his department "had any substantial connection with these matters."

Some of the documents produced in evidence by the Prosecution undoubtedly came under this category. They were, nevertheless, clearly admissible in evidence because all the charges in respect of the extermination and ill-treatment of the Jews alleged that he "conspired with others" to commit these crimes.

Even when a document was clearly proved to have been addressed to him he would frequently attempt to disown it. One such document, addressed to the Accused, and signed by a colleague in the SS, *Sturmbannführer* Höttner, referred to the critical food situation likely to occur in Bohemia and Moravia during the winter of 1941. "Towards winter the danger exists that it will be impossible to feed all the Jews. The question arises, would it not be a more humane solution of the problem to liquidate, by other means, those who are unfit to work. It would be more pleasant than letting them starve to death."

The Accused discounted any possibility of the document ever having reached him because it contained a reference to the physical extermination of the Jews, and he only heard of this for the first time much later when Heydrich mentioned it to him.

Whenever possible, Eichmann insisted, he always took the more humane course, and on the only occasion on which his superiors had given him a free hand to decide the destination of a transport of Jews, he had saved 20,000 from extermination by sending them to an overcrowded ghetto in Lodz over the head of the local Nazi commander. He made this claim when Dr. Servatius called his attention to a document which had been exhibited by the Prosecution.

This was a letter sent to the local German commander by the commander of the same ghetto camp complaining of overcrowding due to the arrival of a large transport of 20,000 Jews and 5,000 gypsies. The complaint was passed on to

Himmler, and Eichmann was accused of "behaving like a horse dealer," whatever that may have meant. When the transport arrived it was discovered that it had not been officially sanctioned in Berlin, but the Accused had claimed that the camp commander or his deputy had agreed to receive it.

Eichmann was asked by Dr. Servatius whether this complaint had been justified and he answered, "Yes, it was." He had just returned from a trip to the East where he had seen the preparations for the physical extermination of the Jews. His orders had been to send the deportees to Lodz, but if any difficulties cropped up he was to move them on to the East. "As I had seen the preparations in the East," he told the Court, "I was determined to send these people to Lodz by every means at my disposal, and I reached an agreement on the spot with the Chief of the Secret Police."

JUDGE HALÉVI: Do you want to say that you employed this method described as "horse-trading" to save Jews?

EICHMANN: I did not want these 20,000 Jews to go to the East because I knew they would face extermination there. I wanted them to go to Lodz where no such preparations were being made.

Eichmann said that this was the only occasion on which he was given the opportunity of deciding the destination of a transport. He was shown another letter which referred to the transfer of more than 50,000 Jews from Bohemia and Moravia to the Riga-Minsk area, and asked by Dr. Servatius whether he had anything to do with the decision to send them there.

He told the Court that the destination of these Jews had already been decided by his superiors and that his Department IV B 4 was never told that they were to be killed. All he had to do was to work out the time-tables and arrange for transport. Evidence had already been given proof, during the presentation of the case for the Prosecution, that all these deportees were later killed in mass shootings by the *Einsatzgrup-*

pen, but Eichmann swore that he had no knowledge of this. He supported this assertion by referring to one of the Prosecution's documentary exhibits, a report made by the SS Commander in Riga, which, he said, proved that these killings had been done on the local Commander's own authority, without reference to anyone else.

Eichmann was then questioned by Judge Halévi about a confidential letter which he had written on 19 November 1941, notifying the German Foreign Office of Himmler's decision to suspend emigration in view of "the approaching final solution of the Jewish problem."

HALÉVI: When you signed this letter did you know what the planned solution of the Jewish problem was?

EICHMANN: I did not know any details of the plan but I knew that one was being drawn because I had seen an exchange of correspondence about it between Heydrich and our Foreign Ministry. . . . It seemed to me that the Madagascar plan, which I had expected to be the final solution, was being abandoned. From this correspondence it became clear to me that, in higher circles, a plan was being prepared to use other means for the solution although the first occasion on which I heard the final solution actually mentioned was the Wannsee Conference.

Another documentary exhibit which, on the face of it, appeared to be incriminating was also shown to the Accused by his Counsel. It was the draft of a letter prepared by the Reich Ministry of Occupied Territories in October 1941 about the erection of gassing installations, and it contained the following sentence: *"Sturmbannführer* Eichmann, who works at the Jewish department of the *Reichssicherheitshauptamt* (RSHA) approves this procedure."

Asked by Dr. Servatius to comment on this document the Accused answered:

In the handwriting draft my name, as well as the name of Wetzel,[3] is left out. In the second typewritten draft my name was

[3] Dr. Ernst Wetzel was Head of the Party's "Race Political Office," and was transferred to Rosenberg's office in 1941. He was the author of

inserted without my authority and it appeared in the third draft, and in the final letter itself. I can only say that it appears to me that the person who actually drafted the letter did not know who took part in the negotiations because the document itself states that the responsible department for this decision was II D 3, not IV B 4.

My name does not appear in any other document as being in any way concerned with these proposals, and I never even met Wetzel until 1942.

With these questions the first week of Eichmann's examination-in-chief came to an end. Its object had been to show that his role, throughout the commission by others of these terrible crimes, had been that of a zealous departmental official, and that not only was he in no way responsible for the measures taken against the Jews but would much rather have been doing something less distasteful. He spoke with a hard rasping voice and many of his answers were interminably long and involved. Although his Judges listened carefully and with studied patience, the Presiding Judge frequently rebuked him for giving prolix and irrelevant replies to the questions put to him by Dr. Servatius, and told him that his examination in court could not be regarded in the same light as his lengthy interrogation by the police while awaiting trial. In court specific questions were asked which required specific answers. In prison when asked a question he had been told to tell all he knew about the subject.

When the Court adjourned on 23 June Eichmann had just been shown the minutes taken at the Wannsee Conference under Heydrich's chairmanship. When the Court reassembled on 26 June the Accused was asked to describe the spirit in which the delegates met and came to such momentous decisions.

---

the famous letter to *Reichskommissar* Lohse in Riga which was the first document that referred to permanent gassing-camps. "I permit myself to observe that *Sturmbannführer* Eichmann is in agreement," he wrote. "To judge from the actual situation one need have no scruples about using this method to liquidate Jews who are unsuitable for work."

When the conference began, Eichmann told the Court, Heydrich had not expected to get his own way so easily. He had anticipated much opposition and many difficulties.

To their joint surprise there was not only an absence of opposition but a general measure of agreement. There was even considerable enthusiasm. As the Accused said in answer to Dr. Servatius:

Contrary to expectation, Secretary of State Bühler, Governor-General Frank's representative, was unflinching in his determination to participate fully in the final solution of the Jewish problem particularly so far as Poland was concerned, and Stuckhart[4] evinced boundless enthusiasm. He was usually hesitant, reserved, reticent and furtive, but all of a sudden he gave expression to boundless enthusiasm, with which he joined the others, with regard to the final solution of the Jewish problem.

The Accused would have liked to create the impression that he was the only gloomy delegate but he did not say this in so many words. He was, however, asked by his Counsel about his own reactions.

Dr. Servatius: From what you said in an interview with Sassen,[5] it seems that you, too, were satisfied with the results of the conference.

Eichmann: Yes, but my joy can be traced to an entirely different source from that of Heydrich and I should like to ask the Court to permit me to make some comments so that my attitude can be seen in a proper light. Heydrich's satisfaction was because of the concrete results of the conference. My joy was quite different. I examined and weighed my character and my personality in the light of the conference. I felt a certain solace and relief at having been able to do my utmost despite my relatively low rank. And I sought a final solution which was not repellent, which was not hideous, and which was feasible and possible.

I say this not because I am being tried by Israeli judges, but be-

[4] Franz Stuckhart, Secretary of State in the Ministry for the Interior, drafted the Nuremberg laws and their later amendments.

[5] This was an allusion to an interview which he gave to a Dutch journalist, named Sassen, in the Argentine in 1957.

cause it is true and can be corroborated by a series of documents which are before the Court.

I had done my level best to turn chaos into order in respect of the deportations and emigration.

My unflinching efforts can be seen from the Radom and Madagascar plans. After all these efforts I could, in the light of the Wannsee Conference, say to myself that in spite of my unflinching determination, *I had to do it, but what was done was not my doing.* I felt like Pontius Pilate who washed his hands before the multitude, saying, "I am innocent of the blood of this just person." I felt that I was not guilty because what was decided at the Wannsee Conference was done by the élite, the veritable Popes of the régime. I had, of course, to toe the line willynilly. This is what I thought in the course of the years which followed, and that is why there is a justification of what I did. What I said to Sassen was said in the Argentine when I never dreamed of being brought to justice here in Israel. Then I wrote about it in a very outspoken manner.

Even after the Wannsee Conference, however, which was the blueprint of the "final solution" and gave the green light to all concerned, Eichmann never took a single step to implement the plan of exterminating, "off his own bat," to use his own words. He always consulted his superiors and decided nothing on his own. Some of his subordinates even criticised this hesitation on his part, and said that he was too much of a bureaucrat and "put too many spokes in the wheel by insisting on so much red tape."

The Defence then proceeded to deal with the allegation, made by the Attorney-General and supported by documentary evidence, that a number of Jewish prisoners in Auschwitz had been killed in order that their skulls might be sent to the Heredity Institute in Strasbourg. A number of the documents produced by the Prosecution to support this charge were put to the Accused by his Counsel. He professed to know nothing about them and told the Court that *if* such a request had been received by him he would undoubtedly have referred it to *Obergruppenführer* Müller.

Eichmann also categorically denied the allegation in the Twelfth Count in the indictment that he ordered the deportation of eighty-one children from Lidice to Poland and arranged for their murder as a reprisal for the assassination of Heydrich in 1942.

A number of documents relating to this were put to the Accused and he was asked by Dr. Servatius to say what he knew about it. The Accused's reply was not very convincing either to the Court or to the spectators in the public gallery.

"I know nothing about this affair and from my own knowledge can contribute nothing to it," Eichmann said. It was clear from the documents, he continued, that he personally had had nothing to do with it. He got the impression that this was yet another occasion on which Günther had received special secret instructions from above, unknown even to the Accused. If the matter had come within his competence he would have immediately answered Krumey's cable asking for instructions and would not have waited twenty days before replying to it.

JUSTICE LANDAU: This is the second time we have heard from you that the fact that there was some delay proves that you had not personally dealt with the matter. Does that mean that you worked much more quickly than the other members of your department?

EICHMANN: No, no! I did not mean to say that. I only wanted to say that it was not clear to me who, in this case, had jurisdiction or competence, and that in all cases where such doubts existed it became necessary to refer the question to the Head of Bureau IV (Gestapo), *Obergruppenführer* Müller, and this, naturally, took some time. Otherwise it would have been dealt with by me personally without any such delay.

Dr. Servatius then announced to the Court that he had just received an affidavit on this particular subject from a Mrs. Freiberg, who lived in Bremen, and he would like to put it in evidence. He had, however, some doubts whether it was relevant, as it referred to Czechoslovak children and the Court was only concerned with offences against the Jewish people. Nevertheless he would make the application that it be admitted in evidence.

The Attorney-General reminded the Court that the affidavit was, clearly, hear-say evidence, for the woman who had sworn to the affidavit had obtained her information about the Lidice children from another woman.

After some argument the Court decided to admit the evidence. The affidavit was then read by Dr. Servatius:

I lived from 1941 to 1945 in Puezikov, near Poznan. I used to see, almost every day, thirty children from Lidice on their way back from school or playing in the garden of the local convent under the protection and supervision of a young lady.

The headmistress of the school told me that they had come from Lidice and their parents had been massacred there. . . . The children were dressed like orphans, but they were clean and tidy and between the ages of four and eleven. I do not know what happened to them after the arrival of the Russians but it would be possible for me to get this information from the Polish nurse who was in charge of them and with whom I am still in correspondence.

On 27 June, the sixth day of his examination-in-chief, Eichmann continued to deny responsibility for anything except the co-ordination of the transport arrangements for the deportations.

When numerous documents addressed to him or signed by him were put to him by Dr. Servatius dealing with large-scale deportations from many of the occupied territories his comment was nearly always the same. "I was not in charge of the operation itself, only with transportation. Müller needed Himmler's consent whilst I was not in a position to make any suggestions; only to obey orders."

The Prosecution had alleged that Eichmann had made a pact with the Mufti of Jerusalem, Haj Amin el Husseini, to close the escape route for all European Jews to Palestine.

Referring to this allegation, Dr. Servatius drew the Accused's attention to a letter, signed by him, and sent to the German Foreign Office on the 4 May 1943, stating that the emigration of Jews to Palestine should be avoided. Eichmann had previously said that he had always advocated emigration to Palestine and Dr. Servatius asked him why he had changed his tactics.

Eichmann's reply to this rather embarrassing question was that until he actually received the orders stopping emigration he had no instructions to stop emigration to Palestine even in the early days of the war. He did not, therefore, stop it; indeed, he encouraged it. But later, when the general order prohibiting emigration was issued, he could no longer do this, and even if he had tried it would never have slipped through the nets of the various regulations and offices.

He denied that he had ever had any official contacts with the Mufti. He could only remember having seen him once on the occasion of a reception given by the SD when most of the departmental heads of RSHA, including himself, were introduced to the Mufti. There was, however, in existence an agreement between Himmler and the Mufti, but neither the Accused nor anyone else in IV B 4 had any contacts with him.

Dr. SERVATIUS: Did the Mufti, or someone on his behalf, ever suggest that you should join his staff as an adviser on Jewish affairs?

EICHMANN: No. I never exchanged any words with the Mufti except on that one evening and then only to tell him my name when I was introduced.

JUDGE HALÉVI: But were you not introduced to him as an expert on Jewish affairs?

EICHMANN: To that I am not in a position to reply "yes," or "no" because I cannot remember. But it is quite possible that our joint hosts, Bureau VI, did introduce me to him as a specialist in Jewish affairs.

On the seventh day of his examination-in-chief Eichmann dealt with the charges in respect of the period during which he served in the Gestapo offices in Austria and Czechoslovakia. He disclaimed any responsibility for "crimes against the Jewish people" in both countries.

These charges covered the deportation of thousands of Jews from Germany, Austria and Czechoslovakia to the ghettos of Riga, Minsk and Kovno where they were exterminated, the pogroms in Germany and Austria carried out after the assassination of vom Rath by Grynszpan, and the confiscation of Jewish property.

The Accused was questioned by Judge Halévi about a document mentioning a change of policy in Austria regarding the Jews. The general trend of Gestapo policy in the pre-war years had been to "lock-up, disperse, arrest and dissolve," but shortly after Eichmann's arrival in Vienna the whole conception of Jewish policy was changed. The SD decided not to dissolve Jewish organisations, but to establish committees which would help with Jewish emigration. To assist with this work, a number of Austrian Jewish leaders were released from the concentration camps and Czechoslovakian leaders were taken to Vienna to see how it was done.

A suggestion was made, while the Accused was stationed in Vienna, that he should be posted to Linz. He was very anxious to secure this posting, for Linz was his home-town and his parents were still living there. He wrote a letter stating that he would regret leaving his work in Vienna on which he was keen and knew so well, but the new appointment meant increased responsibility and, he wrote, "At the age of thirty-two I do not wish to go backwards." The head of Eichmann's section, however, objected to the new posting on the ground that the Accused was "a specialist and experienced." Nevertheless, Eichmann still maintained, "In every matter I had to get my Chief's consent. I had no right whatsoever to undertake any action on my own even so far as the emigration of Jews was concerned." "I had no executive authority. I was always a subordinate and had not even got the power of arrest."

Dr. Servatius asked Eichmann for an explanation of a telegram, which he had sent in February 1941 informing the State Police of a plan to send Jews from Vienna to Poland. Eichmann's reply was that he was, by then, serving in RSHA and that the telegram had been sent by him as the result of a *Führerbefehl* (or order given by Hitler) which, of course, he was bound to obey. He could not fully remember the circumstances but he thought that it was Baldur von Shirach [6] who had asked Hitler to issue such an order to force the hand of Hans Frank, the Governor-General of Poland, who had objected to receiving Jews from Vienna.

The next matter to be dealt with by the Defence was what Dr. Servatius called, "the chapter of the Crystal Night" in Austria. The first document on this subject which Dr. Servatius put to the Accused was a cable reporting damage to certain synagogues and other buildings.

The cable had been sent from Vienna to Eichmann on 10 November 1938 and reported damage to synagogues in Graz Street and public buildings near-by which were gutted by fire. The cable stated that the "operation" had not been organised but was spontaneous, and informed Eichmann that three safes had been recovered from the ruins.

Eichmann told the Court that the only reason the cable was sent to him was so that he could take some action in regard to recovering numerous files of correspondence and other documents which were extremely important for the emigration work to which he had devoted himself. Fortunately as a result of his receiving this information, "part of this material was saved."

Apart from this, Eichmann stated, he had no connection in any way whatsoever with the reprisals taken against the Jews during Crystal Week and issued no orders in respect of them.

[6] Von Shirach was made Leader of Youth in the German Reich and in 1940 was appointed *Gauleiter* of Vienna. He was sentenced by the International Military Tribunal at Nuremberg to 20 years imprisonment.

He was also questioned about the negotiations that took place between himself and a Dr. Löwenherz regarding the exhumation of Theodor Herzl's remains and their despatch to Palestine.

In a memorandum written by Löwenherz, and put to the Accused by his Counsel, it was stated that "SS *Hauptsturmführer* Eichmann expressed his willingness to transfer the remains of Theodor Herzl to Palestine," and Eichmann was asked to give a full explanation.

He told the Court that Dr. Löwenherz approached him on a whole variety of subjects because the Herr Doktor found him a ready listener:

> The same applied to the question of Herzl's remains. Dr. Löwenherz could not find anyone else in Vienna but myself who would listen to him on this subject. He knew my position with regard to the suffering of the Jews, as I had derived it from Adolf Böhm's book, and therefore he turned to me.
>
> I had to apply pressure and intervene with various authorities, for the transferring of Herzl's remains to Palestine was not a matter within my competence. I had to do a lot of running about in Vienna from one authority to another and, particularly, the Ministry of Foreign Affairs. But I told the Doctor that I did not regard the question as a chasm which could not be bridged. I told him, however, that in exchange for this intervention of mine he would have to do something for me—get another 8,000 Jews to emigrate from Vienna.

The deal failed, but Eichmann did not say why. Herzl's remains were not, in fact, removed to Israel until after the formation of the new State.

When the attempt to purge France of Jews was dealt with by Dr. Servatius, the Accused gave the same stereotyped denial that he had already given times without number. It was true, he said, that he instructed his representatives in France to organise Jewish deportations, but he was only passing on orders from Himmler. The only person who could give orders to SS units in France on such matters, he said, was the diplomatic envoy of the Reich, Abetz. This was clearly laid down in a letter from Ribbentrop to the Commander of the German Security Forces which stated that the German Ambassador was appointed by the *Führer* as the sole person authorised "to deal with *all* problems in occupied and unoccupied France."

The Defence then produced a document which had not already been exhibited by the Prosecution. It stated that at a meeting in Paris on 19 August 1940 Abetz proposed that the military forces in France should issue orders that no Jews should be permitted to remain in the occupied zone and that steps should be taken to confiscate all their property before deportation.

Less than a month later, Dr. Martin Luther[7] wrote from the Foreign Office to RSHA asking for Himmler's comments regarding Abetz's proposals. Himmler must have passed the letter on to Heydrich, for Heydrich conveyed his approval of Abetz's proposition and requested that the Commander of the SIPO in France should be instructed to take all the necessary steps to implement it.

Eichmann was asked: who was the expert adviser on Jewish affairs to the Head of the Security Forces in Paris? The answer to this question could have been short and sweet: "Dannecker first and afterwards Röthke." The Accused, however, appeared unable to give a plain unvarnished answer to any question, and his reply was as follows: "As a matter of fact, to be precise, I must point out that this could not be correctly described as a Security service but a special bureau acting for the Security service and the Security police. Nevertheless I can say that the person in charge was originally Dannecker and afterwards *Hauptsturmführer* Röthke."

Frequently the Accused was rebuked by the Presiding Judge for these long complicated replies to simple questions and

[7] Dr. Martin Luther was Director of the Deutschland Department of the German Foreign Office. In April 1943 he was, himself, sent to Sachsenhausen concentration camp from which he never returned. The circumstances of his death are unknown.

warned that if the Court failed to follow his tortuous explanations it would be his fault and not theirs. It was all in vain. According to him every document produced in evidence by the Prosecution was false or misleading; everything that he had said or done was misunderstood; the entire evidence for the Prosecution was either perjured or misconceived, all previous confessions and admissions had been given at a time when he never envisaged, even remotely, the possibility of being brought to trial. Sometimes even his own Counsel's questions were not framed to his liking, and he corrected them.

After the assassination of Heydrich, Himmler gave orders that much sterner measures should be adopted against the Jews. A memorandum written by Dannecker on 21 July 1942 stated that *Obersturmbannführer* Eichmann and *Obersturmführer* Novak [8] had both telephoned from RSHA IV B 4. "The question of the deportation of the children was discussed with Eichmann in this conversation," Dannecker wrote. "He decided that children's transports should recommence as soon as it was possible to start deporting Jews to the General-Government of Poland. Novak promised that by the end of August, or early in September at the latest, it would be possible to send about six transports there, transports which would include all kinds of Jews (even old ones and others not capable of hard work)."

The Accused was asked what he had to say about this memorandum and his answer is given below:

[8] Franz Novak was arrested in Vienna in 1961, where he had been living unperturbed, under his own name, ever since 1957. He had been an Austrian Nazi since the earliest days of the movement there and was deprived of Austrian citizenship in 1934 after the assassination of Dollfuss. After the war he was able to get it back by the simple expedient of applying for it in his native Karinthia, where the records of the provincial Prefecture contained no information which would lead anyone to suppose that his nationality should not be restored to him.

His arrest took place only a few days after a reward of the Austrian equivalent of £900 had been offered for clues leading to his capture. He will be tried in Austria.

Himmler ordered the deportation of the Jews from France. The deportation of all Jews without any limitations or reservations. The French Militia arrested the children along with their parents and the question immediately arose: what was to be done with these children? In answer to that question I wrote (*sic*) what appears in Dannecker's memorandum. If this document is taken separately, out of its context, it undoubtedly appears that I made this decision immediately and on my own responsibility. It would appear that I was the man to make this decision and that I was authorised so to do. In fact the question was originally asked by me by cable on 10 July, eleven days earlier. In the cable Dannecker asked my Department what should be done with children arrested in such circumstances. Were they to be deported or were they not? The very fact that it took eleven days to get a decision proves that I was not the competent authority to make it and that I had to pass it on to my superiors. When the decision was given I passed it on to Paris. Even Müller, the Head of Amt IV, was not empowered to make such an important decision; that is why it took such a long time.

Eichmann then referred to a letter produced in evidence by the Prosecution which contained a report, which was sent to Müller on 12 February 1943 by *Standartenführer* Helmuth Knochen, the Commander of the SIPO in Northern France and Belgium, about a discussion which had taken place between him and Eichmann in connection with the deportation of Jews of French nationality. The subject of the letter was, "Final Solution of the Jewish Problem in France," and it dealt mainly with the difficulties being encountered because of the strong feeling on the part of many Frenchmen against the Nazis' anti-Semitic policy. One paragraph of this letter read as follows: "The report from *Obersturmbannführer* Eichmann and his announcement about the evacuation of all Jews having French nationality causes me to comment briefly on my attitude to this question, and to describe the present situation with regard to this matter and the measures necessary for carrying out this policy, so that there will be as few difficulties with the French Government as possible."

Eichmann was asked by Dr. Servatius whether he had had any negotiations with Knochen on the subject or had sent him any instructions:

EICHMANN: Yes, I had negotiations with Knochen. If one goes into all the details and examines the correspondence, one gets the impression that I disagreed with Himmler's order of September 1942 to the effect that no more deportations of French Jews were to take place, and that I tried to maintain them on my own initiative. Other documents, however, show that Himmler sent General Daluege to Paris and Marseilles to look into the difficulties. When Daluege returned Himmler changed his mind, and I received an order to contact Paris and inform Knochen of the *Reichsführer SS's* fresh instructions that all French Jews were to be deported. It was after receipt of these instructions that Knochen made his report to Müller. The fact that he did so is an additional proof that I was not in a position to issue orders to the Commander of the SD and SIPO, for in that event he would not have reported direct to Müller after his conversation with me.

On the ninth day of the Accused's examination-in-chief the Defence dealt with the deportation of Jews from Belgium, Denmark, Greece, Holland and Yugoslavia. He maintained throughout that in none of those countries did he have any say in the decisions regarding who should be deported. All he did was to arrange transport for them. To support this claim he cited a document, which had been produced in evidence by the Prosecution, recording a decision which had been transmitted to the authorities in Holland by *Gruppenführer* Glücks, to the effect that all furriers would be sent to Auschwitz. Glücks was in the Reich Office for Economic Affairs and this fact, Eichmann said, proved what he had been saying throughout his evidence, namely that it was not RSHA which determined the destination of these people but the Office for Economic Affairs.

Similarly he denied any possibility that he could have ordered the evacuation of the patients in a mental asylum in

Holland, as alleged in one of the Prosecution's documentary exhibits. The reason for the transfer of these unfortunate people to an even less congenial place than their former home was due to a decision, made by *Gauleiter* Seyss-Inquart and Rauter, the SIPO Chief in Holland, to open a sanatorium for SS men and the place chosen was this asylum.

The Accused was also questioned closely about a letter which Felix Benzler, the Nazi envoy in Belgrade, had written in September 1941 to the German Ministry of Foreign Affairs regarding the removal of 1,200 Serbian Jews from the concentration camp at Sabac. Dr. Servatius quoted from the document:

> In present circumstances it is impossible to transfer them into labour camps since it is difficult to provide adequate security measures. Jewish camps create obstacles and dangers even to our own troops. The evacuation of Sabac camp should, therefore, be started immediately, for there are 1,200 Jews among the inmates and it is situated in a combat area where there are numerous bands of partisans. Moreover it has been proved that the presence of Jews in the country contributes considerably to unrest and disturbances. In another area in Serbia, Banat, it was found that the spreading of wild rumours stopped the moment the Jews were removed. . . . For that reason I urgently repeat my previous application. Should it be turned down once more the only alternative left would be deportation to the General-Government of Poland or to Russia. This, however, would probably create transport difficulties. Failing that, all operations against the Jews in Serbia would have to be suspended temporarily, but this would be contrary to the orders which I have received from His Excellency the Foreign Minister.

There was a marginal note in the handwriting of Franz Rademacher [9] stating that according to information received

[9] Rademacher was *Amtsleiter* of Department Deutschland III in the German Foreign Office under Martin Luther from May 1940 to April 1943. He was sentenced by a German Criminal Court in 1952 to three years and five months imprisonment but broke his bail while waiting appeal and succeeded in escaping to the Argentine.

from Eichmann, Department IV B 4, deportation to Poland, Russia or Germany was not possible, and ending with the words, "Eichmann proposes death by shooting."

The Attorney-General had, earlier in the proceedings, produced a statement made by Rademacher on the subject during an interrogation by United States officers after the war in which he stated that he had written this marginal note during a conversation with RSHA about the problem. Rademacher stated that while he was talking to Eichmann on the telephone he wrote notes of what Eichmann was saying. He said that the military authorities were responsible for law and order in Serbia and they would just have to shoot the Jewish rebels. "When I questioned him again," Rademacher said, "he simply repeated 'shoot,' and then hung up the phone."

Eichmann's reply to this serious allegation was, as usual, a complete denial.

I did not say this, I could not have expressed myself so, because that would not have been within my jurisdiction. When I first saw these documents, when preparing my case, I read them through and weighed them carefully, because I knew how serious the charge was. The first thing that struck me was that correspondence between the Foreign Office and RSHA was always conducted, even in less important matters, with bureaucratic accuracy, and it seemed strange to me that such an important question as this should have been dealt with simply by writing a few remarks in the margin of an official document. When I saw this particular document itself I tried to put myself in the same situation as Rademacher.

He has said that he was called upon to report and make proposals, that he was sitting opposite Luther, and that while he was talking to me on the telephone he wrote this note on the document and passed it over to Luther.

He suggested that Rademacher must have inserted these words to protect himself because he and other Foreign Ministry officials had been reprimanded by Baron Ernst von Weizsäcker [1] for "undiplomatic, arrogant action beyond their competence" on a previous occasion, when orders had been given for 1,600 hostages to be executed in Belgrade.

A memorandum written by Eberhard von Thadden to von Ribbentrop on 22 April 1944 was produced as further proof of the truth of Eichmann's insistence, throughout his evidence, that the sole function of his Department in RSHA had been to co-ordinate train time-tables, and that he only obeyed orders and had never initiated them. The relevant contents of this memorandum are as follows:

> The Reich Security Head Office reports that the 50,000 Jews picked out for forced labour are to be taken from the concentration camps in Hungary and deported from there. Details about the time-table and requisitioning railway trucks will be worked out by RSHA. *Obersturmbannführer* Eichmann who is, at present, in Hungary is receiving all necessary instructions from RSHA today.

Suggestions were also made by Dr. Servatius, and supported by new documentary evidence, that the German Foreign Ministry had been pressing, as early as 1942, for the implementation of the *Führer's* final solution plans in Hungary and the removal of the many obstacles that were constantly being put in its way by Admiral Horthy and certain members of his Government. The German Ambassador was also instructed by the Minister for Foreign Affairs to induce the Hungarians to act in accordance with Hitler's wishes by excluding the Jews from economic life, introducing the yellow badge, and deporting them to the East.

The Accused's evidence was interrupted at the commence-

---

[1] Ernst von Weizsäcker was Chief Secretary of State in the German Foreign Office until April 1943. He was sentenced by an American War Crimes Court at Nuremberg in April 1949 to seven years imprisonment but the sentence was reduced to five years and remitted in October 1950. He died at Lindau on 6 August 1951.

ment of the eighty-fifth session of the trial by the production
of evidence from six former Nazis who had worked in close
contact with Eichmann either in the SS or in other Government departments.

In accordance with the undertaking given in June 1960 by
the German Federal Minister of Justice, Dr. Schäffer, that he
would "render Israel justice every legal assistance and place
any material at its disposal," evidence was taken from four of
these witnesses by German courts. The Austrian Government
gave similar assistance by providing Israel with a long statement of evidence given by Dr. Wilhelm Höttl in the District
Court of Bad Aussee before which he appeared on 19 June
1961.

Four of these witnesses had been warned that if they set foot
in Israel they might be prosecuted, under the Nazis and Nazi
Collaborators (Punishment) Law, for war crimes which they
themselves had committed between 1940 and 1945. The other
two had been granted immunity; nevertheless they refused the
invitation to come to Israel.

The first evidence to be given was that of Höttl, who is now
the Principal of Bad Aussee Private Secondary School. The
first time Höttl met the Accused was in the spring of 1938
when he had an office in Vienna. Eichmann introduced himself as an Austrian from Linz, but he spoke with a pronounced
North German accent and "with that superciliousness and
haughtiness so characteristic of North Germany." Höttl spoke
of a conversation which he had with Eichmann just after the
collapse of Rumania and the armistice between the Rumanian
Army and the Red Army. As a result of these events the whole
German Front in that area had crumbled, and Eichmann had
come to get some information about the general military situation which Höttl, by virtue of his appointment, was in a position to give.

Eichmann came to see me late in the afternoon. He was not
wearing the ordinary service uniform which he usually wore
when visiting me. He seemed to be under a great strain, and this

impression was increased after I had described the desperate situation to him. I myself was quite depressed at the time because I feared that the Russian advance through Germany into Austria, my homeland, could not be halted. . . . Later Eichmann gulped down a few brandies and I remember putting a whole bottle down in front of him so that he could help himself. We were alone. Eichmann got up from the table and said, "It looks as though we may not meet again," or words to that effect. Later, realising, perhaps, that such a defeatist attitude needed some explanation he expressed the opinion that the defeat of Germany was now inevitable. When I asked him how he had reached this conclusion he declared that the Allies saw him as one of the chief war criminals because of his role in the plan to exterminate the Jewish race.

On hearing this remark I made an effort to continue the conversation because I was always interested to hear about the extermination plan, especially in regard to the number of Jews exterminated. I wanted to obtain some reliable figures. It is now a long time since this conversation took place but it is indelibly fixed in my memory, although the actual figures were fresher in my mind when I first gave this evidence at Nuremberg in 1945 than they are now. As far as I can now remember, he said that the actual number of Jews murdered was a top secret of the Reich. Nevertheless, as I was a historian, he would tell me the number. He said that, so far as he could tell, up to date 6,000,000 Jews had died. Of this number 4,000,000 had perished in extermination camps and the remaining 2,000,000 were shot by the special operation groups (*Einsatzgruppen*) or died of disease. My reaction to this information must have been very strong because Eichmann immediately added a reservation saying that Himmler's estimate of 6,000,000 Jews having perished could not be taken as correct because the gross total was higher. I cannot remember whether Eichmann gave any explanation or apology in regard to his own part in the affair. He certainly did not say that he felt any guilt. . . . This conversation lasted at least an hour during which he drank several brandies and I warned him not to drive his car when he left, although I would not say that he was drunk. At that time he was known to be drinking heavily.

When I said that 6,000,000 were "murdered" that is not exactly what Eichmann said. He used the words "exterminated" and "liquidated."

Höttl also stated, during his examination by the Judge of the District Court in Bad Aussee, that two statements which he had made on a television programme for the North German Broadcasting Service were true. These were, first, that it was Eichmann who sent hundreds of thousands of Hungarian Jews to extermination camps and, second, that the most suitable way of defining Eichmann's role in the "final solution" was to call him "the great 'expeditor' towards death."

Another former Nazi colleague of Eichmann, Walter Huppenkothen, who had been a counter-espionage officer in the Gestapo, testified in the District Court of Cologne, and the record of his interrogation was also admitted in evidence. When giving evidence at Nuremberg Huppenkothen had stated that Eichmann had a "special status" in RSHA. He now said that it would have been more accurate to have described it as a "special position." Unlike most departmental heads he was not an official, but as an SS Officer held the position of Chief of IV B 4 and had to refer directly to the head of the bureau, Müller, on all matters. Huppenkothen also agreed that Eichmann was correct in describing Müller as an officer who "would not tolerate subordinates who made decisions without consulting his superiors."

In contrast to Huppenkothen's evidence, the testimony of Eberhard von Thadden was not so favourable to the Accused. During the time that he was employed in a department of the German Foreign Office, called Inland Group II, von Thadden had frequent conversations with Eichmann, personally and on the telephone, about Jewish affairs. On one such occasion the Accused had called him weak-kneed when he tried to intercede on behalf of a certain Jew. In the spring of 1944 von Thadden went to Hungary and, while in Budapest, visited the *Sonderkommando* Eichmann.

The real reason for the visit was that his Chief wanted to

give von Thadden a few days' peace away from the almost nightly bombing of Berlin. In his evidence von Thadden stated:

I drew up two reports during my visit, in one of which I expressed the opinion that the *Sonderkommando* Eichmann was working in Hungary in accordance with a defined and cruel plan. I did not know how much of this plan was Eichmann's, but I was shocked when he told me its details. Other members of the Foreign Office staff were of the same opinion; namely, that the implementation of Eichmann's plan must be stopped. So far as I know the plan was not carried out in the way in which Eichmann had described it to me in Budapest. When the deportation of Jews from Hungary was discussed, the East was always mentioned as their destination. Auschwitz camp was also mentioned in the same context.

Another important piece of evidence was contained in the record of the interrogation of former General Hans Jüttner who had been Himmler's aide-de-camp. He spoke of having been an eye-witness to the death march of Jews from Budapest to the Austrian border:

In November 1944 I travelled from Vienna to Budapest in the company of *Obersturmbannführer* Becher. On the road, in German territory, we came across columns of Jews guarded by Hungarian soldiers marching in the direction of Vienna. Becher said to me, "We shall meet the *Standarte* Eichmann." I asked what this meant, because I believed it to be a military unit, and Becher explained that it was a transport of Jews from Budapest to the Austrian border. When I saw those moving columns I went up to an SS man . . . The SS man was a young officer belonging to Eichmann's unit and I told him what I thought about it. He told me that his unit was under the command of RSHA, that orders were issued from there and I had no right to criticise them. He spoke in a very arrogant tone.

In Budapest, I wanted to find out from Winkelmann who was responsible for this march. He told me that he knew about it but had no responsibility for it. It was Eichmann's doing. Then, I asked who Eichmann was and I was told that he was the head of the department dealing with the Jewish problem and that he was not one of Winkelmann's subordinates. In my opinion, from what Winkelmann told me, Eichmann was responsible for this march.

Herr Horst Grell, who had been an SS officer attached to the German Legation in Budapest, when Eichmann was in Hungary, told the District Judge of Berchtesgaden, where he was examined in June 1961, that "it was customary at the time of the Nuremberg and other war-crime trials, held just after the war, for witnesses to palm off as much blame as possible on those who were absent or believed dead." He agreed that Eichmann had said that he was war criminal No. 1 "because he had 6,000,000 lives on his conscience," but, in Grell's opinion, Eichmann was merely boasting.

It was the evidence of Kurt Becher, however, given before the Magistrates' Court of Cologne, which was most damaging to the Defence, and Eichmann's Counsel tried hard to have it excluded on the ground that Becher had been allowed to see the questions and consult his lawyer several days before he gave his evidence. The Court was reminded by the Attorney-General that Kurt Becher's examination had been done at the request of the Defence and if the magistrates in Bremen saw fit to show the questions to him in advance, it was not a matter which came within the jurisdiction of an Israeli court. He asked the Court to admit the evidence.

The Presiding-Judge announced that, in their opinion, the fact that the nature of the questions were revealed to Becher some days before he was interrogated did not invalidate the testimony, but they would, nevertheless, bear it in mind when they came to assess the probative value of the evidence.

Kurt Becher had been a Colonel in the SS and was, for a time, Chief of the Economic Staff of the Field SS in Budapest. He made a number of affidavits which were admitted in evidence at the trial of major war criminals at Nuremberg and played a considerable part in persuading Himmler to bargain with the Jews who still remained alive in 1944, and helped to save the inmates of many concentration camps at the end of the war. "Becher," wrote Gerald Reitlinger in his book *The Final Solution*, "had already had experience in acquiring Jewish property for the SS. A salesman in a Hamburg firm of grain merchants, he became, in the summer of 1942, when he was thirty-three years old, principal horse-buyer for the SS personal department under the jockey, General Fegelein, the brother-in-law of Hitler's mistress, Eva Braun."

He was, without doubt, a peculiar character, and what he says about Eichmann should, perhaps, be accepted with some reserve. There is, however, little reason to doubt his statement that "Eichmann was a convinced National Socialist and a fanatical anti-Semite."

Becher told the magistrates in Bremen about a conversation in his presence between Himmler and Eichmann. For some time Becher had been complaining that Eichmann was trying to get round all instructions then being issued by Himmler, and he asked the *Reichsführer* SS to send for Eichmann and speak to him about this:

I told Himmler that Eichmann was not taking his orders seriously and only carried them out if they were confirmed by his Bureau Chief, Müller. Himmler summoned Eichmann, and Becher was present when the two had a discussion in Himmler's car in the Black Forest. He was very annoyed with Eichmann and reminded him, on this occasion, who was the master and who the servant. "May I remind you," he shouted, "that it was not *Gruppenführer* Müller or you who founded the RSHA and I am the only one who gives orders. If you cannot obey them, you must tell me."

Asked to give the reasons why he had complained to Himmler about Eichmann, Becher said:

On one occasion Himmler had authorised the emigration of 1,700 Jews, in June or July 1944, from Budapest. It was intended that they should go to Switzerland via Vienna. I then heard from Dr. Kastner that Eichmann had given instructions that they should be sent to Bergen-Belsen "for technical reasons."

In reply to my question as to why they were being sent to Bergen-Belsen and not straight to Switzerland, he declared, "First these people must go to Belsen." In reply to another question as to when the transport would be sent Eichmann said, "as soon as there are orders." He went on to say that in the last resort it was left to him to decide when or whether a transport should go, for many things might occur to prevent it, such as an epidemic of spotted fever or the destruction of the railway track by aerial bombardment. Eichmann told me on this occasion, as he did on many others, that even instructions from Himmler would be carried out by him only when they were confirmed by Müller who was his immediate superior.

Becher also spoke of another occasion when he experienced difficulty with Eichmann:

In April 1945 I tried to prevent the extermination of concentration camp inmates and to ensure that they were not adversely affected by the course of the battle. I obtained authority from Himmler to visit Belsen. For technical reasons I thought it desirable to inform Eichmann that I had received Himmler's permission, in order to forestall any possible steps which he might take to prevent my visit. For that reason, before I left for Belsen with Dr. Kastner, I went to Eichmann's office in Berlin. I told him that I was just off to Belsen with Kastner, and that we intended afterwards to visit Neuengamme.[2] At this juncture Eichmann went into a fit of rage. Why was Kastner being taken by me to a concentration camp? He should be sent there as an inmate, not go there as a visitor. In any event he was opposed to my going there. He declared categorically that neither Müller nor he would allow us to go. Nevertheless, we did.

It will be remembered that it was in Hungary that Eichmann was actually in charge of the final solution; on the spot, as it were. Elsewhere he directed all the operations from behind his desk in Amt IV B 4 of RSHA.

[2] Neuengamme concentration camp was situated in the suburbs of Hamburg. It was established in 1938. Altogether 90,000 people passed through the camp, of whom about 40,000 died.

During the eighty-sixth session of the trial, the Defence dealt with what Dr. Servatius called the "Hungarian chapter" and Eichmann was asked:

Q: How did it come about that you were sent to Hungary?

EICHMANN: On 10 March 1944 the head of my office, *Gruppen-führer* Müller, informed me that I must go at once to Mauthausen where I was to report to Doctor Geschke who was then the Chief of the SIPO and SD in Hungary. This posting to Hungary followed an order issued by Himmler for the deportation of all Jews from Hungary and the combing of the whole area, for strategic reasons, from east to west. . . . My duties were then undefined, but my first task was to carry our negotiations with the Hungarian authorities before the deportations of Jews could begin. . . . I was not personally responsible for the arrests of Jews, nor for the confiscation of their property; all this was done by the SIPO and SD. . . .

Eichmann told the Court, in answer to a question put to him by Dr. Servatius, that all he had to do at first, however unbelievable it might sound, was to report to his superiors the progress of the preparations for carrying out Himmler's new order. There was really very little for him or his office staff to do. During the first few days after his arrival, Eichmann stated, he was ordered to move his office to the Majestic Hotel, Schwannenberg. Soon after he installed himself in his new quarters, Kurt Becher came and told Eichmann that he was authorised by Müller to confiscate Jewish property in Hungary. Eichmann discovered during further conversations with Becher that he was proposing to obtain emigration permits for the Jews. This had formerly only been sanctioned by Himmler in very special circumstances. Becher's idea was to trade these permits for foreign currency and/or military equipment.

That Becher intended to intrude into what Eichmann considered to be his own special sphere of activity made him indignant. But that was not all. Becher daily urged Eichmann to speed up the pace of emigration to an unheard-of degree in

order to create tension and facilitate his extortions. Eichmann
told the Court:

I was fed up. Here was someone who did not belong to the
SIPO trying to give instructions to me. There was indignation
in my heart that I should have to take part in this deportation
work whilst a number of my office staff who were my subordinates were doing my work. When I learned that the *Abwehr*
were doing the same thing as Becher my indignation grew. I,
who had been trying, ever since the autumn of 1939, to leave
Amt IV, now had to deal with deportations while others did
my work *in my own sphere.*

I thought it over and sent one of my own men, it was either
Krumey or Wisliceny, to find out what could be obtained in
exchange for emigration permission for one or two hundred
thousand Jews. I did this in order to compete with Becher and
the *Abwehr.*

Then, one day, Yoel Brand came into my office. How and
where he came from I cannot remember. But I clearly recollect
seeing him there, standing in front of me and I agree with his
version, already given in evidence at this trial, of what I then said
to him. I remember mentioning first 100,000, then 200,000, and
subsequently raising it to a million, for reasons of psychology,
so that when I put the scheme to my Chief, Müller, he would be
less likely to throw me out of the room than if I had suggested a
much smaller number. I also invented the ten per cent clause
because I imagined that it would be difficult for Brand to succeed
in raising the money abroad without guarantees of some kind.

I used to visit RSHA at regular intervals, and on my next trip
to Berlin I went to see Müller and put the proposition to him.
It was too big for him to handle and he had to refer it to higher
authority. After two more visits to Berlin I could hardly believe
my ears when I heard that approval had been given. Himmler
already proposed, with the proceeds (10,000 lorries), to motorise
the 22nd and 8th Cavalry Divisions of the *Waffen SS.* . . . I can
honestly say that I did my utmost in order to help Brand carry
out his side of the bargain. . . . I urged him to get going as soon
as possible because I knew that it was not going to be possible
to alter the time-tables of transports for which preparations had

already been made. It was for this same reason that I instructed Krumey to accompany Brand from Budapest to Vienna so that no further delay should occur in transit.

I did not tell Brand, as he gave in evidence during the case for the Prosecution, that I was going to "still the mills of death in Auschwitz." I never said that, or anything like it. In any event it would have been outside the realm of my jurisdiction. Mrs. Hansi Brand's evidence that I had not kept my promise to her is, also, untrue. I made no promises about temporarily holding up the deportations to Brand, to his wife or to Kastner.

I made it clear that the transports would cease as soon as a declaration was made by Brand that the trucks would not be used on the Western Front. . . .

It was in this Court that I learned for the first time why the deal never came off and I regret it very much.

I am bound to admit, however, for I am giving evidence on oath, that it was not out of compassion that I launched this enterprise. After the scheme fell through, I returned to the routine work I had been doing since 1939, co-ordinating the transports to the extermination camps.

With regard to the 50,000 Jews who took part in the well-known death march from Budapest to the Austrian border Eichmann was asked whether it was true, as reported by Veesenmayer, the German Ambassador in Budapest, that it was he, Eichmann, who had negotiated with the Hungarian Government for the deportation of these 50,000 people. The Accused told the Court that he did give instructions to implement these orders after consultation with the Hungarian authorities, but emphasised that the orders themselves came from above. He did not initiate the march, and he took no part in its organisation or supervision.

Dealing with the only charge against the Accused which alleged a killing done by his own hand, Dr. Servatius asked him the following question:

DR. SERVATIUS: Regarding the evidence of the witness Abraham Gordon: you heard him tell the Court about the beating of a

Jewish youth in the garden of the house where you were living
while in Budapest. Do you wish to comment on the evidence and
say whether or not you had a hand in this beating or murder?

EICHMANN: All I can say is, I never killed anyone. I have never
ill-treated or beaten anyone. I can also say in the same breath that
Sergeant Slavic could not have done so either. He had been with
me since 1938, and I knew him well. He would not have dared
to do such a thing. I am amazed at this evidence, and cannot
think what made the witness say it. I emphatically deny the
charge.

DR. SERVATIUS: Do you mean to say that the witness Gordon
deliberately lied when under oath?

EICHMANN: No, I wouldn't say that. I would not say that he
committed perjury, but I do wonder where he could have got his
information, for what he said was certainly untrue. He claims
to have seen what happened, and I ask myself, why is it that no
one else saw it? There were always many people coming to and
going from my house. Someone would have been bound to have
seen it. If this story were true it would surely have come to light
before 1961.

Eichmann also categorically denied that he visited Auschwitz camp in June 1961, after Himmler had decided to make
it "Gas Chamber No. 1," or that he had discussed with the
commandant of Auschwitz, Rudolf Höss, the best method of
carrying out the executions.

On the contrary, he said, he accepted his orders very un-
willingly and on many occasions had asked to be relieved of
his appointment and given another more congenial one.

It was sad, he told the Court, that all this should happen to
him, for he had always been in favour of the plan for the emigration of Jews to Madagascar, and he had never given a
thought to "a blood-soaked solution" of the Jewish problem.

After visiting Kulm, in the Warthe area, where he had
witnessed horrible things happening, he saw Müller and asked
to be given "some other kind of work" because he was "not
suited for that particular kind of activity." Then he had actually seen an infant shot in his mother's arms, and this was as
early as the autumn of 1941.

On another occasion he saw at Lemberg the "so-called fountain of blood." A short time before his arrival a number of Jews had been gassed there, and as a result of the gas used in the gas-chamber, and the hurried burial of the victims, "blood was spouting up through the earth and it looked like a ghoulish fountain." All these things he had seen during his first four visits to the extermination camps. He went reluctantly, but *he had to obey orders.*

Before the close of his examination-in-chief, the Accused was asked by Dr. Servatius about a phrase he used during his lengthy interrogation by the Israeli police while in custody awaiting trial, and by way of reply he read out a prepared statement.

Dr. Servatius: You said during the police interrogation that you carried a burden of guilt. Could you tell the Court how you now regard this question of guilt?

Eichmann: Some sixteen to twenty-four years have elapsed since all these events took place: what existed then exists no longer. It is difficult to say what constitutes guilt, and I must make the distinction between guilt from the legal point of view and from the human aspect. The facts in respect of which I am answerable to this Court concern the role which I played in connection with the deportations. When they took place they were in pursuance of an order given by the Head of the State and the guilt must be borne by those who were responsible for political decisions: when there is no responsibility there can be no guilt or blame. The responsibility must be examined from the legal point of view, and as long as human beings go on living together in society, no global solution can be found except the Government of a State based on law and order and abiding by these orders. . . . In order to safeguard the security of a State, it must find means to bind the individual, and this was done in Germany by making him take the oath. The question of conscience is a matter for the Head of State. One must trust and be loyal to the sovereign power. He who is led by a good Head of State is lucky. I had no luck. The Head of State ordered the deportations, and the part I played in them emanated from the master at the top, the Chief of the SS and the police. He was the man who passed on the orders to the Chief of the SIPO and SD, and he, in his turn, passed them on to Müller, my immediate superior, who passed them on to my department. . . . In the criminal code of the SS, it was laid down that the punishment for disobedience or insubordination would be death. I did all I could by legal means to obtain a transfer to other duties, but I did not succeed, and when in the autumn of 1939 I was transferred to the SIPO and SD this was done against my will and by order from above. I had to obey. I was in uniform at the time and there was a war on. When I went abroad in 1950 it was not because I was afraid of being brought to justice, but for political and family reasons.

My position was similar to that of millions who had to obey. The difference lies only in that my assignment was the most difficult and I had to carry it. All those who say here that it was easy and did not require an effort to disobey orders give no reasons, and do not say what they would themselves have done. It is said that one could have feigned illness. This may have been a way for generals, but not for their subordinates. If it had transpired that the illness was simulated the result would have been extremely serious, and the binding chains of one's oath should be borne in mind.

Himmler said in his famous speech at Poznan that SS generals could ask to be transferred, but that applied only to generals. The small man could not have followed that course, especially when he was the recipient of secret orders. He could have shot himself, but he could not protest. Ethically I condemn myself and try to argue with myself. I wish to say, in conclusion, that I have regret and condemnation for the extermination of the Jewish people which was ordered by the German rulers, but I myself could not have done anything to prevent it. I was a tool in the hands of the strong and the powerful and in the hands of fate itself. That is what I have to say in answer to your question.

Eichmann was then asked by Judge Halévi why he did not give himself up to a court in Germany in 1950 instead of fleeing the country. To this the Accused replied by saying that he felt certain that in his own country he would not be tried in accordance with legal precepts, but according to political principles. It was not that he lacked courage, and he had

repeatedly declared that he was prepared to face trial on condition that he was guaranteed a fair and proper trial uninflu-
enced by political considerations.

After the end of the Accused's examination-in-chief and the
delivery of a minority judgment of the Court (Judge Halévi
dissenting) regarding the admissibility in evidence of certain
extracts from the Sassen document, the Attorney-General rose
to cross-examine. He began dramatically by reminding the
Accused of a statement that he had made to the Israeli police
interrogators when he said, "I am aware that I shall be found
guilty as an accomplice to murder. I am aware that I face the
death penalty and I am not asking for mercy because I don't
deserve it." "You said that you were ready to hang yourself
in public as an atonement for these terrible crimes," said the
Attorney-General, "and this has been recorded, from your
own mouth, on page 360 of your statement."

ATTORNEY-GENERAL: Are you ready to repeat those words
now, here in Court?

EICHMANN: I confirm what I said during my interrogation
and again this morning, in answer to my Counsel's last question.
I have read what I said again and I do not deny it.

ATTORNEY-GENERAL: So you confess to being an accomplice to
the murder of millions of Jews?

EICHMANN: That I cannot admit. So far as my own participation
is concerned, I must point out that I do not consider myself
guilty from the legal point of view. I was only receiving orders
and carrying out orders. . . .

ATTORNEY-GENERAL: Please answer my question. Answer
briefly "Yes" or "No." If an explanation is required you can give
it afterwards. My question is not a legal question. In your heart
do you feel yourself guilty as an accomplice in the murder of millions of Jews?

EICHMANN: Yes, from the human point of view, because I
was guilty of carrying out the deportations.

The Attorney-General then pressed the Accused to ac-
knowledge that towards the end of the war he had said that

he would jump into his grave gladly, knowing that five million Jews would also have lost their lives. The Accused tried to explain that when he used the expression "five million enemies of the Reich," he was referring to the enemy who were storming the capital city of Berlin; the Red Army and the American Air Force. What he said was "not aimed at the Jews." He would not have leaped into his grave gladly because of the Jews.

He went on to explain the circumstances in which he had spoken of these "five million enemies of the Reich." He was saying a final word of farewell to his staff before it broke up, but he never mentioned the Jews at all.

The Attorney-General reminded him that when he had been interrogated by the Israeli police, while in custody awaiting trial, he *had* mentioned five million Jews.

The Accused replied saying that he had already pointed out that he was referring to *all* the foes of the Reich who had been killed in the war and he also mentioned in this connection five million Germans. He had not intended to say that he had killed five million Jews or that he had been instrumental in killing them, although he admitted to the Court that they were on his conscience.

Eichmann was then shown a document in which he had written in his own handwriting that "he who was the *Führer*, Adolf Hitler, stated on many occasions that he had declared war on the Jews . . . the slogan was to exterminate the enemy, root and branch. World Jewry declared war on the German Reich under the leadership of Chaim Weizmann, so the *Führer* ordered the extermination of the Jewish people."

"Was the Jew, therefore, regarded as an enemy?" the Attorney-General asked, and the Accused, after some quibbling, admitted that he was. Nevertheless, he insisted, neither he nor his subordinates in IV B 4 had anything to do with their physical extermination. Asked whether he was a convinced anti-Semite, Eichmann answered, "No. I was a fervent nationalist."

I regarded the Jews as opponents, but not as opponents who must be exterminated. I regarded them as opponents with regard to whom a mutually acceptable and fair solution must be found. That solution I envisaged as putting firm soil under their feet so that they would have a land of their own. And I was working towards such a solution joyfully and I co-operated in obtaining it gladly, because it was the kind of solution which was approved of by the Jews' own organisations, and I regarded it as most appropriate.

This strange picture of Adolf Eichmann as a fervent Zionist produced a gasp of incredulity in the public gallery.

For more than two hours the Attorney-General tried to get the Accused to admit that he was an anti-Semite, but in vain. Finally he gave it up, saying, "I see there is no agreement between us as to what is anti-Semitism and what is not."

Dr. Hausner, however, was not the only one in this battle of words to feel the strain, and when the Court opened the eighty-ninth Session of the trial, the Presiding Judge announced that because of his physical condition the Accused would not be able to face further cross-examination until the afternoon.

On the resumption of the trial, after the Accused had been certified fit to stand up to further cross-examination, he was strenuously questioned about the Nisko affair.

According to the case for the Prosecution, Eichmann was supposed to have sent a large number of Jews to Nisko, which was in the Polish Government-General of which Hans Frank was *Gauleiter*. The Attorney-General suggested to the Accused that he had sent them there because he knew that all the Jews in that part of Poland were to be exterminated but that he had to withdraw them afterwards because of Frank's objections.

Eichmann denied that he had been present at the meeting at which Heydrich had announced this policy, nor had he any knowledge of what the *Einsatzgruppen* were going to do. He rejected the Prosecution's charge that the Jews had been sent there "naked and penniless." He really knew nothing about it. He was only in the district for a couple of days at the most.

ATTORNEY-GENERAL: I put it to you, that everything you have said in this Court about Nisko is one big lie, that you knew that the Jews in the Government-General were to be exterminated and that is why you sent them there.

EICHMANN: Mr. Attorney-General, one of the qualities which Fate has given me is that of truthfulness. My experience in life has taught me that very often this has caused me more damage than gain, but when I say that I did not know at that time about the decision to exterminate the Jews . . . it is the truth.

ATTORNEY-GENERAL: Have you not previously said that any person who is in custody is entitled to lie?

EICHMANN: I agree with that as a matter of principle, but I never personally resorted to it.

ATTORNEY-GENERAL: But you believe in the principle?

EICHMANN: According to the accepted opinion in Germany this is unwritten law. But I am not fighting here for my head or my neck, but to get rid of the lies which have been heaped on me for fifteen years.

Eichmann was closely questioned at great length by the Attorney-General about the autobiography which Rudolf Höss, the commandant of Auschwitz, wrote while in custody in Poland, and he gave another typical example of trying to avoid the issue. "Would you agree with me," Dr. Hausner asked, "that when he wrote the book in which he admitted all the crimes of extermination he had no reason to put blame on others? He was no longer interested in putting the blame on anyone else for these atrocious crimes."

"I am completely convinced, having read the book," Eichmann replied, "that he was trying to transfer the blame from the Office of Economy and Administration to RSHA."

ATTORNEY-GENERAL: Were your relations with Höss good?
EICHMANN: Yes.

Q: Were your relations with Höss better than they were with Müller?

A: No, it is impossible to say that because I was in almost daily contact with Müller, whereas I only saw Höss occasionally.

Q: You have not understood my question, were your relations with Höss better than they were with Müller?

A: Perhaps I can explain it in this way. Müller was too senior for me to be on as friendly terms with him as I could be with Höss, who was more or less my equal and with whom my relations were, shall I say, on a more human level.

JUDGE HALÉVI: Müller was not the superior of Höss, but the question was to compare the relationship of Höss with both of you. Was your relationship with Höss better than the relationship between Höss and Müller?

EICHMANN: I never saw Höss and Müller together.

ATTORNEY-GENERAL: Do you agree that Höss had no reason whatsoever to take the blame off Müller's shoulders and to put it on yours?

EICHMANN: No, there could be no reason for his trying to do that.

Q: When, therefore, Höss wrote that Müller gave Eichmann a free hand in certain matters was he not telling the truth?

A: Müller did not leave me a free hand and Höss was lying. Moreover, I did not want a free hand and I always went to Müller for a decision on everything.

Q: You are saying that Höss was not telling the truth although you agree that he had no reason to lie?

Would you not agree with me that the many witnesses who described you, at the Nuremberg trial, as the central pillar of the extermination policy, could have been more successful, if they were looking for a scape-goat, if they had put the blame on Müller.

A: For that I have a very plausible explanation.

Q: Well, what is it? We are ready to listen.

A: Those witnesses at Nuremberg were trying to create the impression that they were telling the truth. They wanted to give as much veracity to their statements as possible. Therefore they involved some other person about whom they knew most of the details through personal and official contacts whenever their statements about such a person were likely to have the ring of truth. An accused person usually does everything he can to escape from the trap and therefore looks for someone about whom he can testify a lot from his personal knowledge. I was such a person, for I was on their level and not like Müller who was their senior and about whom they did not know so much. I have to admit that to some extent I had a free hand, but that was before anything drastic was really done. I did make suggestions, and I formulated ideas. But later when the plans came to be implemented I did not have a free hand, nor did I want one.

Q: Höss also wrote this about you: "Eichmann was obsessed with his mission and assignment and there was a kind of evil spirit in him. He was convinced that the extermination of the Jews was necessary for the safety of the German people, so he used up all his energy to realise this dream." Is this a correct evaluation of your character by a man who had no reason to invent stories about you?

A: It is not correct.

Q: Did you say in the Argentine that Höss was the personification of correctness and accuracy?

A: If I had said it, it would have been correct.

Q: This same man, this personification of accuracy, wrote this about you: "Eichmann objected to the idea of selection when the question of the transports of Jews-fit-to-work came up for discussion. This was because of the possibility of escape, and other ways and means which might enable Jews to remain alive. In his opinion every Jew should be arrested and everything should be done as speedily as possible because it was impossible to know how the war would end." This referred to 1943. Had you already got doubts about a German victory?

A: This does not correspond with the truth any more than similar remarks that were made by Wisliceny.

Eichmann was also asked by the Attorney-General whether, while he was living in the Argentine, he had read a book entitled *The Last Days of the Reich Chancellery*, written by a former German officer named Gerhard Bolt, a book which contained some criticism of Hitler's conduct.

He admitted having crossed out the description of Bolt as "a young front-line officer," and having substituted the word *Lump*, which is the German for "scoundrel."

He also agreed that he had said, during his interrogation by the special section of police in Israel, while awaiting trial, that the author of that book "should have been skinned alive because it was on account of such filthy scoundrels that Germany lost the war. Bolt was a scoundrel because he violated his oath of loyalty."

The Accused was then questioned further by Judge Halévi and the Attorney-General regarding these previous admissions.

JUDGE HALÉVI: Do you think that a man who takes an oath of loyalty—this oath of loyalty of which you speak—is ever freed from it after Hitler's death?

EICHMANN: After the *Führer's* death, everybody who had pledged allegiance to him was, of course, released from this oath of loyalty.

Q: And this includes you?

A: Yes, I also am free from this oath.

ATTORNEY-GENERAL: But your anger was so great that in 1955, ten years after the war had ended, you still made these disparaging remarks about the author of that book?

EICHMANN: Yes, because I still regard the violation of an oath of loyalty as the greatest crime which a man can possibly commit.

Q: A greater crime than the murder of six million people, including one and a half million children?

A: No, of course not. I ought to say, however, that I was not dealing with extermination. Had I been ordered to do that, I am quite sure that I would have committed suicide. I would have shot myself. I cannot state this with absolute certainty, but as I know my own reactions, I assume that had I known that I had to carry out the exterminations I would have shot myself in order to evade responsibility for them.

Q: Those who did carry out the exterminations, were they criminals in your eyes?

A: They were unfortunate and unhappy.

Q: Did you not regard them as criminals? Answer "yes" or "no."

A: I cannot answer such a question, because I was never personally confronted with the problem.

Q: You saw Höss doing it at Auschwitz. At that time did you regard him as a murderer?

A: I told him that I could never do what he had been ordered to do.

Q: That was not what I asked you. My question was, what did you think about Höss when you saw him butchering the Jews? Did you in your heart regard him as a criminal?

A: I pitied him and I commiserated with him.

Q: But did you regard him as a murderer?

A: I cannot share my inner feelings with anyone and I don't think it is my duty to do so.

Q: You will have to answer my question in Court, here and now. How did you regard the people who were implementing the policy of extermination of the Jews?

A: There are certain situations which bring a man to the verge of insanity, when he may do away with himself. That, however, is purely a personal matter. I can only say how I would have reacted in similar circumstances and I have no right whatsoever to pass judgment on others who had received such orders.

Q: Therefore Höss was not a criminal in your eyes?

A: No, I do not say that.

Q: In your interrogation by the police you said that if you had been told by the *Reichsführer* SS that your father was a traitor you would have shot him with your own hands. Is that true?

A: If he *were* a traitor. . . .

Q: No. If the *Reichsführer* had told you that he was a traitor would you have shot him?

A: In that event the *Reichsführer* would have had to prove to me that my father really was a traitor.

Q: Would you have shot him then, and was it proved to you that the Jews were guilty of anything when you exterminated them?

A: I did not exterminate Jews. Nevertheless I have no wish to evade responsibility or to shirk it in any way. I would like to be allowed to clear up all these matters after the trial, and write a book in which I could call a spade a spade, and so explain it all to the rising generation.

The President of the Court interrupted the cross-examination to tell the Accused that it was equally his duty in this Court to call a spade a spade.

"As you have ordered me to give a clear answer," Eichmann replied, "I must declare that I regard the murder, the extermination of the Jews, as one of the most hideous crimes in the history of mankind." Judge Halévi then asked whether he felt the same at the time when this crime was committed and the Accused replied:

Your Honour, I shall endeavour to answer the question in a few sentences.

When, for the first time, I saw dead Jews I was utterly shattered, and the ghastly sight has never faded and has left an ineffaceable impression on my mind. But I was in the iron grip of orders to continue carrying out my duties despite what I had seen. Many times did I ask the Head of Amt IV to release me from these duties so that I should no longer have to continue to do this work. I have never spoken my mind so clearly before now, because I feared that it might be thought that I was trying to find an easy excuse for my behaviour and endeavouring to influence the final verdict by prevarication. That is not my intention. That is not my aim. My aim is to tell the whole truth whatever my sentence may be. May I say in conclusion that I regarded this violent solution of the Jewish problem as something hideous and heinous but, unfortunately, I was compelled to do what I did because of my oath of loyalty and allegiance.

JUDGE HALÉVI: But my question was, did you regard it as a crime?

EICHMANN: As the Head of the State had ordered it, and as my lawful superiors had passed on the orders to me, I felt that that was like a protective cloak. I would not go so far as to say that I shifted the responsibility on to them, but in my own mind I transferred the thought to them and, in so doing, I found some peace of mind. I felt that I bore no personal guilt, and was relieved by the knowledge that I played no direct part in the physical extermination of the Jews. The part that I did play was quite enough.

The Accused again protested, when questioned by the Attorney-General about the authority he had to make decisions, that he never even made any suggestions to Müller.

The Attorney-General then asked Eichmann whether he was trying to say that, to all intents and purposes, it would have worked equally well, had there been no Eichmann and Müller had given all his orders through a dictaphone.

EICHMANN: No, that is not what I am going to say. It was always my practice to summarise the instructions which came to me from Müller, and I would then re-write it in a few words and act accordingly.

JUDGE LANDAU: And Müller never asked for your opinion? You, the man dealing with these matters day in and day out?

A: Müller knew me very well and he knew full well that I did not take any decisions in the realm of executive measures.

Q: Are you saying that he tried to obtain your opinion but you refused to give it, and he then gave up the idea of consulting you?

A: At first I think he expected me to express my opinion . . . but eventually he realised that I was not prepared to do this and accepted the situation. Afterwards I always consulted him even when it concerned only one transport.

Q: You were completely passive then?

A: That is hardly the right word. I simply obeyed orders without question.

ATTORNEY-GENERAL: Is that why Müller, who knew you well, said, "Had we fifty Eichmanns we would have won the war against Russia, against France, against the whole world." Fifty like you, fifty Eichmanns!

A: This remark was made by Müller in an entirely different context and on another occasion. It was said, after all the files in my office had been burned by incendiary bombs, and he was complimenting us for still carrying on in spite of it all. In any event it was said jocularly. Müller was a Bavarian and the words he used, in the mouth of a Bavarian, had a very different meaning than they would have done had they been spoken officially. It was a casual remark made by a hail-fellow-well-met Bavarian. When the Allied bombers were pounding Berlin it was not easy to sit at one's desk and carry on as usual with everything on fire.

Q: And was it because you were, as you keep on saying, so small, so low, so insignificant that Müller said, referring to you, "We shall send the master himself to Hungary"?

A: This was just a rhetorical phrase such as is habitually used by military men. It was the language of the Services. We used to call it "lavatory slang." What sort of "master" I was in Hungary can easily be found in the official documents. I didn't initiate anything there.

Judge Halévi, expressing some incredulity at these replies, suggested that Eichmann, according to his own evidence, appeared to have carried out his duties so inefficiently that it was a wonder he was not transferred to a less exacting post. The Accused replied by saying that it was because of this lack of initiative that he was never promoted above the rank of *Obersturmbannführer* (Lieutenant-Colonel). Had he shown any initiative he would undoubtedly have been given an independent command of some sort.

Nevertheless, despite his self-confessed diffident manner, he does appear on one occasion, on his own admission, to have protested to *Gruppenführer* Müller about the mass murders being committed in Russia by the *Einsatzgruppen*, and to have urged Müller to find an alternative method of exterminating the Jews other than by gassing. "This cannot go on," he said, "our people are becoming sadists." He then suggested, according to the Attorney-General, that a "more elegant way" must be found, but Eichmann said that he did not remember using those words. What he had always been in favour of was a "political solution," although, after being transferred to Berlin against his will, that was no longer his affair.

When he went on to insist that he had had nothing to do with the introduction of gas-chambers, he was questioned by the Attorney-General about a letter, which had been admitted in evidence at the Nuremberg trial of major war criminals, written by Dr. Ernst Wetzel, an expert on Jewish questions in the Ministry for Eastern Affairs, in October 1941. Wetzel stated that it had been decided that the system of mass shootings was to be discontinued and gassing substituted. "Eichmann, a specialist on Jewish affairs in RSHA," Wetzel wrote, "has given his consent."

Eichmann vigorously denied that he had ever talked to Wetzel about gassing, although the letter never suggested that he had, and he vehemently protested that it was an obvious forgery and that any handwriting expert could easily prove it to be such. The document had, however, only been admitted in evidence by the International Military Tribunal at Nuremberg, after careful scrutiny and after evidence of its origin had been given. The Court indicated, without actually saying it in so many words, that they would be able to make up their own minds about its genuineness and the weight that should be given to it.

The twelfth count of the indictment against the Accused alleged that Hermann Krumey, head of the deportation centre in Lodz, had received orders from Eichmann regarding eighty-nine of the children from Lidice who were to receive "special treatment." They had been arrested after the village had been destroyed and nearly all the adult inhabitants murdered as a reprisal for the assassination of Heydrich in 1942 and, according to the Prosecution, were exterminated in the gas-chambers at Chelmno.

Eichmann was asked by the Attorney-General whether he remembered Krumey telephoning him from Lodz and asking for instructions. The Accused pretended not to remember this, but Dr. Hausner suggested that an atrocity of this kind was not committed every day, even by the Nazis, and the occasion could not have escaped his memory. "Why," the Accused was asked, "did Krumey telephone you for instructions regarding the disposal of these children if you were not, as you keep on telling the Court, a competent authority to give such orders?"

Eichmann refused to admit the possibility that he gave Krumey any orders about the children, although he might have said that he would consult his superiors. "Anyhow," he asked, "why don't you ask Krumey himself? He is in prison in Germany." [3]

A similar disavowal of all responsibility was made by Eichmann when he was questioned about what the Attorney-General referred to as "the skeleton affair."

He told the Court that he remembered someone coming to him and asking for skeletons or skulls, but he could not remember who the person was. The Attorney-General repeatedly asked Eichmann why application should have been made to him for these skulls if it was not his concern. To every such question Dr. Hausner received an evasive answer. "I could no longer remember the details," said the Accused. "It was all very confused in my mind. I could not distinguish between things which were said and things which were done. Anyhow it was not my business and I always kept my finger out of any pie which was not my concern."

It was not a convincing explanation, particularly bearing in mind the contents of the letter written by Dr. Sievers to RSHA, Amt IV B 4, which was clearly marked: "For the attention of SS *Obersturmbannführer* Eichmann: Assembly of skeleton selection." In the opening paragraph, Dr. Sievers wrote, "With reference to your letter of 25 September 1942 IV B 4/3576/42 G 1488, and the personal talks which have taken place between us in the meantime on the above matter.

[3] Krumey was arrested in 1958 but afterwards released in consequence of a decision by the Frankfurt Court of Appeal. Since the capture of Eichmann in 1960 he has again been arrested, and is now at the Ludwigsburg War Crimes Investigation Centre pending his trial.

. . . It is requested that the necessary directions should be issued."

Having regard to the above letter, a memorandum in Sievers' office diary to the effect that he did pay a visit to IV B 4 in this connection, and the fact that the skeletons were later found in Strasbourg, the Court was left with the impression that Eichmann knew much more about these skeletons than he was ready to admit.

The Attorney-General then went on to deal with the Hungarian episode of the Accused's war career and asked him whether it was true, as he had already stated on many occasions during his interrogation by the Israeli police whilst in custody awaiting trial, that the instructions which he received before leaving for Hungary were to bring about, as quickly and as completely as possible, the deportation of Hungarian Jews to the East. When the Accused hesitated before answering this question Dr. Hausner read a passage from Eichmann's own voluntary statement. "The general order from the *Reichsführer SS* and the Chief of the German Police was the evacuation of all Jews from Hungary, to comb Hungary from east to west and the deportation of these Jews to Auschwitz."

Eichmann then admitted that with one exception his previous statement was correct. He was not aware at the time, however, that Auschwitz was the Jews' destination.

The orders regarding the deportation of Jews, the Accused told the Court in answer to a question by the Attorney-General, at first concerned only able-bodied men. Later, when Kaltenbrunner ordered total evacuation, there were no further detailed orders.

The Accused agreed, after some argument, that a member of his staff always had to be present when the Jews were being loaded on to the trains to supervise matters generally, and especially to see that, included among the deportees, there were no Jews of foreign nationality in whose fate Vessenmayer, the German Ambassador in Hungary, had an interest.

Nevertheless, Eichmann still maintained that in Hungary he was in no way concerned with "executive matters." He only dealt with "technical matters."

In this connection the Accused was asked to read out a long passage from the statement he made to Sassen the journalist which afterwards became the basis of a feature article in *Life* magazine. Eichmann, reading from the recorded interview:

Q: Do you know anything in connection with the concentrating of Jews by the Hungarians? Did you ever demand or press for this?

My answer: No, I never watched loading on to trains. This was a matter of secondary importance. I was not authorised and did not have time for it. I saw the loading carried out in various parts of the Reich, but in Hungary—never. This was not my job, it was done by the Hungarian Gendarmerie. They loaded the trains, they supplied rations for the journey. This was by arrangement with the Hungarian Secretary of State for the Interior. I did have at my disposal, however, hundreds of the *Ordnung Polizei* (the ordinary police) to escort the convoys of Jews and they had to see that my orders were carried out. On each train there were thirty police constables and one officer. In Hungary, therefore, though I could privately have watched the loading on to trains, I never did it officially.

ATTORNEY-GENERAL: Did you say that?

EICHMANN: No, there are many inaccuracies in this statement. The statement says that I had "hundreds" of *Ordnung Polizei* at my disposal. I did not even have one hundred.

The Accused, despite further questioning, continued to insist that his sole duties were concerned with transportation. He had to keep in contact with the railway authorities in Budapest and Vienna, to arrange the time-tables, give notice to all concerned of the departure of the transports, and to report their arrival at the destination. He had to render reports on all these matters to the Security Police Office and to RSHA in Berlin. He had no other duties whatsoever!

He admitted, when cross-examined about the offer to

barter a million Jews for 10,000 lorries, that the deportations to Auschwitz still continued without interruption during the time that Yoel Brand was on his way to the Middle East.

He was asked whether he was aware that this would, most likely, render the whole plan abortive. He denied such knowledge but said that he told Brand before leaving that speed was the essence of the contract. In any event, he said, he had never really had his heart in it. He only thought of it, in the first place, because he was annoyed when Colonel Kurt Becher, Himmler's special envoy, arrived in Hungary and began ransoming wealthy Jews. He thought out this more dramatic plan in order to trump Becher's ace.

A secondary reason for his interest in the "barter plan" was because it was intended that fifty per cent of the lorries would be used to mechanise the 22nd Cavalry Division, SS, which was commanded by one of his closest friends. He had always said that it was "a matter of expediency and not of compassion."

On the last day of the Accused's cross-examination by the Attorney-General the position was almost identical with what it had been on the first day. Throughout his career in the SS and particularly during the war years when he was in Amt IV B 4 of RSHA he had done no more than obey superior orders without question. He had never made any decisions on his own responsibility. He had never even made any suggestion to his superiors. He was merely a cog in the machinery of extermination. The Prosecution failed to break him down, but the monotonous regularity with which these protestations were made, during a cross-examination lasting for more than forty-seven hours, lessened, to some extent, their effect.

Before the Attorney-General sat down he asked Eichmann about the part he played in planning the notorious foot-march of Jews, in 1944, from Budapest to the Austrian border.

The Accused denied any responsibility for the march taking place. All he had done was to make arrangements for rationing and accommodation *en route* and "other purely technical matters." But he was not allowed to put these arrangements into effect because, to use his own words, "The entire matter of the foot-march was taken out of our hands and the Hungarians carried it out from A to Z."

It was not true that he celebrated the completion of this march with Endre, the Hungarian Fascist leader, Veesenmayer and Colonel Winkelmann, Chief of the SIPO in Hungary, by drinking brandy and mare's milk. This was on an entirely different occasion totally unconnected with the march.

The re-examination by Dr. Servatius was not lengthy and consisted, almost entirely, of an attempt to discredit parts of the Sassen document which had been admitted in evidence by the Court on the application of the Prosecution. The only portions of the transcript of these conversations between Sassen and the Accused which were held to be admissible were those which had been corrected in the Accused's handwriting. The Court allowed them to be produced in evidence "in order to be able to weigh the probative value of the Accused's words in connection with the contents of those passages."

The examination by the three members of the Court followed, and Judge Raveh was the first to question Eichmann. He began a philosophical discussion with the Accused, prompted by something which Eichmann had said earlier in his evidence about the philosophy of Kant. He had said, during his interrogation by the Israeli police, that throughout his military life he had tried to follow the Kantian philosophy and Judge Raveh asked what he understood its principles to be. Eichmann answered that he had been attracted by the "categorical imperative." [4]

JUDGE RAVEH: Do you contend that your activities in connection with the deportation of Jews corresponded to the imperative premises of Kantian philosophy?

EICHMANN: No. . . . because what I did then was thrust upon

---

[4] Kant's own definition of the "Categorical imperative" was: "Act only on that maxim whereby thou canst, at the same time, *will* that it should become a universal law."

Fundamental Principles of the Metaphysic of Morals, p. 421.

me. I could only follow that particular principle of Kantian philosophy when I could be my own master, when I could follow my own free will and the dictates of my conscience. I could not follow it when I had to bow to the fate which had been thrust upon me. . . . I could not follow it because a superior force prevented me from living that way. It could not be within the framework of the "categorical imperative" to kill people by force of arms, because this was not the will of God. . . .

To this day I still do not understand this moral imperative completely, but I tried to adjust these concepts to my own way of life.

Judge Raveh then questioned the Accused closely about his official relations with his chief, *Gruppenführer* Müller.

Q: In your official contacts with Müller on service matters did you take all your problems to him and ask for his instructions without ever making any suggestions of your own?

A: No. I made no suggestions or recommendations, with one reservation. When it was a border-line case I probably told Müller that there was a previous decision and asked him whether it should be taken as a precedent.

Q: And did Müller never say, "Eichmann, what do you think? What is your opinion?"

A: No, no, no.

Q: When Müller himself did not know the answer what did he do then?

A: He always consulted someone higher up and asked him for instructions.

Q: What you say is difficult to believe. You maintain that a man of Müller's high rank had to take nearly everything to someone above him? He never expressed an opinion and his advice was not solicited at all?

A: One must remember that the Jewish problem was quite different from the other matters dealt with by the various departments. In Jewish questions all the different central authorities intervened, and very often other authorities had already made a decision, and all we had to do was to carry out their policy. It was quite different from other subjects that were within the sphere of competence of Bureau IV where the various departments did have a say of their own.

Judge Raveh also questioned the Accused about his statement that he felt his position to be similar to that of Pontius Pilate. "In spite of everything," Eichmann wrote while he was in Haifa awaiting trial, "I know that I cannot consider myself innocent because the fact that I was the recipient of orders no longer has any meaning."

Asked to explain these two statements the Accused replied, "When I examined and re-examined myself, and when I judged myself, so to speak . . . I came to the conclusion that I had become a tool in the hands of others and could, therefore, from a personal point of view though not from a legal standpoint, wash my hands of all guilt."

The examination of the Accused was then taken up by Judge Halévi who, like Judge Raveh, also questioned Eichmann in German.

Eichmann began by admitting that, although he had been brought to Israel against his will, he was now glad to have had an opportunity to remove the various misunderstandings and misinterpretations which had gathered round him in the course of the last fifteen years. It would enable his family to answer the accusations which were so often falsely made against him by people who had been influenced by distorted propaganda. The Judge then reminded him that this was not a People's Court and he had not been questioned according to Gestapo methods. It depended entirely upon him whether he would have the courage to speak the truth, even if it were damaging, because he could not be forced to do so.

Hans Frank, the Governor-General of Poland, Judge Halévi continued, said at Nuremberg that although the extermination of the Jews was not within his competence he could not dispute that he shared the guilt with others, and that more than a thousand years would pass before this horrible stain would be erased from the German conscience. Furthermore Eichmann himself had proudly declared, more than once, that he did not wish to excuse himself and was determined to speak the truth before the whole world.

The Accused could rest assured, Judge Halévi told him, that the Court had no personal grudge against him, all they wanted was to get at the truth. "This may be your last chance, your only chance to say, in full view of the public, where you stand, what sort of a man you are, and whether you are a man or a person who tries to evade his responsibility."

Eichmann said that he wanted to tell the truth, and began by acknowledging, in answer to a series of questions, that the Nazi treatment of Jews had not originated from a state of war but from Hitler's racial doctrine.

JUDGE HALÉVI: You have often compared the extermination of the Jews with the bombing raids on German cities, and you compared the murder of Jewish women and children with the death of German women in aerial bombardments. Surely it must be clear to you that there is a basic distinction between these two things. On the one hand, the bombing is used as an instrument of forcing the enemy to surrender, just as the Germans tried to force the British to surrender by their bombing, in that case it is a war objective to bring an armed enemy to his knees.

On the other hand, when you take unarmed Jewish men, women and children from their homes, hand them over to the Gestapo and then send them to Auschwitz for extermination, it is an entirely different thing, is it not?

EICHMANN: The difference is enormous.

Q: You want to add something?

A: Whether it is the atom bomb on Hiroshima or Nagasaki, or the bombing of homes in England or Germany, or the gassing of Jews, they are all crimes against humanity, but at that time these crimes had been legalised by the State and the responsibility, therefore, belongs to those who issued the orders.

Q: But you must know, surely, that there are internationally recognised Laws and Customs of War whereby the civilian population is protected from actions which are not essential for the prosecution of the war itself?

A: Yes, I am aware of that.

In order to test the Accused's contention throughout the proceedings that he was not authorised to use his discretion in suitable cases, Judge Halévi asked him about an aunt named Dorsi whom he permitted to leave the Reich for Switzerland in 1943 or 1944.

Eichmann said that some of his stepmother's relatives had married Jews and Jewesses and that Dorsi's daughter, according to the Nuremberg Laws, was regarded as being half-Jewish. It was, therefore, possible for him to "close an eye" in respect of Jews who had not been officially registered.

Judge Halévi suggested that in such cases it would appear that the oath of loyalty to the *Führer*, which the Accused had taken, did not disturb him unduly. To this Eichmann replied that, so far as he could remember, he went afterwards to Müller and confessed what he had done. Had he not done so it might have been difficult for him because he was, at all times, under Müller's strict supervision.

JUDGE HALÉVI: Did you never feel a conflict of loyalties, between your duty and your conscience?

EICHMANN: I suppose one could call it an internal split. It was a personal dilemma when one swayed from one extreme to the other.

Q: One had to overlook and forget one's conscience.

A: Yes, one could put it that way.

Judge Halévi then reminded the Accused that Dr. Grüber had stated in his evidence that in Germany there was very little civic courage. Had there been more, things would have been different. Eichmann agreed, but said that the question how it came about that such large sections of the German nation lost their civic courage during the Nazi régime was a matter for the historians of the future. It was not just fate. It was a question of human conduct. The years during which Hitler was in power were very difficult. Private individuals thought that what they could or might do was of no importance and could not be effective. It would be just like "a drop of water on a hot stone, it would evaporate immediately."

Asked whether, if he searched his conscience seriously, he would have to admit that he, also, lacked civic courage Eichmann said that he shared this deficiency with most others who wore a German uniform.

He then understood his duty to be that of carrying out his obligations as a National Socialist in accordance with his oath of loyalty, but now he realised that excessive nationalism leads to extremism.

On his last day in the witness-box Eichmann made a final attempt, when questioned by the Presiding Judge, Moshe Landau, to convince the Court that he had never been a Jew-hater and intensely disliked the role which he was forced to play in sending millions of Jews to the extermination camps.

Judge Landau had reminded him that Dr. Grüber had told the Court that whenever he went to the Accused's office to plead for a more lenient treatment of the Jews in Berlin, Eichmann always answered him in the first person.

"I refuse," or "I must think it over."

His explanation was that it might well be that on such occasions he "slipped into official German," when it was his duty to notify Dr. Grüber of some official decision. It would have been most unusual to have said, "The decision of Bureau IV is so-and-so." Judge Landau then suggested that, having regard to the fact that Eichmann loathed what he had to do by virtue of his appointment, it would, surely, have been more agreeable if he had made it clear, in the case of a refusal, that the decision was not his but his superior's. The Accused, in reply, said that he was certain that he had not always informed Dr. Grüber of decisions in the first person, because whenever clergymen came to his office he invariably said how sorry he was to have to turn down their requests, because his own father was one of the Presbyters of the Presbyterian community in Linz and, for that reason alone, he would have greatly preferred to say "Yes."

Eichmann specifically denied that he was an anti-Semite, though he admitted that, being a convinced National Socialist, this did not sound very plausible.

He read the *Völkischer Beobachter* regularly and was aware that it was full of Goebbels' anti-Jewish propaganda. He was, however, no more interested in politics than the ordinary "man in the street." He had an office job to do, and kept his nose in his files. Even when the Nuremberg Laws were passed he thought little about them. Like most other Austrians, for he was an Austrian at that time, he never imagined that half the threats against the Jews would ever be carried out. To use a well-known expression, "nothing is ever eaten as hot as it is when being cooked," he said.

Finally Judge Landau asked Eichmann a series of questions about his oath of loyalty and the extent to which he felt it bound him. Would it not have been possible to have relieved himself of this compulsion by leaving the SS and the Party?

The Accused said that it might have been possible to do so prior to the war, but after the outbreak of war this was no longer possible. It was true that he made a mistake when he accepted an appointment in RSHA. He had wanted to be posted to the *Abwehr*. Could he not, however, Judge Landau continued, have arranged a posting to a front-line unit of the *Waffen SS* if he had really pressed for such a posting? Eichmann answered by saying that this would never have been permitted. He was certain of this because he had repeatedly asked for such a transfer.

Judge Landau then reminded him of answers which the Accused had given to the Attorney-General, in cross-examination, when questioned on this very same point.

ATTORNEY-GENERAL: I want to know whether you ever tried to leave the Party and the SS.

EICHMANN: I never tried to leave the Party or the SS.

Q: You stayed on of your own free will and choice?

A: In the SS and the Party, yes; but not in RSHA.

ATTORNEY-GENERAL: I want to know if you ever tried to leave the Party and the SS.

EICHMANN: I never tried to leave the SS or the Party.

Q: You stayed on of your own free will and choice?

A: In the SS and the Party, yes; but not in the functions and assignments I was given.

JUDGE LANDAU: I thought you remained in the ranks of the SS despite your conscience because you knew very well that there was no way of getting out of the Party. That was my impression. Now let me read again what you said in answer to the Attorney-General: "I stayed on in the ranks of the SS of my own free will and choice." Those are your words and must be taken to mean that you did choose to remain in the SS. Is that correct?

A: Yes, that was true. Until 1939 it was possible.

Q: I am not speaking of the years before the war. You are intelligent enough to see the contradiction in your own words. What you say now is that you remained in the SS not of your own free will during the war years?

A: To put it quite frankly, one did not give a thought in those days. It would have been easy for me to answer yes or no, but at the time there was no possibility. It would have been like hitting my head against a brick wall.

JUDGE LANDAU: Are not these answers which were given to the Attorney-General at variance with those which you have just given me?

EICHMANN: Yes, there is a contradiction, but even if a man wanted to leave he could not have done so after the outbreak of war—he was quite powerless. He was entirely dependent on the goodwill and consent of the head of his department.

X

The Final Speeches

AFTER AN ADJOURNMENT of twelve days to enable the Attorney-General and Dr. Servatius to prepare their final addresses, the Court reassembled on 8 August, and Dr. Hausner began his closing speech.

For the last four months, he told the Court, there had been spread before their eyes the picture of a régime which had threatened a whole generation and menaced the freedom of nations and individuals.

Survivors of this terrible holocaust had taken their stand in the witness-box and told a fraction of the story of that appalling tragedy. They spoke of murder, brutality, tortures and other atrocities which, had they not been described by living men and women, it would be impossible to believe were perpetrated by human beings. They spoke of acts of cruelty, the lust for evil, the degradation and oppression of body and soul, the like of which have never been told in the annals of mankind, of Auschwitz from whose soil Jewish blood welled forth like a fountain, of rabbis ordered to put on their phylacteries and praying shawls before being thrust into the flames amid the mockery of their tormentors. They spoke of the camp tortures, the beatings, the degradation and humiliations, showing the depths of wickedness to which men can sink in their behaviour towards their fellow men. They spoke of the rats put into the clothing of prisoners in Chelmno who were then ordered to stand stock-still without moving a muscle. They spoke of the "parachute game," when the camp staff made Jewish inmates of the camp climb up to the roof and jump from it, taking shots at them as they fell. They spoke of the camp staff members' dogs being set upon them, of young boys being hanged to music, and of babies in arms being thrown alive into the crematorium fires after having been saved from asphyxiation in the gas-chambers by their mothers' bodies falling on top of them.

The Accused himself heard all this evidence and saw several films depicting the horrors which, as he knew only too well, took place. It would not have been unreasonable to expect that, sixteen years after the events to which the witness testified, he would have uttered one word of personal regret or repentance, one syllable of remorse.

Apart from declaring that he "regarded the murder, the extermination of the Jews as one of the most hideous crimes in history," he expressed no regret. "It would be childish to do so," he said, "for the dead cannot be restored to life." He still believes that the war was forced upon Germany as was, also, the fight against European Jewry. His oath of allegiance to Hitler, he considers, absolves him from all responsibility for his deeds and completely justifies everything he did.

Dr. Servatius, in his opening speech for the Defence, had spoken of two worlds that faced each other, the depths of suffering and the heights of power. The world of the Caesars, he said, knows no tears. Dr. Hausner reminded the Court of this and said: "Tears are known only to the man who has a human heart within him, and who is capable of being moved by the sufferings of his fellow men. He that has a heart of stone is neither moved nor shocked, even when brought face to face with the horror of his hideous actions."

Dr. Grüber spoke, in his evidence, of the Nazi soldier who cast away his conscience when he put on his uniform and who, from that moment, remained indifferent to the suffering which he inflicted on others. The Attorney-General asked:

Where were the poisonous wells from which these people drew the strength to trample on human beings as on vermin, to tear babies apart limb from limb, to send millions of people to their death over a period of more than five years?

It is a terrible thing to realise that whoever sets his foot on this path can no longer trace the way back to human values, for such a doctrine destroys his heart and transforms him into a chilly block of ice and marble wrapped up in documents, orders, instructions and proclamations. It is with these that the Accused, and others like him, try to protect themselves when in the hands of the law. Truth and falsehood no longer have any meaning for such men. Truth is whatever serves their purpose. Falsehood is whatever hinders them. If there is any regret in their hearts it is because the loathsome work was not completed. If there is sorrow, it is because the means that were chosen were not effective enough to complete the task.

Once this poison had penetrated into the soul and its owner had freed himself from his duty as a human being to weigh moral values and examine his past by the light of conscience, then the ground had been prepared for the Final Solution. There were no longer any moral impediments, no further brake on crime. On the contrary, there was enthusiasm, justification, and the fervent desire to carry out the evil design loyally to the end. The men who raised Hitler to power believed in the doctrine of hatred against whomsoever stood in their path. This was no mass hypnosis in which men were gripped without the possibility of escape. It was a deliberate and conscious act of will. On the crest of this wave of evil there rode to power men who saw in Nazism an opportunity for a career, a good life for their families and comfortable living conditions, men who were prepared, in return for these things, to give their support to any abominable conspiracy. Their hatred knew no bounds, geographical, social or familial. Envy and fanaticism filled their hearts, envy for the belongings of others, lust and thirst for foreign territory and property which was not theirs. . . .

How did this wave of hatred, evil and murder swell up? Why did Adolf Eichmann leave Austria, where he had grown up and been educated, and why was he drawn to Nazi Germany? What attracted him to the false lure of the Nazi doctrine? What induced him to enter their service and to carry out one of their most hideous and heinous projects?

How could a human being do what he did? It would seem that a hatred-ridden dictator when he finds people ready to accept his leadership, can lead them wherever he chooses, even to the depths of hell. Here, too, we have heard from Dr. Grüber of the growing evil of people entangled more and more in the bonds of slavery, the road from which there was no returning. This was the régime which created the cyclists[1] as Dr. Grüber called them, who trampled those under them, displaying joyful, heel-clicking, fawning obedience to their superiors whatever orders they might give.

A complete casting-off of moral restraints, of what they contemptuously called "bourgeois morality," for the achievement of the supreme goal. For this purpose anything was permissible—falsehood, deceit, slander and even murder. In their own eyes, and in those of their friends, they remained decent people and good citizens.

The Attorney-General did not propose to refer again in detail to the atrocities perpetrated by the Nazis during those years. All the facts that had been given in evidence about the ghettos, the tortures, the evil, the malice and the murder in the camps were unchallengeable and the Accused did not attempt to dispute them. What he did do in the witness-box, however, was to deny that he bears any responsibility, and he has tried to put the entire blame on others. It was they who shed all that blood: Hitler, Himmler, Heydrich, Kaltenbrunner, Müller, Pohl and Höss, not he.

The duty of the Prosecution at this stage of the trial was to piece together the evidence of Eichmann's guilt and prove his complicity in the evil conspiracy which was the gravamen of most of the charges preferred against him.

He himself maintained that he was a very small cog in the machinery of destruction. His work was concerned solely

---

[1] Dr. Grüber used the word "cyclists" in order to describe the typical Nazi officials who bowed before those above them and trod on those beneath them.

with the technical aspects of transporting these five million Jews to their place of execution.

It was the case for the Prosecution that Eichmann was a central figure in the Nazi slaughterhouse. The conspiracy to exterminate European Jewry was not drawn up in one day, nor was it implemented in a single night. It was gradual, beginning with enforced emigration and ending with wholesale murder. From the beginning to the end, according to the Prosecution, Eichmann held an executive appointment of the highest importance. He had a hand in all the crimes which were classified in the indictment as war crimes, or as crimes against the Jewish people in particular, and humanity in general. There was ample evidence to support this contention of the Prosecution.

As early as 1938, immediately after the *Anschluss*, Eichmann told the Jewish representatives in Vienna that henceforth he would be the ruler of Jewish life in Austria, that he intended to purge Vienna and Austria of all its Jews, that his orders must be obeyed, and that he would know how to deal with those who did not comply.

On the morning following the "Night of Broken Glass," Eichmann addressed the Jewish leaders who were brought before him after being beaten up by the rabble in the streets of Vienna. They were bloody, shivering with cold, and hungry, for they had eaten nothing for twenty-four hours. "The rate of the disappearance of the Jews from Vienna," he told them, "is not satisfactory. From now on I know what to do."

The Accused's evidence that he was always extremely solicitous about the fate of the Jews and treated them with the utmost politeness and consideration was not corroborated by the evidence of those who had been at the receiving end of his fury.

Dr. Benno Cohen had testified about a meeting which took place in Eichmann's office in Berlin when he threatened all the Jewish leaders and said that if they did not mend their ways they would find themselves in a concentration camp.

The Accused had claimed, throughout his evidence, that the expulsion of the Jews from Germany was a "constructive solution" of the Jewish problem, for it helped them to leave Germany where they were "in a tight spot."

This, Dr. Hausner said, was just a piece of Nazi impertinence, and he likened it to a band of robbers throwing the occupants out of the windows, after setting fire to their house, and then claiming that it was better for them to have been thrown out of the windows than to be burnt alive.

Under Israeli law, which is largely based on English and American law, Eichmann was certainly a conspirator, as alleged in the indictment. By 1938 he had become an acknowledged expert on Jewish affairs, so much so that when he tried to obtain a transfer to another appointment, after being posted to Berlin, Heydrich would not hear of it. He had become, according to one of his superiors, "indispensable on the front of anti-Jewish activity."

Eichmann had an unusually good memory. When he wished he could remember the details of incidents which took place many years ago. It was only necessary to study the first seventy pages of his statement to the Israeli Police, which had been admitted in evidence, in order to understand the amazing capacity of his memory. He was able then to remember details of conversations which many a person would have forgotten. He described the rooms where these interviews took place, the furniture in them, the documents that were discussed and the index files, who attended these meetings, and what they looked like.

It was all the more surprising, therefore, how often, during cross-examination, he had sought refuge in a fictitious "defective memory," how frequently he had told the Attorney-General that he did not remember things which must have remained forever engraved in his memory. He professed to be unable to remember when the decision regarding the Final Solution was made. He said that he had forgotten the details about the supply of gas to the concentration camps, and the skeletons to Strasbourg University. He could not recall whether he had seen Jews being loaded on to any of the trains which he had himself requisitioned, which concentration camps he had visited, what instructions had been given to the *Einsatzgruppen,* and other crucially important matters.

As the Attorney-General said, however: "One vital detail he really did forget, namely, that he had already disclosed, orally and in writing, probably without thinking that it would ever be used against him, the amazing extent of his memory. Now when he tries to seek refuge in forgetfulness, no one can any more believe him."

Dr. Hausner then dealt with the law of conspiracy which is of such great importance in this case. The Supreme Court of Israel, following the common law, defined a criminal conspiracy as follows: It must be proved that two or more people conspired together, and that the aim of the conspiracy was to do some illegal act; the consequence of such a conspiracy is that once a person has entered into a conspiracy with others to perform an illegal act then implicitly he gives his agreement to the fact that his accomplices may use any means needed to carry out the aims of the conspiracy. Moreover, each and every one of the conspirators will be responsible for the acts of all the other accomplices to the extent that such acts are performed to further the objects of the conspiracy.

With regard to the evidence which may be given in support of a charge of conspiracy, the Attorney-General referred to the case of Kaiser v. Attorney-General. "Testimony," he said, "with regard to the commission of any act or the making of any declaration by one of the conspirators may be regarded as admissible evidence in respect of the others, provided there is compliance with the following two conditions:

1. That evidence has been given which is admissible and, *prima facie,* sufficient for a conclusion to be drawn that a criminal plan existed and the conspirators agreed to participate therein.

2. That the act in question shall have been committed at the time of the existence of the conspiracy and in furtherance of it.

"No one disputes that the law of conspiracy applicable to this case, subject to the above two conditions, allows for evidence with regard to the act or acts of one conspirator to be admissible against another conspirator in order to prove the aims of the conspiracy and its very existence.

"Furthermore, where the Prosecution have laid a sufficient foundation by evidence to go to the jury, of several persons having conspired together, the declarations of any conspirator . . . are admissible against all the conspirators even though they were not present at the time."

Another legal principle applicable to all such cases of conspiracy is the elementary and familiar doctrine, applicable alike to crimes and mere civil injuries, that "Every person must be presumed to intend the natural consequences of his acts."

Sometimes the conspiracy may be in respect of a single act, or a predetermined period, but at other times it may carry on for an undetermined period and may be in respect of an objective which is realised by undefined and unexpected acts. The continuity of the criminal conspiracy, however, will be considered as having been proved, *prima facie*, once its existence at any point of time has been proved. One of the fundamental tenets of this principle is the *voluntary adherence* of the criminal to the conspiracy.

In this case, the Attorney-General explained, there arose the question whether Eichmann could still be said in law to have remained a conspirator during such time as he was a soldier acting under orders. For the purpose of his legal argument Dr. Hausner was prepared to assume, in the Accused's favour although he strongly disputed it as a fact, that he was subject to military authority from which he could not extricate himself. The period of his service before the outbreak of war and the war years required separate consideration. It could not be disputed that before September 1939 he belonged to no military formation and was not under any compulsion or duress which prevented him from changing his appointment. During the war, when he was under military discipline, the Accused maintains that he was not in a position to avoid obeying unlawful orders.

A decisive answer was given in this matter in the judgment of the International Military Tribunal when dealing with the conspiracy to wage aggressive war:

The argument that such common planning is not permanent when there exists complete dictatorship is baseless. A plan in the implementation of which several people take part is still a plan, even though it may have been carried out by only one of them. And those who carry out the plan cannot evade responsibility even though they show that they acted upon the instructions of the man who conceived it. Hitler could not have waged aggressive war alone. He had to enlist the co-operation of politicians, military commanders, diplomats and even businessmen. And when they, *knowing his objectives*, gave him this co-operation they became partners in the plan which he had conceived. They cannot be regarded as innocent because they were used by Hitler if they knew what they were doing. . . .

It was not necessary, the Attorney-General told the Court, in this case to rely on the quotation from the Nuremberg judgment given above.

Eichmann was being tried under the Nazi and Nazi Conspirators (Punishment) Law and when this was considered in conjunction with the ordinary criminal law of Israel it was clear that a man who conspired to commit a crime against the Jewish people, or against humanity, or to commit war-crimes must be held responsible for his actions in accordance with the accepted principles of Israeli law.

Dr. Hausner then proceeded to marshal the evidence given by the Prosecution's witnesses and dealt *seriatim* with all the Counts in the indictment.

In case the probative value of some of this evidence should be questioned he explained why the Prosecution had to produce evidence and statements made by those who had been associated with the Accused, as accomplices, in carrying out many of these hideous crimes.

It was not possible to avoid using such evidence, he said, for they undoubtedly knew what was going on in Nazi Germany at all material times, and only they could testify "straight from the horse's mouth," so to speak, about such things. Other witnesses regarding the existence of the conspiracy were not available, for "good men did not sit in Nazi Councils." The Court must not forget for a moment that these witnesses were themselves war criminals, though that did not necessarily mean that the whole of their testimony was a lie, but it was essential that the statements of Wisliceny, Höss, and others should be weighed with the same caution as is the evidence of all accomplices, and if it was found that their statements were corroborated by other admissible evidence whether documentary or otherwise there was no reason why the Court should not give credence to what they had said.

When they made these statements they had nothing to gain, no future to which they could look forward; particularly Wisliceny and Höss whose evidence was the most damaging to the Accused. When Rudolf Höss wrote his autobiography in a Polish prison, he called himself a criminal and had nothing to gain by trying to put the blame on Eichmann's shoulders. When Wisliceny wrote his memoirs in the death-cell in a Bratislava jail he had no axe to grind when accusing Eichmann, because he had already admitted that he was an accomplice.

Eichmann, said the Attorney-General, had murdered with fervour and insatiable lust and his only regret, when interviewed by Sassen in the Argentine in 1957, was that the crematoria ovens had not devoured all the Jews.

That any Jews survived, in spite of his efforts, was due solely to the advance of the Soviet Army which liberated the concentration camps in the East, and the Western Allies who saved tens of thousands of survivors in Dachau, in Neuengamme and many other camps.

Dr. Hausner, in closing, asked the Court to find that the Accused was involved in a conspiracy to commit crimes against the Jewish people and against humanity in all its stages, that he occupied, at all times, a central position in the conspiracy and was, therefore, responsible for all the consequences, for all the acts committed by himself, and by others in furtherance of the conspiracy. He appealed to the "Judges of Israel to render a just and truthful verdict."

The Court then adjourned for three days and reassembled on 14 August to hear the closing speech for the Defence. The Accused, Dr. Servatius said, had to defend himself against all the fifteen counts of the indictment. The last three counts which alleged that Eichmann had been, at all material times, a member of the SS, the SD and Gestapo, which had been declared criminal organisations by the International Military Tribunal at Nuremberg, were dismissed by Dr. Servatius in a few words.

Before the Accused could be awarded any punishment in respect of these counts the Prosecution had to prove that those organisations were criminal. The declaration of the Nuremberg Tribunal did not constitute proof, for their decision included no punishment. No group or organisation could be prosecuted collectively, for guilt is a personal matter. Consequently this ruled out any possibility of the Accused being sentenced in respect of these charges.

Dr. Servatius also said that all the charges which alleged acts against foreigners in countries outside Germany (Counts 9–12) must also be rejected. It was only through the Nazi and Nazi Collaborators (Punishment) Law that an Israeli Court derived jurisdiction to try such charges. International law, however, demanded that there must exist at least one link between the punishing state and the alleged offender. Crimes against the State of Israel or its citizens cannot serve as the link because, at the time when the offences were alleged to have been committed, the State of Israel did not exist.

Nevertheless, Dr. Servatius said, these charges would have

to be defended as they might be used as points for other accusations. He then proceeded to review the evidence given in support of these charges, and submitted that the Court could not properly find the Accused guilty of any of those charges upon such evidence.

Counts 1–6 inclusive, Eichmann's Counsel told the Court, concerned the exterminations in the camps, the killing of Jews by shooting which was carried out by the *Einsatzgruppen*, and the deportations, and in Counts 1–4 it was alleged that these crimes were committed against the Jewish people. It was not clear what, in law, constituted the Jewish nation. International law recognises only the concept of a State and the inhabitants of that State. Since, at the time these crimes were committed, no Jewish State existed, no crime could have been committed against it, even by means of a legal fiction.

In any event it was impossible to incriminate Eichmann because all the final decisions were taken by his superiors, and even if RSHA issued these orders through the instrumentality of the Accused, he could not be said to bear the main responsibility for them. The main charge against Eichmann was, in the opinion of Dr. Servatius, that contained in paragraph F of the first count in which it was alleged that the Accused, together with others, secured the extermination of millions of Jews, by gassing and other means in the extermination camps at Auschwitz, Chelmno, Belzec, Sobibor, Treblinka, and Maidanek from 1941 until the end of January 1945.

The real issue before the Court, in respect of this charge, was, to what extent did the Accused bear responsibility on account of his having sent Jews to the death camps knowing the fate that was in store for them.

The Court should bear in mind, Dr. Servatius said, that these camps were under the control of the Head Office of Economy and Administration, and not under RSHA. No document, he told the Court, was in existence which proved that there was any "co-operation between the Accused and the death camps," and no circumstantial evidence, he argued, could "bridge over this crucial fact."

His Counsel reminded the Court that Eichmann had freely admitted, during his interrogation, that he had repeatedly visited the camps and there was, therefore, no reason why he should not be believed when he insisted that he had been sent there by his superiors to report progress. There was nothing more to it than that. The guilt of the Accused had, once again, not been proved.

Dealing with the probative value of the evidence, Dr. Servatius put forward the documentary evidence as being the most reliable. Without these documents, he said, the Accused would have been deprived of any defence. But they were only fragments saved from the mass of material which was destroyed at the end of the war and this fact had to be borne in mind, as it accounted for the absence of many explanations and the reasons behind some of the decisions which might have been of assistance to the Accused had they been forthcoming.

There were other reservations to be made with regard to the oral evidence which the Court should not forget. After so long an interval of time memory must be hazy on some points and imagination could play some strange tricks on the mind. The risk is even greater when a story is told and retold. The Court should also not forget the position in which some of the Jewish functionaries who gave evidence found themselves. They had to make certain that no suspicion should ever be aroused that they co-operated with the Accused during those terrible times.

And what of the testimony of the German witnesses for the Prosecution?

When this evidence was first given, many of these men were in prison and truth was not important to them. Their evidence, Dr. Servatius warned the Court, should be weighed very carefully and regarded, for the most part, with suspicion.

Eichmann himself, Dr. Servatius insisted, had not had the same opportunities as the Prosecution to obtain documents for his Defence. He did not have the archives of the world at his disposal. Experts who could have supported him did not want to have any dealings with the Defence. The daily fanfares of the Press and the trumpets of the publications made them shy. They closed their ears. This Press campaign against the Accused amounted to contempt of court in an extreme degree, in the face of which the Defence found it very difficult to act.

As for the witnesses whom Eichmann would have liked to call in his defence in this Court, they feared what might happen to them if they were rash enough to set foot in Israel, and they preferred to stay where they were.

The evidence which some of them gave before District Courts in Germany and Austria must be regarded as a poor substitute for the real thing.

The Prosecution claimed, said Dr. Servatius, that the whole testimony of the Accused was a pack of lies, and that the only admissions he ever made were when he was brought face to face with an incriminating document and had his back to the wall and no means of escape. How could he be expected, after a lapse of sixteen years, to remember every single detail?

The Accused was never in a position which could have elevated him into the inner circle of leadership, and it was proved conclusively that his signature on official documents was always on behalf of the Head of Amt IV. His executive power was limited and he could only act on his own in routine matters.

Dr. Servatius then dealt with the Accused's main defence. He relied on the fact that at all times Eichmann was acting on orders received from above. This defence is known as the plea of "superior orders."

Dr. Servatius complained that in the year 1914 the British Manual of Military Law laid it down that members of fighting units who exceeded the orders given them by their commanders were not considered to be war criminals and the enemy could not punish them. Similarly, it was laid down in the United States Rules of Land Warfare of 1915 that "members of fighting units will not be punished for such offences as were committed in accordance with orders or directives issued by their Government or their commander." Those who gave the illegal orders could be punished. Counsel then said that these passages in the two manuals were only altered in 1944 when the Allied victory was certain.[2]

In any event, he affirmed, the basic principle of every State was loyalty and confidence in its leadership. Blind obedience is a virtue upon which a State can build its foundations and upon that alone. Whether such virtue brings its own reward depends on whether it succeeds. If it does not succeed the order is regarded by the victor as a crime. The man who obeyed is unfortunate for he has to pay the price of his loyalty. The gallows or a decoration, those are the alternatives.

Dr. Servatius ended his speech for the Defence with these words:

This trial should not have revenge as its aim, revenge on the Accused for deeds which were, in fact, committed by Germany's political leaders. His conviction cannot serve as expiation for the atrocities committed. This trial can only determine what happened, and serve as a warning for history.

The idea of superannuation found its expression in the earliest history of the Jewish nation when the concept of the "fallow year" was formed. It is a religious concept, that superannuation and the passing of time bring peace and blessings.

We are not asking for forgiveness and forgetfulness, but for thought and truth. The passing of time must bring peace and an end to suffering. A distance must be created between the individual human being and the boundless collective; a return must be made to self-restraint and humanity. Let there be a judgment

[2] Since the last war the impression has gained ground that the statements of law on this subject which were inserted in the British and U.S. Military law-books before the last war did not follow the accepted rules of many years' standing. This is a complete misapprehension and the real position is explained in Appendix II.

given here which will transcend the Eichmann case, a judgment of Solomon which will show the nations of the world the wisdom of the Jewish people. Let there be recognition here of the principle of superannuation which applied in the Argentine, and this will undo the wrong of abduction. It will also serve peace. I submit that the proceedings against the Accused should not be continued, that his file be closed, and that he be judged no more.

The Presiding Judge then announced that the Court would be adjourned until November, at the earliest, when the judgment would be given.

Part 3

THE JUDGMENT

XI

The Judgment and Sentence

WHEN THE COURT reassembled on 11 December 1961, after a four months' adjournment, the Accused was immediately informed that the Court convicted him of committing crimes against the Jewish people, and against humanity, for committing war crimes, and for being a member of criminal organisation as defined by Article 10 of the Nuremberg Charter.

The judgment of the Court was then read by all three judges in turn, beginning with the Presiding Judge, Moshe Landau.

Dealing first with the historical significance of the trial, the Court recalled the fact that the trial of Adolf Eichmann was not the first occasion on which the Jewish catastrophe had been discussed in a court of law. It has been dealt with extensively at the Nuremberg trial of major war criminals, but this was the first occasion on which it had occupied the central place in the proceedings.

That was one of the objects of the trial, namely, to put on record a precise historical description of the events which occurred during the catastrophe and, in so doing, to emphasise the heroic feats performed by the ghetto fighters and the resistance put up by the Jewish partisans in Poland and Russia.

Other questions naturally arose out of the trial. How could such things possibly have happened in the middle of the twentieth century? Could the Nazis have carried out their evil designs without the help given them by other peoples, in whose countries the Jews dwelt? Might the catastrophe have been averted, at least in part, had the Allies displayed a greater will to assist the persecuted Jews.[1] These, and many other questions, undoubtedly have a relevance to the subject matter of the trial, but the Court made it clear that it was not within its province. It was the duty of every criminal court to determine whether the charges in the indictment were satisfactorily proved by the Prosecution, and if the Accused were convicted, to mete out just punishment. Anything which was unnecessary in determining the issue before the Court became irrelevant and formed no part of the proceedings.

The Court emphasised that this did not mean that its members were unaware of the value of the trial from the educational point of view, not only to those living in Israel but to the whole world. The evidence given by many of the prosecution witnesses would, doubtless, provide valuable material to future historians.

The Court then proceeded to give its reasons for holding, as announced during the opening stages of the trial, that it had jurisdiction to try Adolf Eichmann.[2]

One of Dr. Servatius' main arguments, when challenging the Court's jurisdiction, was that the Nazi and Nazi Collaborators (Punishment) Law of 1950 was retroactive and the Israeli Parliament had no power to pass a criminal statute with retroactive effect.

It is not surprising to learn that this question arose, as it was bound to do, very early in the lifetime of the new State. The Court quoted from a judgment of Judge Smoira, then President of the Supreme Court of Israel, in the first criminal appeal ever heard in Israel after its formation in 1948.

[1] See *If I Forget Thee*, by Lord Russell of Liverpool, Chapter X.
[2] The Court gave its reasons at great length for deciding that it had jurisdiction, and cited a very large number of cases in support. Only a short summary is given here.

Judge Smoira referred to an English case in which Mr. Justice Willis distinguished between retroactive and *ex-post-facto* laws and referred to Blackstone's Commentaries.

Mr. Justice Blackstone wrote that *ex-post-facto* laws were objectionable when "after an action indifferent in itself is committed, the legislator then, for the first time declares it to have been a crime and inflicts a punishment upon the person who has committed it.

"Here it is impossible that the party could foresee that an action, innocent when it was done, should afterwards be converted to guilt by a subsequent law. He had, therefore, no cause to abstain from it and all punishment for not abstaining must, in consequence, be cruel and unjust."

Although it will be generally agreed that retrospective legislation is usually inexpedient, it is not always necessarily unjust. There may be special occasions and circumstances for which the law, for want of foresight, has failed to make provision, and this failure may involve practical public inconvenience and wrong. Whether, in such an event, a special and exceptional remedy is called for must depend on the particular circumstances of each case and is a question which must be decided by Parliament.

Justice Smoira followed this case, and stated that the legislation with retrospective effect under which the appellant had been tried did not create a new crime and it could not, therefore, be said that the appellant did not have any criminal intent (*mens rea*) because he could not know that he was committing a criminal act.

This case, the Court said in its judgment, was entirely applicable and relevant to the trial of Adolf Eichmann. No one could argue that the crimes with which the Accused was charged were "indifferent actions" subsequently declared for the first time to constitute a crime. All Eichmann's crimes were recognised as crimes by the laws of all civilised nations, including Germany, before and after the Nazi régime. Nor could it be said that a person who committed such crimes could not have a *mens rea* because he did not and could not know that he was doing a criminal act. The Nazi and Nazi Collaborators (Punishment) Law of 1950 did not conflict with the rules of national justice.

The Court also declared that, in its opinion, the crimes dealt with in Eichmann's case were not crimes under Israeli law only; they were, in essence, offences against the law of nations.

Nor were they merely the figment of the legislator's imagination. They corresponded to the precise pattern of international laws and conventions which defined crimes under the law of nations. Indeed they all had counter-parts in the Nuremberg Charter, the Convention for the Prevention and Punishment of Genocide; they constituted war crimes under accepted international law.

The Court then dealt with Dr. Servatius' argument that all the crimes attributed to the Accused in Counts 1–12 had been committed, as alleged in the charge sheet itself, in the course of duty. They were, therefore, Acts of State, for which only the German State, not Eichmann, could be held responsible.

This plea has been made by the defence at many war-crime trials in which the Accused held an important position in the German armed forces or the SS.

The main argument is that it is the duty of statesmen to make political decisions and the duty of generals, and others in similar positions, to accept these decisions and obey; that whether such a decision did or did not involve a contravention of international law is no concern of the general. It concerns only the Head of State, or the Cabinet from whom he received his orders, and the fact that he is acting under the authority of his government is a complete defence, as being an Act of State.

This defence appears to be based upon what is popularly known as the Caroline Case (People v. McLeod). The Caroline Case was really no case at all, in the sense of being the decision of a Court. It was merely a diplomatic incident. In any event it has nothing to do with the individual responsibility of the armed forces for war crimes, but is an illustration of the doctrine of self-preservation in international law.

This plea of an "Act of State," was repudiated by the International Military Tribunal at Nuremberg and by every other war-crime Court before which it has been raised. The repudiation of this theory was unanimously affirmed by the United Nations Assembly in a Resolution on 11 December 1946 and has since been recognised as a basic principle of international law by the UN International Law Commission.

The fact that a person who committed an act which constitutes a crime under international law acted as Head of State or responsible government official does not relieve him from responsibility under international law.

The Court, in Eichmann's case, followed these precedents, which are now recognised as part of the law of nations, and rejected Dr. Servatius' submission.

The judgment then dealt with another of Defence Counsel's submissions regarding the jurisdiction of the Court to try the Accused.

He had argued that under international law there must be a "linking point" between the State which is prosecuting and the person who is alleged to have committed the crime. In the absence of any such connecting link the State had no legal right to inflict punishment for offences.

This is not a new doctrine, and there has been much controversy between international jurists about it, there being differences of opinion regarding the closeness of the link required. In the case of Eichmann, what was the special connection between the State of Israel and the offences committed by the Accused and, if one existed, was it sufficiently close to form a basis for Israel's right to punish him?

The Court had no doubt that, presented in its widest form, the answer was clear:

The connecting link between Israel and the Accused, or between Israel and any person accused of a crime against the

Jewish people (under the Nazi and Nazi Collaborators (Punishment) Law, is striking and glaring in respect of a crime that has as its intention the extermination of the Jewish people. . . . Provided there is an effective link (not necessarily an identity) between the State of Israel and the Jewish people, then a crime intended to exterminate the Jewish people has a very definite connection with the State of Israel.

The connection between the State of Israel and the Jewish people, the Court stated, did not require any explanation. It was self-evident. Moreover the Declaration of Independence, which was read by Mr. Ben Gurion when the State was proclaimed on 14 May 1948, made special mention of the tragic link between the Nazi crimes set out in the Nazi and Nazi Collaborators Law and the re-establishment of Israel.

"The recent holocaust, which engulfed millions of Jews in Europe, proved anew the need to solve the problem of the homelessness and lack of independence of the Jewish people by means of the re-establishment of the Jewish State, which would open the gates to all Jews and endow the Jewish people with equality of status among the family of nations."

It is an historical fact, of which international law takes notice, that half the citizens of Israel have immigrated from Europe in recent years, some before and some after the Hitler régime. There is hardly one of them who has not lost parents, brothers and sisters, wives or husbands as a result of Nazi anti-Jewish policy.

The Court mentioned this fact and asked whether, in such circumstances which were without precedent in the history of any other nation, there could be any doubt that a satisfactory connecting link existed between the crime of the extermination of European Jewry and the State of Israel which had brought Eichmann to justice.

But the argument put forward by Dr. Servatius went a step further. He had contended that in the absence of a connecting link the case of Eichmann must be governed by the principle of territoriality. Under it at least eighteen countries could try

Eichmann for the offences specified in the indictment, and had any of them prosecuted him for the extermination of the Jews who resided there, the Accused could not have successfully challenged the jurisdiction of the Court that tried him.

It was manifestly unjust, in the opinion of the Court, that eighteen nations had the right to punish Eichmann for the murder of Jews living in their territories while the nation whose members were murdered had no such right because the victims were not exterminated on its territory.

The crimes committed by Eichmann, and those who gave him his orders, most deeply concerned the vital interests of the State of Israel, and in accordance with the protective principle Israel had the right to punish these criminals.

The Court quoted from the work of a well-known authority on this aspect of international law, Dahm.[3] "Penal jurisdiction is not a matter for everyone to exercise. There must be a linking point, a legal connection that links the punisher with the punished. The State may, insofar as there is no rule of international law contradicting this, punish only persons and acts *which concern it more than they concern other States.*"

It could not be disputed, the Court said, that the crimes referred to in the Nazi and Nazi Collaborators (Punishment) Law under which Eichmann was being tried concerned Israel more than they concerned any other country. The punishment of Nazi criminals did not derive from the arbitrariness of a country abusing its sovereignty, but was a legitimate and reasonable exercise of a right to penal jurisdiction.

Dr. Servatius had pointed out that in view of the absence of a sovereign Jewish State at the time of the catastrophe, the victims were not, at the time they were murdered, citizens of the State of Israel. In the opinion of the Court, learned Counsel was mistaken in examining the protective principle in this retroactive statute in relation to the time of the commission of these crimes, as in the case of ordinary law. This statute had been enacted in 1950 with a view to its application during a

[3] *Zur Problematik des Volkerstrafrechts,* 1956, pp. 28, 38.

specified period which had terminated five years earlier. This retroactive application of the law, however, does the Accused no real injury.

Professor Goodhart, the well-known international jurist and Master of University College, Oxford, in an article entitled "The Legality of the Nuremberg Trial," which appeared in the *Juridical Review* of April 1946, wrote: "Many of the national courts now functioning in the liberated countries have been established recently, but no one has argued that they are not competent to try cases that arose before their establishment. . . . No defendant can complain that he is being tried by a Court which did not exist when he committed the act."

In his opening submission to the Court regarding its jurisdiction to try Eichmann, Dr. Servatius had also argued that because the kidnapping and abduction of the Accused was an illegal act it automatically invalidated the legality of his detention and the right to bring him to trial. This does not, in law, constitute a bar to trial, for the method whereby a suspected criminal is brought to trial is of no interest to the Court which tries him.

Under English law it has frequently been held that a Court has no power to go into the question, once an Accused is in lawful custody in this country, of the circumstances in which he may have been brought here. Whatever illegalities may have been committed, and some undoubtedly were committed, in bringing Eichmann to justice, the means used to bring him to trial were no concern of the Court which was trying him and could not rob it of jurisdiction.

As recently as 1949 in *Ex parte* Elliott (1 ALL.E.R. 373) the Court heard an application of a British solider for *habeas corpus*. He had deserted from his unit in 1946, was arrested in Belgium in 1948 by two members of the British Military Police, accompanied by two Belgian gendarmes, and brought back to England where he was in custody awaiting trial by court martial for desertion.

The applicant's Counsel argued that the British authorities

in Belgium had no power to arrest his client and that he was
arrested contrary to Belgian law.

The Lord Chief Justice dismissed the application and said,
in his judgment, that if a person was arrested abroad and
brought before a court in this country, charged with an offence which this court had jurisdiction to try, the court had
no power to go into the question, once the accused was in
lawful custody in this country, of the circumstances in which
he may have been brought here, but the court has jurisdiction
to try him for the offence in question. In this case, he said, the
court martial had jurisdiction to deal with the applicant and
the High Court would not interfere.

Dealing with this point in its judgment the Court cited the
above case and a number of other English cases.

The American law on the subject is similar. The judgments
of many American courts expressly establish the principle that
it makes no difference whether or not the measures whereby
an accused was brought into the area of jurisdiction were unlawful under municipal or international law, and they are all
subject to the rule that the court should not enter into an
examination of this question which is not relevant to the trial
of the accused. The reason for this ruling is that the right to
plead violation of the sovereignty of a State is the exclusive
right of that State. It, alone, may raise or waive that right.
Many judgments of the U.S. Federal and State Courts, following this basic principle, were cited and the Court summed
it up in these words:

> To sum up, the contention of the Accused against the juris-
> diction of the Court by reason of his abduction from Argentina
> is, in essence, nothing but a plea for immunity by a fugitive
> offender on the strength of the refuge given him by a sovereign
> State. The argument does not, however, help the Accused, for
> two reasons:
> (*a*) According to the established rule of law there is no im-
> munity for a fugitive offender save in the one and only case
> where he has been extradited by the country of asylum to the

country applying for extradition by reason of a specific offence, which is not the offence for which he is to be tried. The Accused was not surrendered to Israel by Argentina and the State of Israel is not bound by any agreement with Argentina to try Eichmann for any other specific offence or *not* to try him for the offences which are the subject of this trial.

(*b*) The rights of asylum and immunity belong to the country of asylum and not to the offender, and the Accused cannot ask a foreign sovereign country to give him protection against its will. Eichmann was a wanted war criminal when he escaped to Argentina by concealing his true identity. It was only after he had been captured and brought to Israel that his identity was revealed, and after negotiations between the two Governments, the Government of Argentina waived its demand for his return and declared that it regarded the incident as settled. The Government of Argentina thereby definitely refused to give the Accused any sort of protection. Eichmann has been brought to trial before a Court of a State which accuses him of grave offences against its laws. He has no immunity and must stand trial in accordance with the charge sheet.

The last of the grounds upon which Dr. Servatius based his submission that the Court had no jurisdiction to try his client was the plea of prescription under Argentine law.[4] If that were applicable to this case it meant, according to Dr. Servatius' calculation, that the fifteen years period of limitation would have elapsed on 5 May 1960, a few days before Eichmann's capture. The Court expressed surprise that this flimsy argument had even been raised, as they regarded it as quite untenable. The short answer to it was that even had the Accused been extradited by Argentina to Israel the Argentine law of prescription would not avail him in Israel.

There is a somewhat similar law in Germany and it was doubtless because of this that it was specifically provided in Section 12 (a) of the Nazi and Nazi Collaborators (Punish-

[4] Similar to a Statute of Limitations prescribing that no one can be tried by an Argentine Court after fifteen years have elapsed since the commission of the crime.

ment) Law that "the established laws of prescription shall not apply to offences under this law."

This ended the Court's statement of its reasons for rejecting the Defence submission that it had no jurisdiction to try the Accused upon the charges contained in the indictment.

The Court then dealt with the five categories of evidence which had been tendered in this case, and the respective weight which would be given to them. These categories were five in number:

1. The evidence of the witnesses for the Prosecution and Defence given orally in court.

2. Sworn and unsworn affidavits and the record of evidence given in previous trials by persons no longer living, including convicted war criminals and persons still alive.

Such evidence was admitted by the Court by virtue of the special authority given by Section 15 of the Nazi and Nazi Collaborators (Punishment) Law of 1950. On each occasion when this testimony was admitted in evidence reasons were given by the Court as required by that section. Even so the weight which should be given to this kind of evidence had to be carefully considered by the Court, depending upon the person who gave it. The factors considered in each case were whether he was an accomplice; the special interest he might have in attempting to transfer the blame from himself to the Accused; and the lack of opportunity which the Accused had to challenge the evidence by cross-examination.

3. Evidence given by witnesses in other countries in the German, Austrian and Italian courts.

All these witnesses were interrogated in proper courts-of-law in accordance with detailed questionnaires previously approved by the Court sitting in Jerusalem to try Eichmann, and all of them, with the exception of Höttl, Novak and Slavic, whose evidence was given in Austria, testified in the presence of representatives of both parties.

They could not come to Israel to give their evidence because either they were in custody in a foreign country, or had reason to fear that they themselves might be brought to trial before an Israeli Court if they were to set foot in Israel. The Court felt that it would have been much more satisfactory if these witnesses had come and given their evidence in the presence of the Accused. As this could not be done the Court had no alternative but to accept the evidence as it was tendered. Nevertheless, the Court had exercised great caution before accepting any of the evidence obtained by such means.

4. Hundreds of documents were also submitted in evidence regarding the Accused's activities at all material times. The authenticity of these documents was not frequently disputed but wherever the Defence had denied their authenticity the Court had taken this into account before deciding whether or not to admit the document in question.

5. Finally there was the long statement made by the Accused to Superintendent Less of the Israeli Police, and various notes which Eichmann wrote, of his own volition, while in custody awaiting trial. The Court was of the opinion that all these statements were made voluntarily and, for the most part, the Accused had not disputed this. In regard to a number of incriminating passages, however, Eichmann had argued that what he had said, during interrogation, was incorrect, and that it was only later, when he had had an opportunity of studying all the relevant documents, that he discovered his error. The Court stated that, in each such case, what Eichmann said had been considered most carefully before the evidence was accepted.

The Prosecution had attempted to produce in evidence a copy of a statement which the Accused was said to have made in 1957 to a Dutch journalist, named Sassen. The Court refused, by a majority decision, to admit this document in evidence, for reasons which had been given earlier in the trial. During the Accused's own evidence, however, he had admitted, under cross-examination by the Attorney-General, that some of the statements in the document had, in fact, been made. These became, therefore, part of Eichmann's own evidence to the extent to which he admitted them, either fully or with reservations.

The Court then reviewed the evidence of the Prosecution in support of the charges contained in the indictment.

The persecution of the Jews by Hitler's Germany developed in three principal stages. The first stage lasted from the rise of Hitler to power in 1933 until the outbreak of war in 1939. The second from September 1939 to the middle of 1941. The third and final stage from then until the collapse of the Third Reich in May 1945.

The Court stated that it proposed to describe all three stages in general outline, according to the evidence, for the sole purpose of establishing the place of the Accused, and the degree of his personal responsibility within the régime of persecution, because it would be impossible to understand his real position except against the background of those events.

The method which the Court had chosen in respect of all three stages was to recount the facts in chronological order and deal with the role played by the Accused in regard to them. When dealing with the third and last stage, the physical extermination of the Jews, the story widened out in many directions. After dealing with the facts in each stage the Court would then analyse their legal significance. The next step would be to deal with the various counts in the indictment which referred to the Accused's activities against individuals of other nations and his membership of hostile organisations. Finally the Court would deal with the arguments put forward by the Defence, by which the Accused sought to justify his actions.

As the evidence given by the Prosecution and Eichmann's own testimony has been covered in considerable detail in the preceding chapters, the Court's review of it will not be given here. The remainder of this chapter will be concerned solely with the final part of the judgment in which the Court dealt with the Accused's defence to the charges preferred against him and analysed its findings of fact in the light of the indictment.

The most important fact which the Court had to determine, in order to assess the exact degree of responsibility which Eichmann bore for carrying out the criminal orders of his superiors, was the exact nature of his status within the RSHA machine.

Eichmann himself gave what the Court described as "a truly amazing portrait of himself" during those days. He was in charge of a Department in the RSHA, with the SS rank equivalent to the grade of *Oberregierungsrat* in the general administrative service and the military rank of Lieutenant-Colonel. Subordinate to him in his office in Berlin were many officials, from the lower grades right up to the SS ranks equivalent to the grade of *Regierungsrat* in the administrative service and to the military rank of Major. In addition, he was in control of a group of advisers on Jewish affairs, who were officials of considerable status in the various countries in which they worked. The Accused asked the Court to believe that although he was in such a position, and in spite of his being in such a position, he acted always under explicit instructions in every case, and that it was only when a precedent existed which exactly fitted the case then under consideration that he would refrain from approaching his superiors. On the other hand, he ascribed to his subordinates no small degree of initiative in their specific spheres, for example, in regard to questions of property, which came within the sphere of duty of Suhr and Hünsche. As for his deputy Günther, Eichmann not only said that he possessed considerable initiative but that he even went so far as to take action behind the back of the head of his department. The Court then proceeded, in accordance with the evidence before it, to examine whether that was the way in which work was carried out in the Accused's department IV B 4 and in the RSHA as a whole. The Attorney-General put to the Accused in cross-examination a copy of the 1958 edition of the "Joint Administrative Rules for Ministries of the Federal Republic (Western Germany), General Section." In the preface it was stated that the 1958 edition was based on that of 1927, well before Hitler came to power. When this book was shown to the Accused he did not deny that these rules were in force in the chief ministries of the Reich during the Nazi period, but, with regard to the SS organisations, he said, "in the light of the change in the chain of command and the system prevailing in the Third Reich, the procedure followed in the Weimar Republic was frequently changed. Accordingly, a large number of basic regulations, which had been in force during the Weimar period, were amended." Paragraph 4 of the above publication stated:

"The Ministry is divided into Sections (*Abteilungen*) and the Section into Departments (*Referate*). The basic unit in the organisational structure of the Ministry is the Department. . . . The Head of Department (*Rapporteur*) is a senior service official, who directs the Department on his own responsibility and is directly subordinate to the head of the Section (or to the head of the sub-Section). In his hands lies the first decision on all matters which come within the scope of his Department."

The RSHA, being a central authority (*Hauptamt*), was equivalent, according to this terminology, to a Ministry, and its offices (*Amter*) to Sections.

The following exchange of questions and answers took place between the Attorney-General and the Accused during the latter's cross-examination:

Q: Is it your contention that, whereas all the heads of departments had authority as described in this passage which I have just read, in Bureau IV Müller did not agree that his subordinates should possess such authority, or are you arguing that in the Nazi period none of the heads of departments had authority as stated in this passage?

A: I would not dare to contest the accuracy of the passage which you have read. I am only saying what I know from my own experience and from what I myself went through.

Q: That is to say the head of a department usually had the right of decision but you did not have the right of decision?

A: I think that it would be right to say that at that time it depended upon the personality of one's superiors, in so far as he had, if one may say so, dictatorial qualities.

Q: Did Müller have such qualities?

A: As far as decisions were concerned he was very pedantic and intolerant and reserved to himself all decisive action.

Q: Was this also the case in regard to minor matters and details?

A: Müller took decisions on the most trifling matters. Surprisingly enough this was also true of Himmler who went into the smallest details.

The Accused was, therefore, saying that in principle the Administrative Rules which were in use in 1927 were also valid during the Nazi period and in the RSHA as well. But the scope of a departmental head's powers was governed by the section head, and since Müller, who was the head of Bureau IV, reserved all decisions for himself, Eichmann, as head of Department IV B 4, was not left with any power of decision.

One thing was definitely established. Letters from IV B 4 and the other RSHA departments, as in the case of every department in every ministry of the Reich, were sent out under the name of the head, and if he did not sign himself, which only happened on rare occasions of special significance, another person signed, in his name or on his behalf or "upon his instructions." These letters were always written in the first person, and the "first person" was not necessarily the person who had signed the letter, but the head of the ministry or department in whose name or on whose behalf or upon whose instructions the document had been signed. "The first person" who appears in all the letters which were submitted in evidence, no matter who signed them, was in every case the chief of the SIPO and SD, Heydrich, and after his assassination Kaltenbrunner, and during the interregnum between Heydrich's death and the appointment of his successor Kaltenbrunner, "the first person" was Himmler himself.

The reference number IV B 4 on a document, however, in each case raised a presumption, which the Accused had to rebut, that it was sent on his own responsibility, whether it was signed by one of his subordinates or one of his superiors.

Where the Accused's own signature appeared on a document, it was clear that by signing it he accepted responsibility for any subordinate who had dealt with its contents, but the fact that he had signed it was still not proof that he had made the decision in regard to the subject matter of the document on his own initiative or had acted in accordance with the orders of his superiors.

This did not, of course, mean that either Heydrich or Kaltenbrunner personally dealt with all RSHA matters or initiated all RSHA activities, and the same applies to Müller, as head of Bureau IV. Superintendent Less asked Eichmann what were the matters on which he was normally allowed to make decisions. He replied by saying that he could make personal decisions on any subject provided he was in possession of "the appropriate order, instruction, or directive dealing with the matter from Himmler, Heydrich, Kaltenbrunner or Müller. Failing them I would follow the existing laws or regulations. After that, upon my own authority, in all other cases I could make a decision myself but in that case, if something went wrong, I would have to take the consequences."

What, for example, the Court asked, was the origin of the evacuation instructions which he sent to his representatives in the occupied countries?

In his evidence the Accused tried persistently to limit his personal role and argued that he never made use of the authority which he possessed and never put forward any proposals of his own. At the same time, he admitted that every draft prepared by subordinate officials of his Department had to be approved by him. Accordingly he was asked by the Attorney-General in cross-examination whether every document issued by his Department had first to pass through his hands or, in his absence, through the hands of his deputy and be initialled by one of them. The Accused replied in the affirmative. During the same session the internal correspondence of the German Foreign Ministry with Eichmann's Department was put in evidence and shown to him. It appeared, from one of these documents, that the head of the Department had made a certain proposal which went up to the Foreign Minister via Müller, and was then returned to Eichmann after the Foreign Minister had made a certain correction. Eichmann agreed that in the Foreign Ministry it was usual for the head of Department to make proposals. When it was put to the Accused that it was difficult to understand why the same procedure did not apply to his own Department the only answer he could give was as follows:

On the Jewish question there were so many instructions, so many orders . . . so many points of contact with the principal Ministries and the Party authorities, that it was extremely difficult for the SIPO and SD to do all that was wanted. Its hands were fully occupied with executive work. The orders and the objectives were frequently in contradiction. The various Ministries interfered with everything and made frequent demands and requests. There was never any need to put proposals to them. Not only was my Department not called upon to make proposals, even Müller was seldom asked to make suggestions. All that we did was to carry out the requests and demands of others.

While admitting that there is doubt that other authorities in the Third Reich, besides IV B 4, interfered in the handling of Jewish affairs, the Court did not regard Eichmann's explanation that RSHA was only the servant of others as worthy of serious consideration.

Eichmann also tried to play down the importance of his position by trying to limit the scope of the duties which were within his competence. He repeated his contention that he was only an official who dealt with the preparation of time-tables for the trains which carried the deportees from their homes to the extermination camps. It must have been difficult enough, in any event, to obtain the necessary number of railway trucks required having regard to the Army's needs in time of total war. The Accused's duties, however, did not end there. His chief task was not obtaining the necessary trucks but getting the Jews with which to fill them. The purpose of his office was a single one, namely, to provide the gas-chambers with victims: its duties were many and varied according to the constantly changing circumstances at any given time and place.

The Court found that the Accused's key position in everything relating to the deportation of the Jews to the East was clearly borne out by the evidence:

We reject absolutely the Accused's version that he was not anything more than a "small cog" in the extermination machine. We find that in the RSHA, which was the central authority dealing with the final solution of the Jewish question, the Accused was at the head of those engaged in carrying out the final solution. In fulfilling this task he acted in accordance with general directives from his superiors, but he was still left with wide powers of discretion which included the planning of operations on his own initiative. He was not a puppet in the hands of others: he was one of those who pulled the strings.

The question arose, therefore, if such were the Accused's status, why was he never promoted after his appointment to Amt IV B 4, having regard to his rapid advancement in the preceding years. The Accused gave his own explanation:

It was virtually impossible to promote me further because the post of Departmental Head, according to the office establishment, was that of a *Regierungsrat* or *Oberregierungsrat*, and the equivalent SS ranks were, respectively, *Sturmbannführer* and *Obersturmbannführer*. So long, therefore, as I remained head of my department I could not have gone any higher, even had I stayed there for another twenty years, unless the establishment had been altered.

The Court considered that it should be remembered that in 1944 three decorations were conferred upon him in quick succession, including the Distinguished War Service Cross, First Class with Swords, and thought it not unreasonable that a man in such an important position, especially when there was considerable advantage in anonymity, might be unwilling to be in the public eye and that his superiors might want him to remain inconspicuous for reasons of security and secrecy.

The Court then proceeded to deal with the legal effect of its findings of fact with reference to the indictment. The crimes alleged to have been committed by the Accused against the Jewish people were set out in Counts 1–8 of the indictment. In all these counts the Accused was charged with offences under Section 1 of the Nazi and Nazi Collaborators (Punishment) Law, 1950.

Dealing first with the crimes against the Jewish people referred to in Counts 1–4 the Court stated that the Act specified what were regarded as crimes against the Jewish people:

1. Killing Jews, as alleged in the first count.

2. Keeping Jews in living conditions calculated to bring about their physical destruction, as alleged in the second count.

3. Causing serious bodily or mental harm to Jews as alleged in the third count.

4. Devising measures intended to prevent births among Jews, as alleged in the fourth count.

All these Acts constituted a crime against the Jewish people *only if* they were committed with intent to destroy the Jewish people in whole or in part.

The period during which these crimes were alleged to have been committed was stated in the particulars of the first two counts as 1939–1945 and, from the recital of the facts in the particulars themselves, it appeared that the period referred to commenced from the outbreak of war in September 1939. The offences charged in the third count were alleged to have been committed during "the period of the Nazi régime" and in respect of the charges contained in the fourth count the period is stated to have begun at the beginning of 1942.

The Court stated that it had been proved to its satisfaction that the specific intent to destroy the Jewish people lay at the basis of the "final solution of the Jewish problem" which was Hitler's plan for the extermination of European Jewry. The acts of murder and violence against the Jews, committed by the Nazi régime and under its influence, from the middle of 1941 onwards, were without a shadow of doubt committed with the specific intent to destroy the Jewish people as such, and not only as individuals. Hence the ruthlessness shown even towards little children, because those who sought to strike at the very roots of Jewry did not want the survival of a new generation which would ensure the future and continuity of the Jewish race.

The Court found that the Accused was informed of this plan early in the summer of 1941. Evidence to support this was given by the Accused himself:

It was about two months after the German invasion of Russia that Heydrich sent for me. He then told me that the *Führer* had ordered the physical destruction of the Jews.

During the same interview Heydrich told him to go at once and see Globocnik, who was in Lublin, and to whom Himmler had already given appropriate instructions, and to see what progress had been made. It was also proved that at the end of August 1941 Eichmann tried to prevent the emigration of Jews from German occupied territories, lest they should escape the final solution which was, by then, in the preparatory stage. Sometime in the middle of September 1941 Eichmann paid his first visit to Globocnik, and immediately afterwards took part in discussions about the first deportations from the Reich to the Lodz ghetto. The Court said that it was evident that from the moment he heard of the order for total extermination, the Accused did not sit with his arms folded but, from then onwards, all his activities as *Rapporteur* for

Jewish affairs in the RSHA were co-ordinated and directed towards the target of the final solution.

In the opinion of the Court the evidence had shown not only that the Accused knew of the intent to destroy the Jewish people, which was inherent in the plan for the final solution, but that he personally shared that intent. The very size of the scope of his activities was evidence of this. Moreover, he helped to prepare the brief for Heydrich's speech at the Wannsee Conference by providing statistical material, and data for that part of the speech which dealt with the lessons to be learnt about the Jews from history, and which made it necessary, for the security of the Reich, to exterminate them.

Höss said this about the Accused's attitude on the Jewish question:

Eichmann was permeated with the conviction that if the foundations of Jewry in the East could be destroyed by complete extermination, then world Jewry would never recover from the blow.

The Court also had to decide whether there was evidence that the Accused harboured an intent to destroy the Jewish people at an earlier date, before he was informed in 1941 of the final solution. This was necessary because, in the third count, the Attorney-General had charged the Accused with causing serious bodily and mental harm to millions of Jews, during the whole period of the Nazi régime, with intent to destroy the Jewish people, and, in the particulars of the charge, mention was made of the mass arrests of Jews and their torture in concentration camps like Dachau and Buchenwald, the organisation of mass persecution on Crystal Night, the organisation of a social and economic boycott of Jews, their outlawing as a sub-human racial group, and the implementations of the Nuremberg Laws.

The Court was not satisfied that the Accused helped to organise the persecutions on Crystal Night or that he had taken any part in anti-Jewish measures before he was posted to Vienna after the Anschluss.

With regard to the steps which Eichmann took, in the course of duty, to expel the Jews during the second stage of the Jewish persecution, the Court found that various deportations carried out between September 1939 and June 1941 were organised by the Accused with complete disregard for the health and lives of the deported, but it was not satisfied beyond reasonable doubt that there had been, on Eichmann's part, an intent to exterminate them, and although what he did amounted to a crime against humanity it could not be said to constitute a crime against the Jewish people.

The Court then dealt with the legal aspects of the Accused's acts during the third and final stage, "the final solution." The Attorney-General had submitted that the plan of the final solution must be regarded as a criminal conspiracy to carry out numberless criminal acts connected with the extermination of the Jews in the Greater Reich and occupied Europe. As the Accused participated in this criminal conspiracy, Dr. Hausner argued, he must be held liable, *ipso facto*, for all the offences committed to bring about its implementation. He based his argument on the judgment of the Supreme Court of Israel in the case of Kaiser and, especially, on the following passage:

> Sections 35 and 36 of the Criminal Code Ordinance of 1936 stand by themselves in their definition of a specific crime. We are bound by virtue of Section 4 of the Ordinance to interpret in accordance with English law. In my opinion, under English law, the offence of conspiracy connotes a substantive rule of law whereby the conspirators are jointly liable, and this without having regard to the general rules as to complicity.

The Court considered that the Kaiser case was not on all fours with the case of Adolf Eichmann and it hesitated to accept the proposition put forward by the Attorney-General as a general rule in all cases.

Nevertheless, although the Court did not accept the Attorney-General's argument, it was of the opinion that his general approach was correct, namely, that all the acts perpetrated during the implementation of the final solution should be regarded as a single whole, and the Accused's responsibility determined accordingly. The Court came to this conclusion not because of the law regarding criminal conspiracy but from the very nature of the "final solution" as being a crime against the Jewish people in accordance with the legal definition of that crime.

The basis of the crime law was Hitler's order for the physical extermination of the Jews. It was not a series of separate orders for the extermination of the Jews in Germany, Poland, France, Soviet Russia and Hungary. It was not an order to exterminate first, one million Jews, and later, another million and so on: it was a comprehensive order and the desire of the main conspirators and perpetrators was identical with the wish of the originator of the plan. Their criminal intention did not renew itself from time to time, it was continuous, and embraced all activities until the whole operation was completed.

When the order to exterminate was given it was at once obvious that it would be an extremely complicated operation.

In the words of the judgment:

It was not easy to kill millions of people dispersed amongst the population. The victims had to be found and isolated. Not every place is convenient for killing. Not everywhere will the population submit to the killing of their neighbours. Therefore the victims had to be transferred to suitable places. It was war-time. Labour was needed and labour was scarce. Manpower should not be wasted, so the working capacity of the victims themselves had to be exploited so long as their muscles could function. It was, therefore, clear from the outset that a complicated machine would be needed to carry out the task. Everyone who had been "put into the picture," from a certain rank upwards, was aware too that the machinery existed and was functioning, although not all of them knew how each part of the machine operated, with what means, at what pace, and where.

The campaign for extermination, therefore, was one single comprehensive act which cannot be divided into acts or operations carried out by various people, at various times and at different places. One team of people carried it out jointly, at all times and in all places.

Hence, everyone who took part in the extermination of the Jews, with knowledge of the existence of the plan for the final solution and its implementation, is to be regarded as an accomplice in the killing of the millions who were exterminated during the years 1941–45. . . .

The Accused was privy to the extermination secret as from June 1941. By August 1941 he had begun to be active in the furtherance of the plan and occupied a central place in it. From then on all Eichmann's activities in rounding up the Jews and transporting them to the extermination camps, including all the planning and essential organisation, were directed not only towards an isolated incident such as the gassing at Auschwitz of a batch of Jews deported by him in a certain convoy. They were done within the general framework concisely expressed in Hitler's order and passed on by Heydrich at the Wannsee Conference.

The Court, therefore, found Eichmann guilty, as an accomplice, of the general crime of the "final solution" in all its forms. The verdict of guilty extended to all the many acts forming part of that crime, both those in which he took an active part in his own Department IV B 4 and the acts committed by his accomplices in pursuance of the common conspiracy. This verdict covered the first two counts in the Indictment which specifically referred to the "final solution."

The third count in the indictment referred to the whole period of the Nazi régime and ought, in the Court's opinion, to have been divided into two periods of time:

1. To include the first two stages of the persecution of the Jews mentioned earlier.

2. The third stage which only began in the summer of 1941.

The charge was that he had committed a crime against the Jewish people by causing serious bodily or mental harm to the Jews, and the particulars alleged that Eichmann had, together with others, caused serious harm by the enslavement, starvation, deportation and persecution of them, and by their detention in ghettos, transit and concentration camps in conditions which were designed to cause degradation, to deprive them of their rights as human beings and to suppress them and cause them inhuman suffering and torture. It was further alleged that all this had been done with the intention of exterminating the Jewish people.

There was ample evidence to support this charge, and the only question about which there could be any doubt was the exact period during which the Accused had been proved to have participated in these crimes.

The Court had already mentioned, earlier in the judgment, that it had not been proved that Eichmann was criminally responsible for what he was alleged to have done, prior to the outbreak of war, in Vienna, Prague, or Berlin. The Court now found, "because of doubt," that during the period covered by the second stage of the persecution, the intention to exterminate did not yet exist in the mind of the Accused.

There was, however, no doubt with regard to the third and last stage, beginning in August 1941, that the causing of serious bodily harm to Jews was a *direct and unavoidable result* of the activities which were carried out with the intention of exterminating those Jews who still remained alive, including the witnesses who had given evidence against Eichmann.

The fourth count alleged that the Accused had devised methods intended to prevent child-bearing among the Jews, including, among other things, sterilisation. The Court considered that there was no proof that Eichmann had put any of these measures into effect, and the only part of the charge in respect of which a conviction would be proper was the allegation that he gave orders to prevent child-bearing in the ghetto at Theresienstadt of which there was satisfactory proof.

The next three counts all charged the Accused with crimes against humanity, which includes all or any of the following acts: murder, extermination, enslavement, starvation, deportation of the civilian population, and persecution on national, racial, religious or political grounds.

The Court found that, with effect from August 1941, Eichmann participated in all these inhuman acts and that it was all done with the necessary intent.

The only possible difficulty arose with regard to the seventh count, in respect of which Counsel for the Defence had submitted that the "plunder of property" was not included in the definition, in the Nazi and Nazi Collaborators (Punishment) Law, of what constitutes a crime against humanity. The Attorney-General argued that it was covered by the words "any other inhuman act committed against any civilian population," as defined elsewhere in the same statute.

A similar problem had come before the United States Military Tribunal at Nuremberg during the trial of Friedrich Flick and five other leading German industrialists. That Court expressed the opinion that the plunder of Jewish industrial property could not be considered a crime against humanity; although a distinction could possibly be made between industrial property and the dwellings, household goods and food supplies of a persecuted people. In another famous war-crime case however, the opposite view was held by a majority of judges.

After considering both these cases and others, the Court came to the conclusion that the plunder of property could be considered an inhuman act only if it were carried out under the pressure of mass terror against the civilian population, or linked to any of the other acts of violence which, under the statute, constituted crimes against humanity, i.e., murder, starvation or deportation, etc. In this way the confiscation of Jewish property in Austria, through the agency of the Centres for Jewish Emigration, in the organisation of which the Accused played a leading role, could properly be regarded as a crime against humanity in which he participated, because it was carried out by means of terror against the Jews as a community.

The methods which Eichmann had used in Vienna and Prague he later put into operation from his office in Berlin, and in Germany, also, the Jews lived in permanent state of fear. The terror began the very moment Hitler came to power, and it intensified daily after the happenings of Crystal Night.

In the Court's opinion all this applied with even greater force to the Jews who were deported during the second stage of the persecution. It made no difference whether the property of these Jews fell into the hands of the Germans themselves, or whether it was left in the hands of the satellite governments of the countries in which the victims lived, in accordance with the "territorial principle" which had been invented for the purpose.

In all these instances the Accused participated *by the very act of deporting the victims* which rendered the confiscation of their property a foregone conclusion.

Finally the Accused also had a hand in the abominable desecration of the victims' corpses, the extraction of gold from their teeth and the cutting of the hair from women's heads, for it was he who had been responsible for bringing the victims to the extermination camps, well knowing what their fate would be. The Court, therefore, found the Accused guilty of the seventh count.

No legal questions arose in regard to the eighth count. There was no disputing that what was alleged in this charge, namely, the ill-treatment and deportation of Jews from the occupied territories during World War II, constituted a war crime. There was, furthermore, ample evidence that Eichmann had played an important role in carrying out these deportations in circumstances which involved gross ill-treatment, and the Court found him guilty of the charge.

The ninth count alleged that the Accused caused the deportation of over half a million Polish citizens from their homes with intent to settle German families in their stead.

Dr. Servatius had argued that the Poles were not deported but resettled in a way which did not constitute a crime against humanity.

Having regard to this submission the Court thought it necessary to examine, at some length, the nature of the activities mentioned in the particulars of the charge. Most of the evidence relevant to this count was documentary except for that given by Eichmann himself, that taken from Krumey in Germany, and certain extracts from a statement made by Höss.

The activities of the Accused in this connection concern two separate waves of deportation:

1. The transfer of Poles from the Warthe district to the area of the Government-General, i.e. from West to East, which started at the end of 1939 and went on until 1943.

2. The transfer of Poles from the Zamocz district to the West. This began at the end of 1942 and continued, as far as is known, for several months.

The foundations for the first transfer of population were laid by Heydrich at a meeting held on 21 September 1939 at which Eichmann was present in an official capacity.

The Court quoted from Heydrich's speech on this occasion, for it happens to contain the answer to the above-mentioned argument put forward by Dr. Servatius. This is part of what Heydrich said:

The solution of the Polish problem will be carried out by distinguishing between the higher and lower social strata. The leaders on the one hand, the labourers on the other. Of the political leaders in the occupied part of Poland not more than three per cent remain. They must be rendered harmless and will be taken to concentration camps. Lists are to be made of outstanding leaders and of the less important teachers, clergy, nobility, and retired officers. These, also, will be arrested and sent away. The care of the souls of the Poles will be placed in the hands of Catholic priests from the West, but they will not be allowed to speak Polish.

Primitive Poles will be included in the forced labour units as nomadic labourers and gradually they will be evacuated from the German area and moved into the foreign language area. The aim and object is that the Pole shall be nothing more than a seasonal labourer, always on the move: an eternal wanderer.

Anyone who listened to Heydrich's speech outlining that plan, and later participated in any form whatsoever in the operation of uprooting the Polish population, the Court stated in its judgment, "will not be allowed to argue that this was an innocent operation of 'resettlement.' This was a plain and simple expulsion, accompanied by degradation of the people, and aimed, with malicious intent, especially against the educated class."

The Accused, as usual, stated in evidence that his role in the "resettlement" plan was limited to obtaining and organising the necessary transport. That admission alone, in the Court's opinion, was sufficient to convict him of complicity in the deportation of the civilian population according to a plan of which he had full knowledge only three weeks after the invasion of Poland by Germany on 1 September 1939.

Having considered the documents in evidence, however, the Court came to the conclusion that the Accused's evidence was untrue, and that the deportations were organised and supervised by IV B 4 under Adolf Eichmann himself. The Court convicted him upon this count.

The tenth count charged the Accused with the commission of a similar offence to that alleged in the ninth count in respect of the deportation of over 14,000 Slovenes.

In respect of this charge, also, Eichmann did not seek to deny that he was responsible for arranging the transportation of these unhappy people, but his Counsel again argued that it had not been proved that the deportation had been carried out in an inhuman way. All the evidence, however, forced the Court to the inevitable conclusion that it was an enforced deportation and not a planned and orderly exchange of populations.

Every forced deportation of a civilian population was, in itself, in the opinion of the Court, a crime against humanity. The fact that at the end of 1942, more than eighteen months after the operation started, thousands of Slovenes had still not found any permanent dwelling place for themselves proves that the deportations brought much human suffering in their wake.

In respect of the eleventh count, which alleged that Eichmann had caused the deportation of tens of thousands of gypsies to extermination camps *for the purpose of their being murdered,* there was a special finding.

There was evidence to prove the Accused's complicity in the commission of a crime against humanity by virtue of his participation in the deportation of gypsies. There was ample evidence to prove that many of the gypsies so deported were exterminated by gassing in Auschwitz and Chelmno, but the Court found that there was no reliable proof that Eichmann knew that the gypsies transported by his department to Auschwitz were to be exterminated there. The Court, therefore, convicted him of causing their deportation, but *not* "for the purpose of their being murdered."

The twelfth count concerned one hundred children from Lidice whose deportation to Poland, and murder there, were alleged to have been caused by the Accused.

Eichmann strenuously denied all knowledge of this, and Dr. Servatius contended that the murder of these children had not been proved. There was a great deal of contradictory evidence called by both the Prosecution and Defence, but after careful consideration the Court was satisfied that the following facts had been satisfactorily established:

After the Lidice massacre two transports of children were sent to Lodz. The first consisted of ninety-one children, but only eighty-eight arrived, for three were taken out of the party being considered "fit for Germanisation." While at Lodz another seven were removed on the same grounds. The remaining eighty-one were put into a camp in Lodz from which they were removed on 2 July 1942. It was contended by the Attorney-General that these eighty-one were then transferred to the East, and he produced a document in evidence on which was written: "To the Government-General, eighty-one Czechs." The Court, however, was not convinced of the accuracy of this document and felt unable to say with certainty where these children were sent. Nevertheless, the Court was satisfied from another document attached to the evidence of Eichmann's colleague, Krumey, that they were handed over to the Lodz Gestapo.

This document reads as follows:

Confirmation: In accordance with a cable from RSHA, eighty-one Czech children, who were temporarily lodged at the camp at 41 Gneisenau St., were handed over today, 2.7.42, to the Litzmannstadt Gestapo.

The second transport consisted of eighteen children, six of whom were destined for Germanisation, and all of whom were admitted to a children's home. The total number of children sent from Lidice, therefore, amounted to a hundred and nine, of whom sixteen were retained for Germanisation. It will be remembered that an affidavit made by a Frau Freiberg was tendered in evidence by Dr. Servatius to the effect that she had seen a number of children, supposed to come from Lidice, in a school in Germany.

The Court assumed, therefore, as there was no reason to doubt Frau Freiberg's truthfulness or accuracy, that the children whom she saw must have been those who were selected for Germanisation.

The Court was in no doubt about the total number of children who were sent from Lidice or the fact that the Accused took part in their deportation. But it was not proved to the Court's satisfaction that either he or his office had any part in the children's murder nor had it been proved beyond reasonable doubt that they were murdered.

Eichmann, therefore, was only convicted, in respect of the

twelfth count, of committing a crime against humanity by participating in the expulsion of the ninety-three children of Lidice from their homeland.

The last three counts in the indictment (13, 14 and 15) charged the Accused, under Section 3 of the Nazi and Nazi Collaborators (Punishment) Law, with being a member of three "hostile organisations," the SS, SD, and the Gestapo. That Eichmann was a member of these organisations was not disputed but the Defence submitted:

1. That the Prosecution must prove the organisations were criminal, and this had not been done.

2. That as the Statute under which the prosecution had been brought obliged the Court to punish without proof of guilt, the Court should refrain from so doing and ought not to fill in any gaps by searching for, and perhaps finding guilt, where the law itself ignored its existence.

The Court referred to the fact that in the definition of a hostile organisation in the Statute in question reference was made to the findings of the International Military Tribunal which tried the major German war criminals at Nuremberg. When declaring the SS, SD, and Gestapo to be criminal organisations the Tribunal laid down certain conditions without which no one could be made liable on account of his membership of any of them.

The relevant extracts from the Tribunal's judgment are set out below:

The Tribunal declares to be criminal within the meaning of the Charter the group composed of those persons who had been officially accepted as members of the SS as enumerated in the preceding paragraph who became or remained members of the organisation with knowledge that it was being used for the commission of acts declared criminal by Article 6 of the Charter, or *who were personally implicated as members of the organisation in the commission of such crimes.* . . .

The Tribunal declares to be criminal within the meaning of the Charter the group composed of those members of the

Gestapo and SD holding the positions enumerated in the preceding paragraph who became or remained members of the organisation with the knowledge that it was being used for the commission of acts declared criminal by Article 6 of the Charter *or who were personally implicated as members of the organisation in the commission of such crimes.*

The words in italics were underlined in both findings in the written judgment of the Court because it was upon them that the conviction of Eichmann on these last three counts was based.

The crime of the extermination of the Jews during the war, the Court stated, was expressly declared by the International Military Tribunal to be also a crime within the meaning of the London Charter. The Court had already found that the Accused personally participated in the commission of this crime, and there was no doubt that he did this in his capacity as a member of all three organisations. Hence his criminal responsibility as a member of them.

The rest of the judgment dealt with the Accused's principal defence to all the charges and his "inner attitude" towards what he had done. This defence was, of course, the threadbare plea of superior orders [5] which, the Court said, Eichmann regarded as full justification for all his deeds. He explained that his SS training inculcated in him the idea that blind obedience is of primary importance, obedience based on boundless confidence in the wise judgment of the leadership, which will always know what the good of the Reich demands, and will give its orders accordingly.

The rejection of this plea, the Court said, as exempting an accused completely from criminal responsibility has now become general, if not universal, in all civilised countries. It has also been acknowledged as a principle of international law by the General Assembly of the United Nations.

Even the jurists of the Third Reich did not dare to put on

[5] This defence is discussed at length in Appendix II.

paper that obedience to orders transcends all else. They never repealed Section 47 (2) of the German Military Criminal Code which stated that whoever committed an offence against the criminal law, through obedience to a superior's order, was punishable as an accomplice to a criminal act, if he knew that the order concerned an act which was a crime or an offence according to military law. This Section was also applicable to the SS.

The Accused well knew that the order for the physical extermination of the Jews was manifestly unlawful, and that by carrying it out he was committing criminal acts on a gigantic scale. Eichmann's own words are proof of his guilty knowledge:

Your Honour, President of the Court, since you call upon me to give a clear answer I must declare that I see in this murder, this extermination of Jews, one of the gravest crimes in the history of humanity.

And in answer to Judge Halévi:

. . . I already realised then that this solution by the use of force was something unlawful, something terrible, but to my regret I was obliged to deal with it in matters of transportation, because of my oath of loyalty from which I was not released.

Although the Accused's attempt to rely on superior orders for the justification of his acts or even in mitigation of his punishment, in accordance with Section 11 of the statute, was already doomed to failure, the Court proposed to examine the Accused's "inner attitude" to the orders within the framework of which he acted:

Did they disturb his conscience so that he acted throughout under a compulsion from which he saw no escape, or did he act with inner indifference like an obedient automaton, or did he identify himself, within his heart, with the purpose of the orders. Although this makes no difference as regards convicting the Accused it is important to go into these questions in order to determine the measure of the Accused's moral responsibility for his acts.

The Court recalled that even before the Wannsee Conference Eichmann had already seen with his own eyes what was happening in Eastern Poland and had begun sending German Jews to the slaughter, yet in spite of it all he felt like Pontius Pilate, able to find an easy way of soothing his conscience by passing the responsibility on to someone else. No wonder Dr. Grüber called Eichmann a typical *Landsknecht*, a person who the minute he dons a uniform deposits his mind and his conscience in the cloakroom.

Why, if he so much disliked what he had to do, did he not apply for a transfer? The Attorney-General submitted that had Eichmann really wished to be released from his murderous task he could have found a way to do so. He could have applied for a posting to a front-line unit of the *Waffen SS*. He could have made various excuses to get away as others did, or he could have stated openly that he disliked the job assigned to him.

The Court considered that there were good grounds for this submission. It is known that men were sometimes released from service in the *Einsatzgruppen* when it became clear that they did not have the heart or the stomach to commit cold-blooded murder. The fact remains that Eichmann preferred to remain in his office job, sitting behind a desk, transporting millions of innocent men, women and children to their death.

It was strangely inconsistent that he admitted being a zealous National Socialist yet, in the same breath, he denied being an anti-Semite. Dr. Grüber could not distinguish between the two. "National Socialist zeal," he said, "was always connected with strong anti-Semitism. The two elements were always bound together and always went hand in hand."

It is, surely, common knowledge, the Court said, that in Hitler's crazy ideology the elevation of the German nation to the position of "master-race" was bound together with hatred of the Jews and their degradation to the rank of sub-human.

In the opinion of the Court the Accused successfully closed his ears to the voice of his conscience, as the régime to which he had sold himself body and soul demanded he should do. Dr. Grüber's description of Eichmann as a *Landsknecht* could not have been more apt. In the words of the judgment:

Thus he sank from one depth to another until, in the implementation of the "final solution" he reached the nethermost hell. But it is not to be said of him that his mind ceased to function or that it only functioned out of blind obedience. He believed wholeheartedly in the National Socialist bogus ideology that the Jews were enemies of the Reich and that they must be destroyed without mercy. His hatred was cold and calculated, aimed rather against the Jewish people as a whole than as individuals . . . to this task he devoted his alert mind, his great cunning, and his organising skill. He acted within the general frame-work of the orders which were given to him, but within that frame-work he went to every extreme to bring about the speedy and complete extermination of all Jews in the territories under German rule and influence. In saying this we do not mean that the Accused's viciousness was unusual within the régime which had raised him. He was a loyal disciple of a régime which was wholly evil and malicious.

The Court said that it was not disputed that in all his activities Eichmann always acted in concert with others, and that is how he was charged in the indictment. It would be quite wrong to place the entire responsibility for the extermination campaign on the shoulders of the Accused. Above him were the big men of the Leadership Corps with Hitler at their head. It was they who initiated the "final solution," they who issued the basic orders which the Accused implemented.

It is also true that there were other ministries, offices and organisations that took a hand in the persecution of the Jews and helped to prepare the way.

Nevertheless, this does not detract from the fact that RSHA was at the very centre of the final solution and the guilt of the others does not lessen by one iota the personal guilt of the Accused. The Court could not accept Eichmann's evidence.

His entire testimony was nothing but one consistent attempt to deny the truth and to conceal his real share of the responsibility, or at least to reduce it to a minimum. His attempt was not unskilful, due to those qualities which he had shown when he was committing those crimes. An alert mind, the ability to adapt himself to difficult situations, cunning, and a glib tongue. But he did not have the courage to tell the truth either about what actually happened or about his innermost feelings about what he did. We saw him, again and again, twisting and turning under the impact of the cross-examination, retreating from complete to partial denial and only, when left with no alternative, admitting anything, but always, of course, taking refuge in the plea that in all matters great or small he was acting on explicit orders.

The Court then announced its verdict on all fifteen counts.[6]

When the Court re-assembled on the following day the Attorney-General, in a long speech, asked for the death penalty to be imposed, and after Dr. Servatius had pleaded for a more lenient punishment, Eichmann addressed the Court:

I have heard the severe judgment of the Court and my hopes for justice have been disappointed. I cannot accept the judgment.

I fully understand that the crimes committed against the Jews must be atoned for. The evidence given in this Court by witnesses has again shocked me considerably, just as I was profoundly shaken at the time when, under orders, I was once obliged to witness such horrors. I had the misfortune to have been involved in these horrors. But these misdeeds were committed against my will. I did not will the murder of human beings. This mass slaughter is solely the responsibility of the political leaders.

I tried to get away from my desk, to front-line fighting, to an honest fight, but my dark duties kept me in my place. I wish to emphasise once more, my guilt lies in my obedience, my re-

[6] These, with the Court's reasons, have already been given in detail on pages 320–333.

spect for discipline, and my military obligations in time of war, my allegiance to the colours and to the service.

To that end, martial law had been in force since the outbreak of the war.

Such obedience at no time came easily, and both those who issued orders and those who had to obey them knew full well the limits to which a person can be driven. It is not I who persecuted Jews with avidity and fervour, this was done by the Government. The whole persecution could only have been carried out by a government, never by me.

I accuse those in power of abuse of my obedience. Obedience was exacted then, just as it will be exacted also in the future, from those under orders.

Obedience is praised as a virtue. I would therefore request that my having obeyed be the sole factor to be taken into account, while sight should be lost of those whom I obeyed.

As I have already stated it was the ruling circles, to whose ranks I did not belong, who issued the orders; it is they who, in my view, justly deserve punishment for the horrors perpetrated against the victims upon their orders. But now, the underlings too are amongst the victims. I am such a victim. This cannot be ignored.

It is said I might have refused to obey and indeed should have done so. This, however, is thought of only now. Under the circumstances at the time, such behaviour was impossible. Nobody acted this way.

I know, from experience, that the theory so widely propounded, but only after the war, that it might have been possible to refuse to obey an order, is merely a fable invented for the purposes of protection.

Only a few were able to do so, but I was not amongst those who believed that this was possible.

It is a great mistake to assume that I was fanatical in my persecution of Jews. Throughout the whole post-war period I have been tormented and enraged by the fact that all blame was transferred to me from my superiors . . . and others. In fact I have made no statements which might have indicated any fanaticism on my part and the guilt for the bloodshed does not rest with me.

The witnesses have here been most untruthful, and although

the summing-up of the testimonies and documents by the Court may, at first sight, seem convincing, it is in fact deceptive and misleading. . . .

My guiding principle in life, from my earliest days, has been the desire to strive for the realisation of ethical values. At a given moment, however, I was prevented, through the intervention of the State, from living up to these principles. From ethics I had to shift to one of the many facets of morality. I had to bow to the reversal of values as dictated by the State. This search for self-knowledge was confined solely to the innermost recesses of my being. In the course of this soul-searching, I have not taken into account the innocence which I believe is mine, from the legal point of view.

Today, of my own free will, I would ask the Jewish people for pardon and would confess that I am bowed down with shame at the thought of the iniquities committed against the Jews and the injustices done to them, but in the light of the Court's judgment, this would, in all probability, be construed as hypocrisy.

I am not the monster I am made out to be. I am the victim of a misconception. I was attacked in Buenos Aires, chained to my bed for a week, and doped by injections in the arm, and brought to the airport at Buenos Aires; thence I was flown out of the Argentine Republic. This is quite obviously the result of my having been held to be the all-responsible one.

The reason for this lies in the fact that some of the National Socialists of those days, as well as others, had been spreading untruths about me. They endeavoured to rid themselves of responsibility at my expense, or were seeking to create confusion for reasons unknown to me. That is why I am here today. It is my profound conviction that I must suffer for the acts of others, and carry the burden imposed upon me by fate.

The Court then adjourned until Friday 15 December to consider the sentence, and on re-assembly the Presiding Judge sentenced the Accused to death:

With a deep sense of responsibility lying upon us, we have considered what is the proper penalty to be meted out to the Accused, and have arrived at the conclusion that, for the due punishment of the Accused, and for the deterrence of others, the maximum penalty of the law has to be imposed in this case. In our judgment we have described the crimes in which the Accused participated, crimes of unparalleled enormity in their nature and their extent. The aim of the crimes against the Jewish people, of which the Accused has been convicted, was to blot out an entire people from the face of the earth, and that is what distinguishes them from crimes against persons as individuals. It may be said that such crimes against humanity, which are directed against a group of people as such, are of an even graver nature than the sum total of the criminal acts against individuals of which they are composed. But at this stage, when the sentence is to be considered, we have to take into account also, and perhaps first and foremost, the injury to the victims as individuals which was involved in these crimes, and the untold suffering which they and their families have undergone, and continue to undergo, as the result of these crimes. Indeed, the despatch by the Accused of every train carrying a thousand souls to Auschwitz, or to any of the other places of extermination, amounted to direct participation by him in one thousand acts of premeditated murder, and his legal and moral responsibility for those murders is in no way less than the measure of liability of him who with his own hands put those persons into the gas-chambers.

Even had we found that the Accused acted out of blind obedience, as he alleges, we would still have said that one who had participated in crimes of such dimensions, for years on end, must undergo the greatest punishment known to the Law, and no order given to him could be a ground even for mitigating his punishment. But in fact we have found that in acting as he did, the Accused identified himself in his heart with the orders received by him and he was actuated by an ardent desire to attain the criminal objective. The Court sentences Adolf Eichmann to death for the crimes against the Jewish people, the crimes against humanity, and the war crimes of which he has been found guilty.

The Court then informed Eichmann that he was entitled to appeal against both judgment and sentence, should he so wish, in which event notice of appeal must be filed within ten days and his reasons for appeal given within fifteen days.

EPILOGUE

AND SO, almost nineteen months after the capture of Eichmann in the Argentine and eight months after the commencement of the trial, Adolf Eichmann was convicted of nearly all the charges preferred against him and sentenced to death.

Before the trial opened there were, as I wrote in the Prologue, two main criticisms against it, apart from the complicated legal question whether an Israeli Court had jurisdiction to try Eichmann. Many Jews feared that the trial might react unfavourably on Jews everywhere. Might not the spectacle of the Jews stripping and showing their scars to the world like old beggars, years after the sores have healed, lead to a resurgence of anti-Semitism?

There is no evidence, at the moment, that the trial has resuscitated any anti-Jewish feeling.

In Germany, for example, where many Jews feared otherwise, the reaction has been, generally, favourable. A West German public opinion research institute, during the long adjournment during which the Court was preparing its judgment, conducted an investigation into the effect on viewers of the thirty-two television programmes, each of half an hour's duration, which were shown by all West German Stations at peak-viewing hours. This series of programmes was preceded by a lengthy documentary giving the background of the trial, and they had a tremendous impact on the youth of Germany. How were such crimes possible? Why has there been such a conspiracy of silence about them in Germany? How can one believe that millions of Germans knew hardly anything about these crimes? Such are the questions which these young people have been asking.

Not all Germans, of course, have reacted in this way. Many, over forty-five years of age, said that they would be glad when they had heard the last of it and that it was high time "these things" were forgotten. Such a reaction from those who are so heavily compromised by the past is not altogether surprising, but it was outweighed by opinions like the following: "It is a good thing to present these reports so that there may be no repetition of such events. We should be ashamed that such things were allowed to happen. Such events should never be forgotten."

Nor have the fears of some people that Eichmann could not expect a fair trial in Jerusalem been justified by events. No one who has attended the trial and followed the transcript of the proceedings day by day can have any doubt that it has been scrupulously fair.

"It cannot be denied," the President of the Court said at the opening of the trial, "that the memory of the Nazi holocaust stirs every Jew, but while this case is being tried before us it will be our duty to restrain those feelings and this duty we shall honour." Eichmann's judges kept their word.

From the historical point of view, also, the trial has been useful. There have been other war-crime trials in which evidence has been given of the "final solution" of the Jewish question, the physical extermination of European Jewry, but this was the only trial which has dealt solely with the Jewish catastrophe, and the full and terrible story is now on record for present and future generations to read and remember.

This was, as the Prime Minister of Israel intended it should be, the trial of a régime, not an individual. Whether Eichmann was a large or small cog in the Nazi machinery of extermination is of little or no importance. Whatever he was, it appears that he did his work thoroughly and, if the evidence of some of his colleagues is to be believed, with no little enthusiasm. Yet, when all is said and done, had he been successful in getting transferred to another post, as he said he would have liked to have done, it would not have saved the life of a single Jew. Someone else would have taken his place and the slaughter would have continued. Therein lies the real object lesson of this trial.

Eichmann, under considerable pressure in the witness-box, eventually admitted that he regarded the extermination of the Jews as one of the most hideous crimes in history, but that he should have refused to carry out such criminal orders never, for a moment, crossed his mind. Although at the end of the trial he appeared to realise the enormity of what he did, he nevertheless took pride in doing it well. That the head of a small department in the Reich Security Head Office felt able to implement Hitler's criminal plans, without so much as a protest, is a reminder, never to be forgotten, of the appalling and disastrous effects of totalitarianism on men's minds.

LONDON, 20 DECEMBER 1961

APPENDIX I

Untersturmführer	2nd Lieutenant
Obersturmführer	Lieutenant
Hauptsturmführer	Captain
Sturmbannführer	Major
Obersturmbannführer	Lieutenant-Colonel
Standartenführer	Colonel (*Oberst*)
Oberführer	Brigadier-General
Brigadeführer	Major-General
Gruppenführer	Lieutenant-General
Obergruppenführer	General
Oberstgruppenführer	Colonel-General (*General Oberst*)

Himmler held the special supreme rank of *Reichsführer SS*, equivalent to Goering's rank of *Reichsmarshal*.

APPENDIX II

THE DEFENCE OF "SUPERIOR ORDERS"

Theirs not to reason why,
Theirs but to do and die.

THE PLEA of "superior orders" has been raised by the defence in war-crime trials more frequently than any other. To understand the doctrine it is necessary to know something of the history of its evolution. In 1919 an International Commission was appointed to consider and report to the Allied powers on the question of the immunity of Heads of State in respect of the conduct of war. This body was known as the "1919 Commission on Responsibilities," and when recommending the trial of Heads of State and other high State administrators, they made these observations:

"We desire to say that civil and military authorities cannot be relieved from responsibility by the mere fact that a higher authority might have been convicted of the same offence. It will be for the Court to decide whether a plea of superior orders is sufficient to acquit the person charged from responsibility."

Although there was not at that time any international judicial authority on the subject, there were few writers on international law who had not rejected the doctrine that the receipt of superior orders was a complete justification of war crimes. The German Code of Military Law provided that a soldier must execute all orders undeterred by the fear of legal consequences, but it added that this would not excuse him in cases where he must have known *with certainty* that the order was illegal.

This view was held and expressed by the German Supreme

Court in Leipzig in 1921. The Court was trying two lieutenants, part of the ship's company of a German U-boat which, during the period of hostilities, had sunk the *Llandovery Castle*, a British hospital ship. In accordance with the orders of the submarine's Commander to leave no trace, the two junior officers gave orders to fire on the hospital ship's lifeboats.

The judgment of the Court is of tremendous importance, for this reason. Since the last war ended the impression has gained ground that the statements of the law on this subject, which were inserted in the British and American Manuals of Military Law in 1944, did not follow the accepted rule of many years' standing. Although this impression is mistaken, there are understandable reasons for its existence. In the British Manual of Military Law certain revisions and amplifications were made in 1914. In a chapter headed "The Laws and Usages of War on Land," the doctrine regarding superior orders was declared to be as follows: "Members of the armed forces who commit such violations of the recognised rules of warfare as are ordered by their Government or their commander are not war criminals and cannot therefore be punished by the enemy. He may punish the officials or commanders responsible for such orders if they fall into his hands, but otherwise he may only resort to other means of obtaining redress."

A similar statement appeared in the United States Rules of Land Warfare.

The statement which appeared in the 1914 Manual, and remained without amendment until 1944, was based on the fifth edition of Oppenheim's International Law, which was corrected in the sixth edition published in 1940. It was not only inconsistent with the view of most writers upon the subject, but also with the decision of the German Supreme Court in the above case.

The Court, applying the German Military Penal Code, which has already been referred to above, stated in its judgment that the Commander's order to leave no trace did not free the Accused from guilt. A subordinate who obeyed the order of his superior officer was liable to punishment if it were known to him that such order involved a contravention of the law, in this case international law. This applied to the two Accused, the judgment continued, though it should be urged in favour of military subordinates that they are under no obligation to question the order of a superior officer and they can count on its legality, but no such confidence can be held to exist if such an order is universally known to everybody, including the Accused, to be without any doubt whatever against the law. This happens only in rare and exceptional cases, but this case is precisely one of them, for in the present instance it was perfectly clear to the Accused that killing defenceless people in the lifeboats could be nothing else but a breach of the law.

"In estimating the punishment it should be borne in mind that the principal guilt rests with the submarine's Commander under whose orders the Accused acted. They should certainly have refused to obey the order. This would have required a specially high degree of resolution, and this fact therefore justifies the recognition of mitigating circumstances in determining the punishment under the State Penal Code. A severe sentence must, however, be passed."

In order to appreciate how fantastic is the claim that the statement in the 1914 Manual of Military Law had been the accepted rule for so many years, it is only necessary to remember that the above judgment showed that as early as 1921 it was not the accepted doctrine in Germany.

It is true that it remained unamended in the British Manual of Military Law until 1944, though it is difficult to understand why. One explanation is that it related to a subject which between 1918 and 1940 was of no immediate concern to the Army, and its inadequacy only became apparent when renewed interest naturally arose during the last war. That it was not amended until the tide of war was flowing strongly in our favour is extremely unfortunate, for this has persuaded some people, including Dr. Servatius, that it was the law which had been conveniently changed rather than its mis-statement corrected. Nevertheless, this does not alter the fact that it was an incorrect statement of the almost universally accepted law.

The German Supreme Court's judgment shows that German law is in line on this subject with international law as accepted in other countries, and in itself is a refutation of the argument put forward by many German counsel at the various war-crime trials since the war; namely, that British Military Courts who followed the amended version of Chapter XIV, para. 443, in the Manual of Military Law, were applying *ex post facto* legislation. The Manual has no legislative authority, and the fact that for some reason a mis-statement of the law therein remained so long uncorrected is no justification for such argument.

The amendment to the 1914 statement in the Manual of Military Law, which was so belatedly promulgated, is set out below:

The fact that a rule of warfare has been violated in pursuance of an order of the belligerent government or of an individual belligerent commander does not deprive the act in question of its character as a war crime; neither does it, in principle, confer upon the perpetrator immunity from punishment by the injured belligerent. Undoubtedly a Court confronted with the plea of superior orders adduced in justification of a war crime is bound to take into consideration the fact that obedience to military orders, *not obviously unlawful*, is the duty of every member of the armed forces, and that the latter cannot, in conditions of war discipline, be expected to weigh scrupulously the legal merits of the order received. The question, however, is governed by the main principle that members of the armed forces are bound to obey lawful orders only, and that they cannot escape liability if, in obedience to a command, they commit acts which both violate the unchallenged rules of warfare and outrage the general sentiment of humanity.

That passage, it is true, does not in so many words make ignorance of the illegality of an order a complete legal defence.

Nevertheless, it indicates to the Court that they should not convict an accused of a war crime committed in consequence of the order of a superior, unless satisfied that he *well knew* he was committing an act which both violated the unchallenged rules of warfare and outraged the general sentiment of humanity. In a somewhat extensive experience of British war-crime trials, I know of none in which the Judge Advocate, or if there was no Judge Advocate then the law member, failed to remind the Court of their duty to satisfy themselves of the Accused's knowledge of the illegality of the order before convicting him.

In practice, therefore, ignorance of the order's illegality did furnish a complete defence, and it is a pity that the Amendment of 1944 to the Manual of Military Law did not say so categorically. The general upshot of the many judicial decisions on this plea of superior orders is that if the order in question was, or must be presumed to have been, known to the Accused as illegal, or was illegal on its face, the Accused cannot then rely on the defence of "superior orders." My own opinion is that ignorance of the illegality of the order should constitute a legal excuse, but the onus should be on the Accused to satisfy the Court, having regard to all the circumstances, that he could not reasonably have known that it was illegal.

At the trial of the major war criminals by the International Military Tribunal at Nuremberg the plea was raised on behalf of most of the Accused on the ground that everything they had done was in obedience to a *Führerbefehl*, an order from Hitler himself. In their judgment the Tribunal referred to the Article of the Charter regarding this subject, which stated that the fact that the defendant acted in pursuance of an order of his government or of a superior does not free him from responsibility, but may be considered in mitigation of punishment. They stated that this Article was in conformity with the law of all nations. That a soldier was ordered to kill or torture in violation of the international law of war has never been recognised as a defence to such acts of brutality, but could be regarded as a mitigating factor. The true test, according to the Tribunal, was not the existence of the order but whether moral choice was, in fact, possible.

The defence of "superior orders" was also raised and dismissed at a number of other trials, and in the famous *"Einsatzgruppen* Case," tried by an American Military Tribunal, in which the Accused were charged with the extermination of over a million inhabitants of the occupied territories, the Court dismissed the plea in these words: "The obedience of a soldier is not the obedience of an automaton. A soldier is a reasoning agent. It is a fallacy of widespread consumption that a soldier is required to do everything his superior officer orders him to do. The subordinate is bound only to obey the lawful orders of his superior."

The Germans have really no cause for complaint regarding that attitude of Allied Military Courts to the plea of "superior orders." The approach was the same as that of their own Supreme Court in 1921, and the principle on which these Courts dealt with such pleas had the approval of no less a person than Goebbels himself. In an article in the German Press on 28 May 1944 he wrote: "No international law of warfare is in existence which provides that a soldier who has committed a mean crime can escape punishment by pleading as his defence that he followed the commands of his superiors. This holds particularly true if those commands are contrary to all human ethics and opposed to the well-established international usage of warfare." It was, of course, the bombing of Germany by the Allies to which Goebbels was referring, and he was attempting to justify the growing Nazi practice of shooting captured Allied airmen. When, some two years later, the Allied Military Courts for the trial of war criminals applied the same law, there could not possibly be any cause for complaint.

Index

A Note about the Author

Edward Frederick Langley Russell, Russell of Liverpool, 2nd Baron, C.B.E. 1945, was educated at Liverpool College and St. John's College, Oxford, and is Barrister at Law, Gray's Inn. He is Brigadier (retired), and saw service in both world wars. In World War II he was First Deputy Judge Advocate General of the British First Army and was attached to Allied Force Headquarters, G.H.Q. Middle East Forces, and H.Q. British Army of the Rhine, in which he served as legal adviser at the Nuremberg Trials. From 1951 to 1954 Lord Russell was Assistant Judge Advocate General of Great Britain. His most widely known previous book was *The Scourge of the Swastika.*

December 1962

A Note on the Type

THE TEXT of this book was set on the Linotype in JAN-
SON, a recutting made direct from type cast from ma-
trices long thought to have been made by the Dutchman
Anton Janson, who was a practicing type founder in
Leipzig during the years 1668–87. However, it has been
conclusively demonstrated that these types are actually
the work of Nicholas Kis (1650–1702), a Hungarian, who
most probably learned his trade from the master Dutch
type founder Dirk Voskens. The type is an excellent example of the influential and sturdy Dutch types that prevailed in England up to the time William Caslon developed his own incomparable designs from these Dutch
faces.

Composed, printed, and bound by
Kingsport Press, Inc., Kingsport, Tennessee.
Typography by Anita Karl